# Tutor Ted

## guide to the ACT

Ted Dorsey, M.A.

Alice Humbracht

Martha Marion

Del Nakhi

Stephen Black

Ryan Harrison

Maryann Dorsey, M.A.

# Tutor Ted.

For more information, visit our website: **www.tutorted.com**

Book Design: Sherri Nielsen

ISBN: 978-0-9834471-3-9

## STAY CONNECTED!
**We love to connect with our students!**
Follow us on Twitter, add us on Facebook, or just send us an old-fashioned email!

 TWITTER @tutorted

 FACEBOOK /tutorted

 INSTAGRAM @tutorted

 YOUTUBE /tutorted

 EMAIL sayhello@tutorted.com

## Special Thanks!

Special Thanks to:
Matt Casper
Noah Dzuba
Evan Endicott
Andy Featherston
Maryann Dorsey
Asa Anderson
Monica Miklas
Brigid Miklas

# Table of Contents

A Note from Ted                                           5

## 🚀 PREPARE FOR LIFTOFF
How to Use This Book                                       6
Short and Sweet Advice                                     7
The Myth of the Bad Test Taker                             8
Prep Strategies                                            9
Before, During, and After the Test                        10
Score Deletion and Superscore                             13
Official Stuff                                            14

## ✎ ENGLISH
The Breakdown                                             16
Usage / Mechanics
   Independent and Dependent Clauses        20
   Comma Rules                               23
   Semicolons, Colons, and Dashes            26
   Apostrophes/Possessives                   28
   Subject-Verb Agreement                    30
   Verb Tense                                32
   Pronouns                                  34
   Object Pronouns                           36
Rhetorical Skills
   Shorter is Better                         40
   Sentence Logic                            42
   Relevance                                 46
   Redundancy                                51
   Author's Intent                           54
   Diction                                   58
   Organization and Flow                     61
   Style                                     70
   Rhetorical Skills Exercise                72
Answers & Solutions                                       78

## 🔬 MATH
The Breakdown                                             84
Formulas                                                  88
MathCabulary                                              91
Strategies
   Calculators                               95
   Wordy Word Problems                       99
   Plugging In                              101
   Reality Math                             106
   Geometry                                 110
   Eyeballing                               113
   Play Around                              116
   Using the Answer Choices                 118
Basic Math
   Circles                                  124
   Triangles                                129
   Percents                                 133
   Proportions and Ratios                   137
   Distance and Midpoint                    140
   Slope                                    143

Intermediate Math
   Foiling, Factoring, and Quadratics       148
   Inequalities                             152
   Absolute Value                           154
   Trigonometry                             158
   Lines and Angles                         163
   Mean, Median, Mode                       166
   Probability                              171
Advanced Math
   Functions                                174
   Exponents and Scientific Notation        177
   Imaginary and Complex Numbers            182
   Three Dimensional Geometry               185
   Advanced Trigonometry                    188
   Logic                                    195
   Combinations and Permutations            198
Answers & Solutions                                      203

## 📚 READING
The Breakdown                                            230
Key Strategies                                           234
Passage Types                                            242
9 Essential Question Types                               244
Wrong Answer Traps                                       252
Reading Exercise                                         256
Answers & Solutions                                      266

## ⚕ SCIENCE
The Breakdown                                            272
Strategies                                               276
Think Through Exercise                                   284
Passage Types                                            288
Conflicting Viewpoints Exercise                          290
How to Be a Science Ninja                                292
ACT Science Knowledge                                    295
Answers & Solutions                                      301

## ✎ WRITING
The Breakdown                                            304
Two Rules                                                307
Sample Prompt                                            309
Have a Plan                                              310
Sample Essays                                            315
Additional Prompts                                       322

TUTOR TED'S GUIDE TO THE ACT

# A Note from Ted

One day soon, a group of people you don't know will sit around a table and shuffle through a file of information that represents you: an application, a transcript, letters of recommendation, an essay... and an official score report from **ACT**.

After they review those documents, those people will make a decision that will affect the rest of your life.

**You can alter the conversation those people have about you.** You can distinguish yourself, impress the admissions officers, and become **the one they put in the YES pile. We're here to help you do that. That's our job: to help YOU improve your ACT score.**

When you study with Tutor Ted, improving your **ACT** score is not just possible, it is expected. The **ACT** tests your content knowledge. This book contains that knowledge. The **ACT** asks you to think in a specific way. This book gives you strategies to think that way. When you know that content and apply those strategies, your **ACT** score will go up.

It really
is
that
simple.

So let's get started!

TED

# How to use This Book

Here it is:

## 1 📚 READ THE CHAPTERS

**Use them to learn the stuff you don't know.** Semicolons, for example. Be honest: do you really know how to use a semicolon? *Are you sure?*

You should also use the chapters to review concepts you haven't thought about since 4th grade. It may have been awhile since you've seen a ratio. Time to refresh your memory on that.

## 2 🧩 APPLY THE STRATEGIES.

**Just as important as learning all of the content of the test is finding your own personal test-taking approach.** We've got effective strategies for attacking all sections of the **ACT**. Read the strategies, try them out for yourself, and find the approach that works for you.

## 3 ⏱ PRACTICE AT THE SPEED OF THE TEST.

**Our companion book, "Tutor Ted's ACT Practice Tests," includes three full-length practice tests.** As you work through this book, take the tests from that book. Study between your practice tests so that you always expect to improve your score. Whenever you take a practice test, **use a timer.** Speed is a factor on the **ACT**, so you want to get used to the pace of the test.

**Practice tests tell you which topics you've mastered and which ones you need to study more.** In addition, they help you figure out whether your strategy is working. Can you get through the Reading and Science in time, or do you need to work faster? Do you need to be more careful to avoid careless math errors? How much time is the right amount of time to spend planning your essay?

**In addition to the three practice tests in "Tutor Ted's ACT Practice Tests," you can find a free practice test online at www.actstudent.org/testprep**

Does that plan sound more like common sense and less like **magic?** **If so...good!** ACT improvement is simple: know the stuff, have a strategy, and practice. We give you expert advice, you do the work, and your ACT score improves. **That is how the magic happens.**

## Now let's get into some details.

**Your job on the ACT is to answer 215 multiple-choice questions and write one essay.** Yes, the essay is technically optional, but like everything else in the college admissions process that's optional, **it's mandatory.**

## Are you ready for the world's shortest, simplest, most effective ACT advice?

**You should always answer all of the questions.** You do not get penalized for wrong answers, so even if you have to guess you should answer all of the questions.

**You have to work quickly.** The pace of the test is fast, so you'll have to practice working at the right pace. Even though it's a quick test, keep this in mind: it is designed for you to finish it in time.

**Every correct answer is right for a reason.** Keep it simple. Don't overcomplicate or overthink these questions. Find a reason to pick an answer and move on.

**OK, there is a little more to it than that.** Just take our word for it: this really is a simple, straightforward test. **Let's get into why that's true.**

*And that's pretty much all you need to know!*

*End book now.*

 Here is an overview of the sections of the **ACT.**

**The English Test asks 75 questions in 45 minutes.** Even though that is a quite a number of questions to answer in a short amount of time, this is often the easiest section to finish in time. 40 questions test you on technical grammar stuff like commas and verb conjugation, and 35 of them test you on flow, organization, and content.

**The Math Test asks 60 questions in 60 minutes.** The content covers your entire math education to date. That means everything from adding fractions up through functions is fair game. The Math Test measures how much you know and how precisely you can solve problems.

**The Reading Test asks 40 questions in 35 minutes.** The questions will be based on passages within four different topics: Prose Fiction (or Literary Narrative), Social Science, Humanities, and Natural Science. Within one of those topics you are likely to see a set of double passages—two passages that relate to each other. Speed and timing are the biggest challenges on this section—you should practice Reading passages until you find the pace that works for you.

**The Science Test asks 40 questions in 35 minutes.** There are passages in three different categories: Data Representation, Research Summaries, and Conflicting Viewpoints. **The #1 most important thing to keep in mind on the Science? You don't need to know very much science.** Fewer than 10% of the questions rely on specific science knowledge. Most questions just test your ability to interpret charts and graphs.

**The Writing Test is a 40-minute essay test *(technically optional, but plan to write it)*.** You'll be given a general prompt on a topic of debate plus three perspectives on that topic. Your job is to analyze the given perspectives and present your own based on your analysis.

## THE MYTH OF THE BAD TEST TAKER

**Before we go any further, we've got something important to say. Ready? OK.**
**There is no such thing as a Bad Test Taker.** There is no chromosome that predisposes you to perform poorly on tests. There is such a thing as an unprepared test taker, but that's different. Students are labeled as Bad Test Takers when they fail to perform at a certain level during a timed test. They are told that they can't manage their time well or that they get too anxious/nervous.

**First off, let's talk about anxiety. Take a look at this graph:**

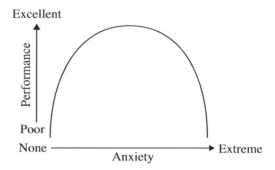

**Consider this a warm-up for the Science Test—and by the way, if you can handle this graph, then you can handle the Science Test. What does this graph mean?**

**What it shows is a classic finding of psychology.** The graph shows that at either extremely high or extremely low levels of anxiety, performance is poor. However, at moderate levels of anxiety, performance is at its peak! This has been proven to be true in academics, athletics, and every other performance setting.

*Pretty crazy, huh?*

**Anxiety is actually your friend.** You WANT to be somewhat anxious/nervous. It is not a lot of fun to feel anxious or nervous...but it is actually beneficial to you if you are.

**Now let's talk about confidence.** When will you perform your best on the **ACT**, or on any other test you ever have to take? When you know the content of the test and have done enough practice to work out your approach to the test. **Let's put it another way.**

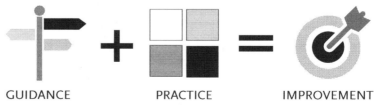

GUIDANCE + PRACTICE = IMPROVEMENT

Think about it. If you learn the material and concepts on the test, and familiarize yourself with the strategies and techniques necessary to do well, you will come out on the other side with confidence, ready to face the test. As a result, you'll earn a higher score.

**There is no such thing as a Bad Test Taker, just test takers who are unprepared. And you're not going to be one of those people.**

## PRACTICE, PRACTICE, PRACTICE...PRACTICE?

**What's the right amount of time to devote to ACT prep?** There isn't one answer that's right for everyone, but we've got some guidelines. We recommend that all students take a minimum of four practice tests before their actual exam. The companion to this book, "Tutor Ted's **ACT** Practice Tests," contains three tests. Those three tests, plus the free test you can download from **ACT** (www.actstudent.org/testprep) makes four tests you can use to practice—and improve.

**When should you take those practice tests?** Take one at the very beginning of your prep. That will help you establish a baseline score and show you where you need to focus your energy during prep. Take the other tests as you study. **Our rule of thumb is that you shouldn't take another practice test until you think you'll do better on the next test than on the previous one.**

Also, don't wait till just before your actual **ACT** to take all of your practice tests—you'll get more benefit when you have some time between practice tests.

## DO I NEED A TUTOR?

**The decision to work with a tutor is a personal one for each individual student.** It is a matter of how you study and learn best. Some students are independent and can manage their time and practice diligently until they understand a concept or problem. Others can use guidance and encouragement along the way, and might better understand a problem by talking it through with a tutor. You can always start with self-study and work with a tutor later on.

**If you decide you would like to work with someone, Tutor Ted is here to help.** Our expert tutors are equipped with the best technology and will work with you one-on-one online, just as they would in person. The difference? You can connect from anywhere, at any time, on any device, to get the support you need. Visit our website *(www.tutorted.com)* for additional information about our services.

## THE NEED FOR SPEED

With 215 multiple choice questions to complete in about three hours, you don't want to waste any time trying to figure out how many minutes you have remaining in a section. The **ACT** proctors will give you a 10-minute and a 5-minute warning. That's helpful, but it's not as much info as you would like to have.

**One really bad option is to rely on the clock in the classroom.** Sure, you COULD use it to figure out that if it is 9:18 am now and the section ends at 9:55am, you have 37 minutes remaining. But when you're frazzled and anxious and racing against the clock do you really want to? **Silent digital watches are a great option to help you keep an eye on the clock, and they are allowed in the test room.**

THE **"BIG RED BOOK"** The Real **ACT** Prep Guide *(or, as we call it, the Big Red Book)* was created by the folks who make the **ACT**.

We recommend it as a great additional resource. It includes five previously administered **ACT**s.

Whether you complete timed sections or sit down for a full-length test at once, the **Big Red Book** is a great resource for additional practice material.

⏱ **Want to improve your ACT timing? Get the Tutor Ted—Test Buddy Watch for ACT.**
Check it out on Amazon.com! It's a timer/watch that shows you how much time has elapsed, how much total time there is in each section, and what question you should be on in order to finish in time. And because it is silent, you can use it during the actual test! Get yours now and use it as you complete timed sections or full-length practice tests during your prep.

## BEFORE THE TEST

**What should you do in the days leading up to the test?** Hopefully you've already completed at least four practice tests and feel confident that you know what to expect on the real exam. The heavy studying should be out of the way by now, but we do recommend you look back at your practice tests from our companion book ("Tutor Ted's **ACT** Practice Tests") to review the problems you've learned how to solve. Remind yourself of the strategies that have worked for you. If you feel like you have to, you could do a timed section or two, but in those last couple of days, focus on reviewing and relaxing!

## WALK IN YOUR OWN SHOES

**A great way to ease your nerves before the test is to visualize what you will do on the actual test day. This might sound silly but it really does help!**

Picture yourself arriving at the test center a little early. You are certain that you have your admission ticket, ID card, pencils, digital watch, and calculator because you packed them the night before. You sign in and find a seat. You take out your pencils and calculator, put your watch on your wrist, and put everything else under your seat. Everyone settles in and the proctor reads the long list of instructions. Later, he/she starts the timer or writes the end time for the first section. You are working at a good pace as you move through each section. You might have a moment of panic here and there, but overall you can feel that the work you put into preparing for the test is paying off now. Before you know it the test is over and you breathe a huge sigh of relief.

**Give this visualization a try!** It can help calm you during the week of the test and boost your performance on test day too.

## THE **ACT** DIET

**What is the magical meal you can eat that will give you a 36 on the test guaranteed?**
Unfortunately, that meal does not exist. However, you can eat in a way that will put you in the best possible performance shape for the test. Here are the rules:

- ✯ Eat a well-balanced dinner the night before the test.
- ✯ Eat a breakfast the morning of the test that includes protein. You need long-term fuel!
- ✯ Don't eat a sugary or heavy breakfast that will make you crash.
- ✯ Bring a snack with you to the test—something healthy and substantial, like a Clif bar. **It's going to be a long morning and you'll want to refuel during your break.**

## GET SOME SLEEP!

**Is this the most obvious advice ever given? Well, maybe...but there is a twist.** You want to get not just ONE good night of sleep before the test but TWO. If you're testing on a Saturday, that means getting good sleep on Thursday night AND Friday night.

**One more piece of sleep advice:** don't try to go to bed at 6:30pm or anything crazy. Go to bed at a time that will let you get eight solid hours of sleep.

## DURING THE TEST

**Remember first that anxiety, while not fun at all, is not your enemy.** That said, you want to have a strategy to calm yourself down if you feel overly anxious. Feel free to use our tip or find another that works for you. *Ready?*

*Slow your roll.*

*Okay, here it is:*
**Put your pencil down. Go on. It's okay. Now close your eyes and visualize your favorite beach.** Here are a few suggestions: Waikiki. Paradise Beach. Bora Bora. Can you picture it? Good. Now, with that image in mind, count to five. Take deep, slow breaths as you listen to sound of the waves crashing, smell the salty air, and dig your toes into the warm, grainy salt. **Feels good, right?** Now open your eyes, pick up your pencil, and keep plugging along. Repeat as necessary.

## WHAT TO DO WHEN YOU'RE STUCK

**Here is a great way to get un-stuck:**
- ✔ Write down all of the given information in a math problem.
- ✔ Refer back to the passage even if you think you remember something.
- ✔ Glance back at the introduction to a Science passage to see if you missed anything.
- ✔ Remember that the right answer to the question is in front of you.

If, after a minute goes by, you still can't solve it, follow the next step:

**YOU GOTTA KNOW WHEN TO FOLD 'EM**
**The ACT is a weird, fast test.** Tests in school usually provide you enough time to think your way through a tricky question. On the **ACT**, you have to pick your battles and move on quickly.

**Don't spend 2-3 minutes on a hard question—even if you get it right, it may cost you the time you need to answer several easier questions at the end of the section**. When you feel like you can't find the right answer, try to eliminate answer choices and make a good guess. **Circle the question number in your test booklet and return to it if you have time at the end of the section.**

## WHEREVER YOU GO, THERE YOU ARE

**Keep this in mind: you can only answer one question at a time.** That means that it is not beneficial to stress about a question that came before or one that will come next. Focus on the question that you're on and remember: you are allowed to make mistakes. **Your job is to do your best, not to be perfect.**

## TAKE A BREAK

**The Gods of the ACT, in a rare act of kindness, have granted you a 10-minute break between the Math and the Reading Tests.** How should you spend your 10 minutes? Use this time to refuel. Eat that snack bar or sandwich you brought with you. Walk around a bit. Get some water. Use the bathroom. Just get up and move around a bit—you want to get your blood flowing.

**Oh, and stay away from the people who are obsessively discussing the first two sections.** There will be plenty of time to talk about the test later.

Clear your mind so you can come back to the test focused and calm.

## AFTER THE TEST

*Patience, grasshopper.*

**One funny thing about the ACT is that the scores don't all come back at the same time.** Sometimes our students receive their scores within two weeks of the test date. Other times, it takes more than six weeks for them to come back. During the two to six week wait, it's your job to chill and not think about the **ACT**. You've already done your part.

## IF AT FIRST YOU DON'T SUCCEED…

**…try, try again! One of the best things about this test is that you can take it multiple times.** People typically do better on something when they've done it once before. The experience of taking the test the first time, spending time doing some additional practice work, focusing on your schoolwork to get even smarter than you were—these factors will most likely lead you to a higher score on your second attempt at the **ACT**.

**If you didn't reach your target score by the spring of junior year, we highly recommend re-testing in the fall of your senior year.** 90% of our students earn their highest score in the fall of senior year. Join that group by taking the **ACT** at that time.

**How many times can you re-test?** College admissions officers we have spoken to say that seeing three or fewer test dates on a student's record is totally normal. Four or more test scores starts to look fishy. Here's the thing: you don't really want to take the **ACT** more than three times. If you do the prep—you work through this book and take at least four practice tests from the **ACT** website and our companion book—you won't need more than three shots at the test.

## UNHAPPY WITH YOUR SCORE? **DELETE IT!**

**We've got a little secret to share... there is a way to take as many ACTs as you like and only have your best test score appear on the record.** *Ready?*
**ACT** allows you to delete any of your test scores.

**They don't advertise this widely, but they tell you clearly how you can do it on this web page:**
http://www.actstudent.org/faq/delete.html

**This is pretty amazing, right?** You can take an **ACT**, get your score back, and then decide at any point that you'd like to delete it. When you do, your score goes away...

*poof, like magic!*

**Even with this option available, we still recommend you take the test a maximum of three times.** Plan ahead and do the prep and you'll get the score you want in one of those three sittings. It is nice to know that you can get rid of any scores you don't like, though, isn't it?

## MIXED RESULTS? **SUPERSCORE!**

**Many colleges now superscore the ACT.** That means that they will cherry-pick your highest section scores from multiple test dates and consider you based on those highest scores.

**Here's an example:**

| FIRST TEST | SECOND TEST | SUPERSCORE |
|---|---|---|
| English: 33 | English: 28 | English: 33 |
| Math: 27 | Math: 30 | Math: 30 |
| Reading: 29 | Reading: 30 | Reading: 30 |
| Science: 27 | Science: 29 | Science: 29 |
| *Composite: 29* | *Composite: 29* | *Composite: 31* |

*This student got a 29 on both his first and second test... but his superscore is a 31!*

*Now THAT is magic.*

To find out whether the schools you are applying to look at **ACT** superscores, search the web for **"Which colleges superscore the ACT?"** The list of schools that do is growing every year.

## OFFICIAL STUFF

**Sign up for the actual exam at actstudent.org.**

That's also where you'll go to check your scores and send score reports to colleges.

For more **ACT** info from **Tutor Ted** as well as information about our online and in-person **ACT** tutoring, visit **tutorted.com**.

For printable answer sheets to use when you complete practice tests or sections, visit **tutorted.com/resources.**

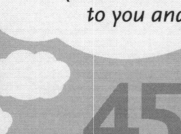

**0.6 minutes per question**
*(that's 36 seconds
to you and me)*

**1**_punctuation

**?**

**2**_grammar
& usage

# HOW MANY?
**45** minutes
**75** questions
**5** passages
**15** questions each

**3**_sentence structure

## USAGE/MECHANICS
**40** questions

## RHETORICAL SKILLS
**35** questions

**4**_strategy

# ENGLISH

**The Breakdown**

## 6 THINGS TO THINK about...

> punctuation
> grammar & usage
> sentence structure
> strategy
> organization
> style

5_organization

**6**_style

### Do...
know the essential **RULES OF GRAMMAR.**

### Don't... overthink it.
The right answer to each of these questions is **correct** in an absolute, **BLACK**-&-**WHITE** way.

NOTES:

## The ACT English Test might seem intimidating: 75 questions to answer in just 45 minutes.

As it turns out, this is the easiest section to improve your score. Why? Because it tests the same dang stuff over and over again.

We will teach you stuff like the difference between **"it's"** and **"its,"** the proper use of a semicolon, and how to answer questions about the content of the passage. Once you know that stuff, guess what? It never changes. The rules of grammar are constant. When they become second nature to you, you'll be able to answer 70+ questions right out of 75 right without breaking a sweat. Oh, and you'll become a better writer as a result.

## The English Test asks two types of questions:

### ✎ Usage / Mechanics (40 questions)
These questions test your technical know-how—stuff like punctuation, grammar, and sentence structure. Because these questions are based on fixed rules, you can learn literally all of this stuff. Once you do, you can reduce the likelihood of making an error to nearly zero.

### ✎ Rhetorical Skills (35 questions)
These guys ask you to think about how well an essay communicated what it was trying to communicate. You'll answer questions about how the essay should be organized, whether it accomplished a certain goal, and whether the author should make revisions. We have very specific ways of approaching these questions that can lead you to the right answer quickly and reliably.

**This section of the book is separated into two big chapters based on those two types of questions.**

*Turn the page, and let's get going with some Usage & Mechanics!*

# Independent and Dependent Clauses

**Let's start with a simple question: how do you make a sentence?**

*and, arguably, a very dumb question...*

A sentence needs a subject and a verb, and it needs to express a complete thought. The phrase, **"I grilled a big fat piece of tofu,"** is a sentence because it's got a subject *("I")*, a verb *("grilled")*, and it expresses a complete thought. On the other hand, the phrase, **"because my girlfriend is a vegetarian,"** is not a sentence, because it doesn't express a complete thought.

**Now, let's get a little more technical.**

## INDEPENDENT AND DEPENDENT CLAUSES

**An independent clause** is a clause *(a group of words with a subject and verb)* that can stand alone as a sentence.

 **Here are some examples of independent clauses:**

I never learned to read.
Smoking kills.
Sarah went to the market to stock up on Vitamin C.
My math teacher is a CIA operative.

**A dependent clause** is what you might expect:
a clause that expresses an incomplete thought and therefore cannot stand alone as a sentence.

 **Check out the examples below:**

Whether you're riding in a car or talking on the phone
If you find a letter in the mailbox today
Because George felt bad about hurting Malia's feelings
Before we start today's lesson

Those dependent clauses can't stand on their own, but that doesn't mean they can't be part of a sentence.

Here are some of the ways you can combine clauses to create what's called **a complex sentence.**

## DEPENDENT CLAUSE + COMMA + INDEPENDENT CLAUSE

**When you start a sentence with a dependent clause, you have to put a comma after it before you get to the independent clause. Just like I just did!** That was accidental...but let's pretend it was a really, really good teaching moment instead.

1

Before we start today's lesson, I must tell you about the hilarious thing I found in my bed this morning.

If you find a letter in the mailbox today, don't open it under any circumstances.

## INDEPENDENT CLAUSE + DEPENDENT CLAUSE

**We don't have to use a comma when we put the independent clause first and follow it with the dependent clause.** This is really good training not just for your **ACT** test but also for your own writing.

2

I'd like to tell you a joke before we get started today.

Tony ran to the store because he desperately needed supplies to build his diorama.

## INDEPENDENT CLAUSE + SEMICOLON + INDEPENDENT CLAUSE

**This is a funky little way of combining two independent clauses.** The semicolon functions exactly the way that a period does. Some people say **"then why don't you just use a period?"** Those people actually have a point. **Kurt Vonnegut** said that the only thing semicolons do is prove you went to college. The grammar snobs among us would say that a semicolon separates two closely related ideas—so closely related that we don't want to break them apart with a period.

3

Some people find the pop song catchy; others say that it's mushy and annoying.

*Take that, Vonnegut.*

## INDEPENDENT CLAUSE + COMMA + COORDINATING CONJUNCTION + INDEPENDENT CLAUSE

4

**The coordinating conjunctions are these seven words: For, And, Nor, But, Or, Yet, So.** The easiest way to remember them is **the acronym "FANBOYS."**

**We're getting just a little bit technical here.** Believe me when I say that we try to keep our grammar prep as non-technical as possible. If we ever do introduce a technical term, it's because it's actually really helpful to know it. *So, there you go.*

*Are you asking yourself now what the **** is a coordinating conjunction? If so... good question!*

The student council attempted to set a World Record for the **"largest ice cream sundae,"** but the attempt just resulted in a sticky mess and a huge grocery bill.

**Here is one way that you CANNOT build a sentence.** *Ready for this?*

My dad says that this rash is not contagious, he's a doctor so he should know.

**That's called a comma splice,** which is two independent clauses separated by just a comma can't do that. **Don't do that.**

OKAY. See if you can
# fix the punctuation
of these sentences.

## EXERCISE

**Instructions:** Insert commas, semicolons, and/or conjunctions to fix the following sentences. **Warning:** some sentences may be correct as written. On this and all other exercise pages, you'll find the right answers in the Answers & Solutions chapter at the end of the English section.

1. The game was over, but the crowd refused to leave.

2. While I was making dinner, my dog started barking outside.

3. The band played for three hours and never took a set break.

4. If you are sick, you shouldn't ride the subway.

5. He followed the team for fifty years; it hardly mattered whether the team won or lost.

6. It isn't easy being tall, but it's even harder to be short.

7. Maria is my only sister; she is dutiful and decent.

8. Because Lana was so difficult to work with, the studio decided to hire another actress.

9. This Twitter feed doesn't make any sense; it reads like it is written by a computer.

10. The city could no longer call on Batman when local criminals began to cause problems.

11. To get a ticket, you'd better buy online.

12. The famous designer decided that the town needed something really grand at its center; he proposed a rose garden flanked by cascading waterfalls.

# COMMA RULES

The **ACT** is crazy for comma questions. If comma questions were chocolates, the **ACT** would open a candy store. If commas were llamas, the **ACT** could open a petting zoo. If commas were... well, you get it.

*or should I say commas rule!!*

**The most basic rule when it comes to commas on the ACT is this: get rid of as many commas as possible.** That said, there are times when we need to use a comma. Here are **the four main rules for comma usage** on the **ACT**.

## USE A COMMA AND A COORDINATING CONJUNCTION (FANBOYS) WHEN LINKING TWO INDEPENDENT CLAUSES. 1

This is one of the ways we built a sentence in the last section. You just insert a comma and a coordinating conjunction to link two independent clauses.

🔍 **Check 'em out:**

Maria went to the market to buy groceries, but she forgot to bring her shopping list.

Professor Thompson loved the idea of teaching English full time, so he begged the president of the university to give him a chance to prove himself.

Noami Foner wrote the screenplay to *Losing Isaiah* and *Running on Empty*, but her son, Jake Gyllenhaal, is far more well known.

## USE A COMMA WHEN A SENTENCE STARTS WITH A DEPENDENT CLAUSE FOLLOWED BY AN INDEPENDENT CLAUSE. 2

Normal people start their sentences with an independent clause and follow it with a dependent clause.

🔍 **Like this:**

I jogged to work because my car had broken down.

Creative, eccentric, and/or unstable people reverse the order and put the dependent clause first. When they do so, they have to include a comma after the dependent clause.

Because my car had broken down, I jogged to work.

Although I am a pretty fast runner, I was still 10 minutes late to the morning meeting.

**Instructions:** Insert commas where they are needed in the following sentences.

*Try these out, play-ya!*

**1.** While the Senator made his speech on Capitol Hill, the activists organized outside.

**2.** After succumbing to pressure from animal rights activists, the amusement park agreed not to keep Orca whales in captivity.

**3.** If the chef finds even the smallest objection to the dish, he will send it back to the kitchen in anger.

# 3  USE COMMAS TO SEPARATE EITHER ITEMS IN A LIST OR MULTIPLE ADJECTIVES THAT EACH DESCRIBE THE SAME SUBJECT.

As you probably know, commas are handy for separating items in a list.

### For example, this sentence...

"The doctor recommended plenty of rest some crackers and soda and a warm bath."

**...is in desperate need of some commas, right?** One after rest, and one after soda? You also use commas to separate multiple adjectives that describe something separately from each other. For example, **"a dusty heavy book"** should be **"a dusty, heavy book,"** because those two adjectives each describe the book.

*Can we take a quick pause to look at the word "comma" and agree on how weird it is?*

**There is a case when you do not use a comma to separate multiple adjectives that describe a noun :** when one of the adjectives is so connected to the noun that together they become a unit.

### An example of that:

**"the organic grocery store."** You don't need a comma between **"organic"** and **"grocery"** because **"grocery"** and **"store"** together are a single thing: **a grocery store.**

A trick to decide whether you need a comma between adjectives is to ask yourself if you would include the word **"and"** between them. If the answer is yes (**"a dusty and heavy book"**), then include the comma; if the answer is no (**"the organic and grocery store"**), then you don't need a comma.

*Comma. Comma. Comma.*

*Super weird.*

**Instructions:** Insert commas where they are needed in the following sentences.

**1.** I picked up grapefruit juice, salt, and soda from the local grocery store.

**2.** I never had a mom, a dad, a dog, a friend, or a good night's sleep.

**3.** When I looked into her eyes, I saw a wild, angry animal.

**4.** To think clearly, to feel deeply, to love constantly: these are the objectives of an evolved human being.

**5.** My silent, happy sister simply nodded her head in amazement.

## USE COMMAS TO BRACKET OFF **"UNNECESSARY INFORMATION."** 4

By **"unnecessary information,"** we mean clauses (or words) that could be removed from the sentence without destroying the main idea of the sentence.

🔍 **Take a look at this sentence:**

"The Statue of Liberty, which sits in New York Harbor, is a cherished symbol of freedom."

The phrase **"which sits in New York Harbor"** is inessential in that sentence because it could be taken out without disrupting the functional parts of the sentence: **"The Statue of Liberty is a cherished symbol of freedom."**

I KNOW I promised not to get too technical... but I can't help myself here. **Inessential phrases like these are called "appositive phrases." FYI.**

*You will blow your teachers' (and professors') minds if you start using commas correctly.*

**Instructions:** Use a pair of commas to bracket off these types of clauses or words.

1. My cousin Jared, who I had never met until I was an adult, plays soccer for the L.A. Galaxy.

2. I took a trip to New Orleans, the birthplace of jazz, to celebrate my graduation from music school.

3. Irving's novel, which took him twelve years to write, suffers from its long, poetic passages.

Those are the **four major ways** that commas are used. **If one of these four situations DOES NOT APPLY** to a sentence on the **ACT, get rid of those commas!**

*Keep this phrase in mind regarding commas:*

## "When in doubt, take it out!"

# Semicolons, Colons, and Dashes

## 1 THE SEMICOLON

Like we mentioned in the first section, **the semicolon (;) functions just like a period:** you have to have an independent clause *(aka a complete sentence)* on either side. The only difference is that **the two clauses on either side of the semicolon are more closely related than the sentences on either side of a period.**

**Here are some examples of semicolons at work:**

Sarah lost a lot of money in Las Vegas this weekend; it's an easy thing to do.

The first time I fell into the pool it was funny; the second time it was embarrassing.

Carl Pumphrey was an honorable man; nevertheless, he occasionally told a white lie if it happened to suit his purposes.

> 🔥 **HOT TIP**
> You will frequently see **semicolons before clauses that begin with** words such as **"however," "moreover," "nevertheless," "thus," "therefore,"** etc.

🔎 **For example, take the sentence:**
Jethro really wanted a double chili cheeseburger; however, he ordered a sensible salad.

🔎 **If you wanted to, you could also write that as:**
Jethro really wanted a double chili cheeseburger. However, he ordered a sensible salad.

*Don't do it!*  **What you CANNOT do is this:**
Jethro really wanted a double chili cheeseburger, however, he ordered a sensible salad.

**The last one is that comma splice thing: two separate sentences separated with just a comma.**

**Here's one other way we use the word, "however"** and its cousins, like **"thus"** and **"therefore."**

🔎 **First, look at this sample sentence:**
Mr. Neilson, who is my college counselor, has advised me to look at Engineering programs.

Just as **"who is my college counselor"** is simply an appositive clause within an independent clause, words like **"however"** can also be used between commas when they are unnecessary and removable within a sentence.

The reality, however, was much different.
The election results, therefore, were deemed invalid.

**When you use words like "however" and "therefore" as removable, appositive-like phrases in the sentence, you need a comma on both sides.**

## THE COLON

2

The colon is an essential part of your digestive system. It is also a piece of punctuation. It always has to follow an independent clause, and it **can be used in two different ways**.

 **The first is to introduce a list.**

The students were asked to bring only three things on the camping trip: a flashlight, a change of clothes, and a pocketknife.

Here's what you need to do in order to impress your boss: show up early, dress nicely, and speak your mind.

**A colon can also be used to extend, illustrate, or amplify an idea from the beginning of a sentence.**

 **Like so:**

Samantha knew there was only one way to defeat the beast: punch it in its eye.

The magazine followed one simple rule: Mock all people and cultures equally and relentlessly.

Keep in mind that the phrase that comes after the colon here can be an **independent clause** or **a dependent one**. The rules for using the colon aren't as strict as those of the semicolon.

## THE DASH

3

**The dash can be used in a number of ways,** but on the **ACT**, dashes **are usually used to set off "inessential" information** in a sentence (*just like commas!*).

Jared spent time on Oahu—the most populous of the Hawaiian Islands—before deciding to move back to Montana.

**We call the information between the two dashes "inessential" because if we removed it, the sentence would still express a complete thought.**

**Dashes can also be used to express a sudden change in tone or thought within a sentence.**

I hope we can stay in Philadelphia for a little longer—or never leave at all!

And that is sentence punctuation, y'all.

# Apostrophes/Possessives

## APOSTROPHES

**Of course you know that apostrophes can be used to form contractions** like **"don't,"** or **"can't."** In this case, the apostrophe replaces the missing letter
*(the words **"do not"** become **"don't"** when the second **"o"** is replaced with an apostrophe).*

**You may also know that apostrophes can also be used to show possession.**

If Charlie owns a hat, **you can say that it's Charlie's hat.** If Lisa owns a scarf, then **that's Lisa's scarf.** If Lisa thinks that she's the rightful owner of Charlie's hat, then Charlie might say that **that's Lisa's problem.**

And people aren't the only ones that can possess other things.

⊕ **For instance, you can say**
"**the painting's brilliant colors**" or the "**fire's warm glow,**" or the "**day's end.**"

**But what if you have a subject that's already plural?** What if there are two boys that own hats? In that case you start with the plural noun *(boys)*, and add an apostrophe at the end of the word *(boys')*. You don't need to bother adding another **"s."** You simply write the **"boys' hats."**

### It's a Special Occasion: IT'S vs. ITS

The difference between these two can trip some folks up because it's an exception to the rules laid out above.

**Here are the goods:**
It's  = "it is," -or- "it has"
Its  = possessive form of "it"

**Got it?** So if you want to say,
"It is a good idea to invest in the stock market,"
**you would say**
"it's a good idea."
**If, on the other hand, you wanted to say**
"how much you loved a painting's beautiful colors",
**you would say,**
"I sure do love its beautiful colors."

*It hurts my eyes to look at it. Let's move on.* On the **ACT**, you will sometimes see this: **its'** That is not a word. Not ever.

**Instructions:** Choose between "it's" and "its" in the following sentences.

1. _It's_ time to go home.

2. This house has _its_ own power plant.

3. _It's_ a good idea to wear a shirt if you go to the opera.

4. Do you think _it's_ ready?

5. I saw the play during _its_ initial run.

6. _It's_ been a long, hot summer.

# THEIR, THERE, AND THEY'RE; YOU'RE AND YOUR; WHO, WHOM, WHO'S, AND WHOSE

Here are a few more words that can trip folks up. Let's break these down:

**THEY'RE** = **"they are"**—it's a conjunction
**THERE** = a place or position *(over there)*
**THEIR** = the possessive form of **"they"**

**YOU'RE** = **"you are"**
**YOUR** = the possessive form of **"you"**

**WHO** = a pronoun that represents a person who is the subject of a clause, i.e. **"who wrote the letter."**

**WHOM** = a pronoun that represents a person who is the object of a clause, i.e. **"the letter was addressed to whom."**

**WHO'S** = **"who is"**–or– **"who has"**

**WHOSE** = the possessive form of **"who"**

**Instructions:** Pick a word to correctly complete these sentenes. In some cases, more than one answer may work.

1. I wonder who _they're_ talking to.

2. _Whose_ sweatshirt is that?

3. _Your_ cat is pregnant again.

4. _You're_ going to need stitches on _your_ forehead.

5. We are going to _their_ house next time.

6. Do you have any idea _who_ my father is?

7. _Who's_ coming over for lunch.

8. To _whom_ are you referring?

9. Have you seen _their_ new Buick?

10. _Who's_ invited to the party?

29

# Subject-Verb Agreement

This is the basic building block of English: every sentence needs a subject and a verb, and the verb has to match the subject.

DUH.  **For example:**
"**We is hungry**" is wrong, and "**We are hungry**" is correct.

**Here's the harder version: which of these is correct?**
"Research into cosmic rays use the surface of the moon as a detector."
"Research into cosmic rays uses the surface of the moon as a detector."

**This is a classic subject-verb agreement trick. What's the subject of that sentence?** It's the first word of the sentence, "**research.**" All that stuff that comes after "**research**" serves as an adjective—that is, it describes "**research**"—but it doesn't change the fact that "**research**" is the subject. That's why the subject and verb should be "**research uses.**"

**Here's another trick when it comes to subject-verb agreement:** Certain sneaky words *(called collective nouns)* represent groups but function as singular nouns. Words like **team, family, gang, swarm, and bunch** fit this category.

 **Here's a sample:**
A bunch of bananas is sitting on the hood of my car.

That sentence is puzzling in a number of ways, but grammatically it is sound. That bunch of bananas operates as ONE thing, so the singular verb "**is**" is correct.

**One more trick: Certain pronouns are always singular.** "Each," "every," and "any" are pronouns that are referring to one item within a group. If you see one of those words, then that subject is singular.

 **Example:**
Each of the men was too terrified to enter the dance circle.

This sentence might sound strange because the plural "**men**" is right next to the singular verb "**was.**" Since we're talking about "**each**" of the men, the singular verb is actually correct.

**Keep in mind that some subjects are compound subjects.** When two or more singular subjects are added together using the word "**and,**" they become a plural subject.

 **For example:**
Andy and Shannon
Benny and the Jets
George, Bill, and Roger

# EXERCISE

**Instructions:** Underline the subject and circle the form of the verb that agrees with it.

1. Anne and her family (**live**, **lives**) in that house.

2. The siding on the houses (**has**, **have**) been painted purple.

3. The basketball team (**hope**, **hopes**) to earn a trip to the playoffs this year.

4. Each of the songs on his record (**is**, **are**) an instant party-starter.

5. Economics (**was**, **were**) his declared major when he entered college.

6. The committee investigating differences in economic equality between racial and ethnic groups (**is**, **are**) organized by the state university.

# Verb Tense

**Verbs have to match their subjects.** The other thing they do is express a sense of timing. We call that **"tense."**

**For example, we might say:**
"Thomas Jefferson WROTE The Declaration of Independence in 1776."

or

"Yesterday, I ATE a sandwich."

or

"I currently AM EATING another, even more delicious sandwich."

or

"Tomorrow, I WILL EAT the greatest sandwich ever made by human hands."

**Whenever the ACT wants to test you on verb tense, they have to give you some sort of sense of timing.** That could be a date, or another verb in the sentence that's in a certain tense.

**Check it out:**
"Since 1965, the percentage of non-European immigrants to the United States HAS GROWN steadily."

"Candy bars HAVE BEEN ENJOYED by millions ever since Joseph Fry introduced the first 'bar chocolate' to the world in 1847."

"By the time Marcel arrived, we HAD BEEN WAITING for over three hours."

Don't get tensed up!

# EXERCISE

**Instructions:** Pick the version of the verb that supplies the appropriate tense.

||||||||||||||||||||||||||||||||||||||||||||||||||||||||||||||||||||||||||||||||||||||||||||||||||||||||||||||||||||||||||||||||||

1. By next Tuesday, I <u>wrote</u> the entire essay.
   A. NO CHANGE
   B. have written
   C. will have written
   D. had written

2. Protozoa <u>are</u> single cell microorganisms.
   F. NO CHANGE
   G. were
   H. have been
   J. will have been

3. I toured Romania for six straight years after I <u>become</u> a pop star there.
   A. NO CHANGE
   B. have become
   C. will have become
   D. became

4. The musicians rehearsed long into the night, only realizing that they <u>had been playing</u> for three straight hours when they looked at the clock.
   F. NO CHANGE
   G. play
   H. has played
   J. will play

5. Although Martin once <u>has been</u> a staunch advocate of the death penalty, years of experience as a public defender have made him reconsider its efficacy and fairness.
   A. NO CHANGE
   B. is
   C. would have been
   D. was

6. When we finally get flying cars, it <u>will be</u> pretty sweet.
   F. NO CHANGE
   G. is
   H. was
   J. would be

# Pronouns

Pronouns are stand-ins for nouns: he, she, it, they, etc. That way, instead of always having to say, "that handsome devil of a man, Tutor Ted," we can just say, "him."

### Here is how they can get screwed up:
**Unclear reference:** pronouns always have an antecedent, the noun that they stand in for. If it's not clear which noun a pronoun represents, you got a problem, bub.

> ### Here's an example:
> The debt crisis created controversy in both Greece and Germany because it had not anticipated a downturn in economic growth.

**What does "it" refer to in that sentence?** We don't know! That's a problem. In that sentence, we'd have to restate the country we're talking about because the pronoun doesn't refer clearly to one country.

### Pronoun Agreement:
If you've got a singular subject, it has to have a singular pronoun *(like "it")*, and if you have a plural subject you have to have a plural pronoun *(like "they")*.

The easiest quiz in the history of the world: tell me if the following nouns are plural or singular.

1. Zebras

2. My cat T.K.

3. The Crab Nebula          *Hey, good job.*

Pronoun agreement gets tricky when it comes to certain types of words, like collective nouns. As we mentioned in the section on subject-verb agreement, collective nouns are words that describe a group but function as a singular noun, like **"team"** or **"family."** You have to be careful with these because they seem plural but function like singular nouns.

> ### Example:
> The company insisted that they had no knowledge of the purported price fixing.

The pronoun **"they"** is incorrect there. It wants to refer to the **"company,"** which is made up of a bunch of people but functions like a singular thing. Instead of **"they"** you need to use **"it."**

# EXERCISE

**Instructions:** Underline the antecedent for each pronoun then circle the pronoun that agrees with it.

1. <u>Fans</u> of the winning team showed (its/**their**) pride in a ticker tape parade down Main Street.

2. Some social conservatives argue that the traditional family <u>model</u>, and (**it**/they) alone, provides children with the best chance for future success.

3. While the debut <u>album</u> from the <u>band</u> was largely panned, (**its**/their) sophomore album has been touted as one of the best punk records in decades.

4. Colin's <u>collection</u> of meteorites was sought after by astronomers who thought (**it**/they) could be put to better use in a laboratory.

5. The Coachella concert goers rushed the stage as Jay-Z emerged from the shadows; (**it**/they) would be a good <u>night</u>.

6. The <u>city</u> had a reputation for exceptional hospitality that was put to test when (**it**/they) hosted football's Super Bowl in 2013.

# Object Pronouns

One more pronoun issue to tackle: subject and object pronouns.

**Which of these is correct:**
"Me am happy" or "I am happy"?

OK good, you know the difference between subject and object pronouns.

**Here is a list of both:**
**Subject: I, he/she, we, they, who**
**Object:  me, him/her, us, them, whom**

We pick which one to use based on whether the pronoun is the subject of the verb *(the thing that's doing something)* or is the object of the verb *(the thing that's receiving the action)*.

**For Example:**
I do things, but things happen to me.

**These can get tricky when pronouns are compounded.**
When you were young, your mom and dad would often correct you for saying

"Brian and me." But "Brian and me" is not always wrong.

**Here's an example of that:**
The sudden increase in business for our lemonade stand came as a surprise to Brian and me.

**Your instinct might be to change that "me" to "I," but "me" is actually correct here.** One easy way to determine that is to take Brian out of the sentence and then ask yourself how you should write it. Did it come as a surprise to me, or did it come as a surprise to I? **"Me"** sounds a lot better in that version, and that's because **"me"** is the right pronoun.

So when you're in doubt about
a subject or object pronoun,
make your decision based on
**how the sentence sounds**
when you remove the other noun.

# EXERCISE

**Instructions:** Pick which pronoun is the correct one to use in the following sentences.

1. They told the children that (**he**/**him**) is on a long vacation rather than in prison.

2. To Jeff and (**I**/**me**), the news came as a surprise.

3. The committee finally agreed that the prize should be awarded to both (**we**/**us**) and (**they**/**them**).

4. They gave the new blueprints to the development office and (**we**/**us**).

5. Written by (**he**/**him**) and (**I**/**me**), the new pamphlet is sure to revolutionize the world of 21$^{st}$ century pamphlets.

6. In the event of an evacuation, (**who**/**whom**) should I contact first?

7. For (**us**/**we**) teachers, the new world of education technology is both exciting and overwhelming.

8. You have to choose between Susie and (**I**/**me**).

# EXERCISE

**Instructions:** Punctuate these sentences using commas, semicolons, colons or dashes as necessary.

1. The greatest resolution, 100 meters, is found in the upper left portion of the image.

2. When I speak of modern sculpture, I do not refer to every sculptor of our age.

3. Maybe that is so; I couldn't say.

4. The saleswoman started by describing the best television, so I quickly interrupted her to say she should begin with the cheapest offer.

5. It looked like an ordinary pot: squat and light brown with a small amount of blue glaze as trim.

6. In all fairness, I have to admit that Jesse, or someone calling himself Jesse, has done a wonderful job with the building's interior.

7. I was no longer unwilling to go north; on the contrary, the proposed journey excited me.

8. Whenever a new scholar came to our school, I used to confront him at recess to find out as much as I could about him.

9. The horse's name was Triste, which is Spanish for "sadness", so I called her Sadie.

10. Though the experts called themselves "doctors", only one of them had ever gone to medical school.

11. For example, should a product be in excess production, its price in the market would fall, providing incentive for the public to purchase it, thus reducing the value of the stock.

12. Early in the morning, before the orphans awake, Charlize plans the day's activities.

13. Mrs. Endman wore too much make-up; women always put on too much make-up when someone dies.

14. Humors theory was first developed by the Greek physician Hippocrates, the founder of western medicine, and later expanded upon by Galen.

15. When Grandpa first decided to fly, his dream had been to fly planes; he desperately wanted to be on the front line of the air defense.

16. I'm interested in a career in nursing; I decided to try to secure a spot as a volunteer at a hospital

17. I took golf lessons for several years but never improved very much.

18. Dr. Stone wasn't insane; he was a healer.

19. Venus's atmosphere contains higher concentrations of inert or "noble" gases, especially gases like neon and argan.

20. The Army provided tents, showers, mess halls, and latrines and, waiving the age restriction, invited members as young as seventeen years old to join.

**Tutor Ted.**

NOTES:

# Rhetorical Skills

This is Part II of the English test—the section that pertains to the **"Rhetorical Skills"** questions. These questions *(35 of them scattered throughout the test)* ask you to think about how well the author communicated what he/she intended to communicate.

You'll have to assess the logical relationships between sentences or paragraphs, or decide if a particular sentence is relevant, or select a good sentence to conclude a passage, among other things. We've got exercises and strategies for tackling these questions, so let's stop wasting time and get right to it!

The first *(and easiest)* tip is that **when it comes to style,** the **ACT** prefers fewer words. In other words, **shorter is better!** When you're choosing between three longer answer choices and one that only consists of one word, you can bet that it's probably going to be the one word answer.

### Take a look at this, for example:

1.  The Kennedy Center works all over the globe to eradicate <u>poverty</u>.
    A.  NO CHANGE
    B.  poverty around the world.
    C.  poverty both at home and abroad.
    D.  poverty at an international level.

**Notice that all of the answer choices are grammatically fine.** That means that the grammar is not the problem. The right answer here is (**A**), and here's why: the sentence says that **the Kennedy Center works "all over the globe."** If you say that, you sure don't need to say **"around the world,"** or any of the other choices. **The shorter, one word version is the correct one.**

*Is there an easier strategy to use than "shorter is better"?*

# EXERCISE: SHORTER IS BETTER!

**INSTRUCTIONS:** Choose the most concise version from within each set of answers.

1. As I looked at all the unfamiliar maps and graphs, I felt very <u>confused.</u>
   **A.** NO CHANGE
   **B.** confused and uncertain.
   **C.** confused without clear understanding.
   **D.** confused like my mind couldn't make sense of anything.

2. <u>I cannot explain</u> the mysteries of the Ouiji board.
   **F.** NO CHANGE
   **G.** cannot explain or fully articulate
   **H.** cannot explain or describe in any detail
   **J.** cannot explain and also cannot describe

3. That summer proved to be very <u>memorable.</u>
   **A.** NO CHANGE
   **B.** memorable and difficult to forget.
   **C.** memorable as some things can be.
   **D.** memorable and unforgettable.

4. When I went to Chicago after graduating high school, I didn't consider myself a <u>skilled rider of underground trains.</u>
   **F.** NO CHANGE
   **G.** person who knew everything there was to know about underground trains.
   **H.** master of the art of traveling by public transportation.
   **J.** veteran subway rider.

5. Though the car is energy-efficient, it can only travel the very <u>shortest distances.</u>
   **A.** NO CHANGE
   **B.** distances that are shortest in length.
   **C.** shortest and least long distances.
   **D.** smallest distances in length.

*If you went through those questions and just picked the shortest one by sight...*

*I respect that. You got them all right.*

# Sentence Logic

A number of questions in the **ACT** English section test your ability to decipher the relationship between two consecutive thoughts or clauses.

**For instance:**

1.  Kenneth is academically unqualified for the job at the university; _____, he has exhibited a terrible attitude towards the other professors and staff.
    A.  moreover
    B.  however
    C.  therefore
    D.  even so

**On these questions, you need to think about what the author says in each part of the sentence and how those ideas relate to each other.** In the first part of this sample sentence, we learn that Kenneth is unqualified. In the second, we learn that he also has a bad attitude. These two things obviously do not reflect terribly well on Kenneth. Not only that, those two thoughts are related to each other—they each make the point that Kenneth probably should be fired.

The word **"moreover"** *(which means the same as **"furthermore"**)* is the right choice to link those two ideas together.

The most important thing you'll need to know in order to get these questions right **is the definition of the words and phrases** they're going to give you as answer choices. The good news is that a lot of these words mean basically the same thing, and can be put into the same category.

## HERE IS A SELECTION OF THE MOST COMMON WORDS, LINKED BY COMMON MEANING:

- ✎ Moreover – Furthermore – Additionally – Likewise
- ✎ For example – For instance – In fact
- ✎ Nevertheless – Even so – In spite of – Nonetheless – However – Though – Otherwise
- ✎ Therefore – Consequently – Because of – Thus – As a result
- ✎ Subsequently – Ultimately – Finally – Eventually

### ✎ Moreover – Furthermore – Additionally – Likewise

These all have to do with addition or continuation.

> Kenneth is academically unqualified for the job at the university; moreover, he has exhibited a terrible attitude towards the other professors on staff

### ✎ For example – For instance – In fact

Use these when the clause or sentence that follows provides specific evidence to justify the claim that came just before it.

> Turtles have long lifespans; in fact, they can live longer than one hundred and ninety years.

### ✎ Nevertheless – Even so – In spite of – Nonetheless – However – Though – Otherwise

Other words show a negative relationship between the ideas of a sentence—in other words, the ideas in the sentence work in different or surprising ways from each other.

> His visit was unexpected; nevertheless, I was pleased to see him.

> I could see that the professor was doing his best to explain the theory to me; however, I continued to find the idea utterly baffling.

> My grandfather's comment angered me; even so, I decided to respond calmly.

### ✎ Therefore – Consequently – Because of – Thus – As a result

Some sentences have a cause and effect relationship, meaning that the second thing happens because of the first thing. These are the words you would use to imply that kind of relationship.

> I think, therefore I am.

> There has been a great deal of rain this season; as a result, the reservoirs are full.

> The American public loves a lowbrow summer comedy; thus, American Pie 8 has done big business at the box-office.

### ✎ Subsequently – Ultimately – Finally – Eventually

Lastly, there are words that connect two ideas or events that happen before and after one another. These words signify a temporal relationship **("temporal" means "related to time")**.

> The monkeys were the first to climb aboard the ark, then the lions and tigers, and, finally the goats; eventually, all the animals found their way onto Noah's ship.

---

### 🔥 HOT TIP

If you see two words among the answer choices that both signify the same type of relationship between the two clauses *(for example **"furthermore"** and **"moreover"**)*, you can get rid of them because they are both wrong. If they mean the exact same thing, then neither one of them can be the one right answer.

# EXERCISE: SENTENCE LOGIC

**INSTRUCTIONS:** Pick the best word(s) to link the ideas of the sentence(s) together.

1. Every day thereafter, I would spend the morning with my three comrades; _____, we'd go our separate ways for the rest of the day.
   A. since
   B. so
   C. then
   D. therefore

2. _____ our dogs are dependent on us, traveling is not an option.
   F. Because
   G. In spite of the fact that
   H. So
   J. Moreover

3. Many construction projects across the city are in need of laborers; _____ there's a shortage of workers throughout the region.
   A. instead,
   B. in fact,
   C. consequently,
   D. however,

4. It is important to mix the batter thoroughly; _____ the muffins will come out lumpy and bitter.
   E. whereas
   G. otherwise
   H. in fact
   J. then

5. It can be difficult to travel to distant reaches of the globe; _____, it was far more difficult for people of the 19th century.
   A. again
   B. however
   C. in that case
   D. unfortunately

6. There is nothing quite like driving a convertible on a quiet ocean road _____ cruising through the city on a summer night with the top down.
   F. while
   G. whereas
   H. or
   J. because

7. Traditional basket-weaving is based on the same idea _____ it requires a good deal more time and energy.
   A. although
   B. while
   C. therefore
   D. because

8. The organizers of the festival feel that each film must meet the high standards of quality typical of high-profile film festivals. _____, they want the filmmakers to directly participate in promoting the festival.
   F. For example
   G. In addition
   H. However
   J. For instance

||||||||||||||||||||||||||||||||||||||||||||||||||||||||||||||||||||||

**NOTES:**

9. Self-appreciation and self-discipline are the cen-
tral principles of the technique, _____
Barrani claims has a success rate of over ninety
percent.
A. which
B. considering
C. through
D. despite

10. I've always considered cats to be lazy animals. On
a recent trip to Africa, _____, I encoun-
tered some cats that made me reconsider my point
of view.
F. nevertheless
G. thus
H. moreover
J. however

11. Positive reinforcement of good behavior can lead
to serious improvement in the behavior of prison
inmates; _____, negative reinforcement
can cause frustration, isolation, and eventually
violence.
A. consequently
B. conversely
C. therefore
D. as a result

12. School counselors requested that all students
submit a full inventory of career interests but
_____ loosened that requirement when
it proved to generate more paperwork than the
office could handle.
F. therefore
G. ultimately
H. furthermore
J. even so

# Relevance

Information within a piece of writing can be completely true but have no important connection to the topic at hand. The oldest known bowhead whale lived until it was at least 211 years old.

**See what happened there?** We're talking about rhetorical strategies and then **BAM!** Out of nowhere, a bowhead whale shows up and interrupts the flow.

**This section is all about finding those sentences that diverge from the topic at hand and getting rid of them as fast as possible.**
Frequently, at the end of an English passage the **ACT** will ask you whether or not the author should add a new sentence to a passage. To decide, you need to know what the intent of the passage was. Try to summarize the passage in one sentence. A great trick to help with that is to look back at the title of the passage—whatever the author called the passage is likely a strong clue about what the passage is about.

**Here's another trick: a change in point of view can indicate irrelevance.**
If an entire essay is written in the third person, as in, **"Cats were give special status in Ancient Egyptian culture,"** and suddenly you see a sentence like, **"My cousin has two cats named Fluffy and Mr. Mittens,"** it's probably irrelevant.

# LET'S TRY SOME EXERCISES!

**INSTRUCTIONS:** In this exercise, underline **KEEP** if the bold portion of each mini-essay is relevant to the essay and should remain or **DELETE** if it is irrelevant and should go bye-bye.

|||||||||||||||||||||||||||||||||||||||||||||||||||||||||||||||||||||||||||||||||||||||||||||||||||||||||||||||

1. In "Harry Potter" lore, J.K. Rowling, then a struggling, single mom, first started writing the Harry Potter series on cocktail napkins in a bar. She may still be a single mom **whose children's names are David, Mackenzie, and Jessica,** but she is no longer struggling. Between book sales, merchandise, and film revenue, Harry Potter is one of the most successful franchises in history, having generated revenues of over 20 billion dollars.

   KEEP   DELETE

2. The room seemed to have been frozen in time. Everything, from his well-worn little league cap to the signed photo of Kobe Bryant telling him to "Stay in School," was exactly as it had been when he'd last inhabited the space between these four walls. **Only the view from the window had changed.** The large willow, which used to mesmerize him during the day with its hypnotic swaying then frighten him at night with branches that turned into long, reaching fingers, was no longer there. "The roots were starting to tear up the sidewalk, so the city cut it down," his mother had informed him casually as she unloaded the dishwasher.

   KEEP   DELETE

3. By June of 1907, when Mark Twain sailed from New York to London to receive the honorary degree of Literary Doctor from Oxford University, he was already one of the most famous authors in the world. **While many writers die in obscurity only to have the world discover their genius posthumously, Twain cultivated then fastidiously maintained his celebrity while he was alive.** The one thing he hadn't achieved, up to this point, was official acknowledgment from the world of academia. Despite his public statements to the contrary, he really did care what others thought—especially those in ivory towers.

   KEEP   DELETE

4. Did you know that you can make your own massive soap bubbles at home? You can! All you need is dishwater detergent, water, and glycern, **which you can find at your local drugstore.** Mix ½ cup of detergent, 4 cups of water, and 4 tablespoons of glycerin in a container. Then dip a bubble wand into the mixture and blow!

   KEEP   DELETE

5. Originating in South America, the tomato has become one of the world's staple fruits. The tomato began to spread to almost every part of the world following the colonization of the Americas by the Spanish. **The fruit contains large amounts of lycopene, which is now known to have health benefits.** The earliest known European reference to the tomato can be found in a description of plants written in 1554 which names the tomato the *"pomo d'oro,"* or "golden apple." Today, whether it's being used in Italian sauces or in the classic BLT, modern world cuisine, it seems, would be lost without the tomato.

   KEEP   DELETE

# EXERCISE 2

**INSTRUCTIONS:** Read the passage and think about what the main idea is, then **cross out** the part of the passage that is irrelevant.

1. The first Women's World Cup was held in 1991 in China, and it included 12 teams. Since then, the competition has grown in popularity and skill level. The 2011 Women's World Cup Final, between the U.S. and Japan, was widely seen to have demonstrated the highest level of play in WWC history, and Homare Sawa of Japan became the oldest player to score a goal.

2. How many people are on Facebook? The number grows every day. What started as a way for college students to keep track of their friends online has turned into something that everybody and her mother (and even her grandmother) is using. Mark Zuckerberg recently settled a lawsuit with the Winklevoss twins regarding the founding of Facebook. Whether or not it was Mark Zuckerberg's original intention, Facebook is now a way for young and old alike to communicate online.

3. "One man's trash is another man's treasure." There is no better example of this aphorism than that of the makers of "found object" art. One time I found a fifty-dollar bill on the street and used it to buy a new pair of skinny jeans. The found objects art scene, of course, is not uniform or exclusive; it includes anyone who takes lost or discarded items—from bicycle chains to old tires to faded photographs of complete strangers—and turns them into things of beauty.

4. When the Super Bowl is the most watched event in American Broadcasting, can we really still say that baseball is "America's Pastime"? Many Major League Baseball players come from Latin America and the Caribbean. Even basketball is now more popular than baseball. The question is: did baseball change? Or did we?

5. Some people don't pay their taxes, and these people are called scofflaws. The American tax code does not pretend to be simple. There are different tax rates for different income brackets, as well as a host of tax breaks and deductions that a taxpayer can itemize. Some say that this complexity reflects the natural complexity of society; others argue that it is unfair and basically amounts to a government subsidy to the tax accounting industry.

6. Behind the barn, which was built in 1873 by a Danish farmer by the name Viktor Schmeichel, flowed a creek that changed personas with the seasons. In winter it was a stoic, old man who kept his secrets, but in the spring it became a giddy child, skipping about in wonder at every twist of light and air. In the summer the creek became a loudmouth drunk, holding court in the middle of a party while others were having their first glass of wine. But the one you waited for was the autumn creek, the mother, who would hold you to her bosom, calm and strong, just as she caught and cradled the most magnificent of leaves.

7. The term "prom" comes from the word "promenade," a dance step practiced in classic English and American social dances. Movies about high school tell you that prom is supposed to be the greatest night of your life, but where they got that I'll never know. It seems to me that if you go into anything thinking it's got to be the "best ever," you're only setting yourself up for disappointment. Luckily, if you go into it just trying to live in the moment and have a good time, it's likely that you will.

**NOTES:**

8. In his Drivers' Ed class, Ryan had seen the videos of the horrible wrecks and mangled bodies, cautionary tales meant to scare kids into good driving habits. But he had never seen anything like this. The entire highway was paved with broken glass; the smell of burning gasoline invaded his nostrils. Drivers' Ed is a mandatory class in some school districts, but others treat it as an extracurricular or private activity.

9. By now most people know that reality TV is somewhat scripted, but I never understood how much until a friend of mine was on a reality show. It was a show on which a group of supposed friends allow the viewing public into their social scene. But the "reality" in my friend's case was that none of the people even knew one another before they were cast as friends, and casting is the process by which producers find people to be on their shows. The producers told these "friends" what to talk about, and writers edited scenes together to manufacture the juiciest narratives.

10. Many absurd things happened during the Cold War, but one of the most absurd occurred on the streets of a small town in the former East German Republic (or GDR) in 1989. This was an era in which a West German official setting even a toe down in East German soil made international headlines. Therefore, the news that the Prime Minister of West Germany would be going to the GDR in order to view the work of an artist became a sensation. The East German government, determined that the international media covering the event, which took place on a Tuesday, would witness only scenes of prosperity and communist utopia, ordered all real citizens of the town to stay in their homes. Meanwhile, it filled the town square with government officials and their families pretending to be residents.

# EXERCISE 3

**INSTRUCTIONS:** Sometimes the underlined portion of an **ACT** English essay is relevant to the essay as a whole, but is located in the wrong spot. So let's add a layer of complexity. In this exercise, if the underlined portion of each mini-essay is relevant and should stay where it is, circle **"KEEP."** If it is irrelevant and should be deleted, underline **"DELETE."** If it is relevant information that the essay would lack if it were deleted but doesn't make sense where it is, underline **"MOVE."**

1. The Salton Sea is not technically a "sea," but it certainly is as salty as one. Geographically speaking, it is a saline, endorheic rift lake. It is the largest lake in California, and its salt concentration makes it saltier than the Pacific Ocean (though less salty than the Great Salt Lake in Utah). Did you know that there is a sea in the middle of the desert in California? Throughout the Spanish period of California history, the Salton Sea was used as a salt mine, but since the 1920s it has primarily served as a tourist attraction and recreation area.

    KEEP    DELETE    MOVE

2. As both a former diver and volleyball player, I believe it is important for kids to engage in both individual and group activities. From diving I learned that sometimes responsibility rests on me alone. When I succeeded, it was because I was at my best; when I failed, I was the only one to blame. Volleyball, on the other hand, taught me how to check my ego. It taught me that we are part of a community, and we all have to work together to get things done. Being a member of a team taught me communication skills, and it taught me to appreciate the skills of others that I may not possess myself. At 5 feet, 2 inches, I could serve and defend, but no one in their right mind would ask me to jump above an eight foot net to block a spike.

    KEEP    DELETE    MOVE

3. The crowd moved like a tidal wave, pushing relentlessly forward like a single entity. Who would have thought that the release of a mere video game could cause such a crush of humanity outside a Best Buy at six in the morning? Most Best Buy stores are open from 10am until 9 or 10pm. You could see fevered anticipation in the eyes of those first few customers, many of whom had camped out in the parking lot the night before, as they exited cradling the thin, rectangular video game box like a newborn child.

    KEEP    DELETE    MOVE

# Redundancy

Very rarely is the problem with writing that there's not enough of it. Grammatically speaking, **if given the choice between using one word and six words to accomplish the same thing, use one.**

**This is another explanation for why "shorter is better."**
When the test asks you whether to include or omit a phrase or sentence, ask yourself, *"does this provide new, relevant information without which the essay would suffer? Or does it provide information we already know, in which case it would be redundant."*

## EXERCISE 1
**Instructions:** Circle the phrases that include redundancy.

1. my rich, wealthy uncle

2. the captivating, hilarious story

3. the unprecedented accomplishment that had never happened before

4. the threatening, ominous clouds

5. a vague, indirect question

6. I was terrified and quite afraid

7. the group that met and gathered

8. the students who fought and persevered

9. who finally accepted and came to terms with the settlement

10. the inventive, entrancing film

# EXERCISE 2

**INSTRUCTIONS:** Pick **"KEEP"** or **"DELETE."** Pretty self-explanatory.

1. In this day and age, the County Fair can seem like somewhat of an antiquity. <u>It can also seem out of date and old-fashioned.</u> A throwback to earlier days when more Americans lived on farms than in cities, the fair was a way to bring far-flung neighbors together to celebrate the bounty of the land and spirit of community. But the modern County Fair is becoming something of a beautiful hybrid, keeping all of our nostalgic favorites (funnel cakes, deep-fried everything, questionably safe rides), and updating those features that seem dated.

    KEEP    DELETE

2. I have always been an adventurous eater. As my mother tells it, when I was only two years old I was already asking for snacks like chicken liver. <u>That may not be the craziest food on the planet, but ask any parent of a two-year old and you'll find it's a rare request.</u> Now when I watch food shows like Andrew Zimmern's Bizarre Foods, I don't think, "how could he eat tofu that was marinated in fish intestines," but "how do I get my hands on some of that?!"

    KEEP    DELETE

3. Studies show that a sizable percentage of young adults get their news from comedy news programs like "The Daily Show." Some criticize this phenomenon as evidence that younger generations are not engaged with the political process in a serious way, while defenders say that these programs are some of the only sources of media that explain the news in an honest, unbiased, <u>neutral</u> way.

    KEEP    DELETE

4. The Mars rovers called Spirit and Opportunity were only supposed to last three months but ended up traveling the "red planet" for over five years. Among the things they discovered include signs of water erosion and <u>pure silica, most likely formed by hot springs,</u> indicating that Mars used to be wet and could have potentially sustained life as we know it.

    KEEP    DELETE

5. The saying goes, "falling in love is easy; staying in love is hard." Apparently when we "fall in love," something chemical happens in our brains that scientists claim most closely resembles a drug interaction. We literally become "high on love." When this initial period naturally ends <u>or reaches a conclusion,</u> couples break up.

    KEEP    DELETE

# EXERCISE 3

**INSTRUCTIONS:** Choose the best version of the underlined portion in each mini-essay.

|||||||||||||||||||||||||||||||||||||||||||||||||||||||||||||||||||||||||||||||||||||||||||||||||||||||||||||||||||||||||||||||

1. Puerto Rico became an "unincorporated territory" of the United States at the end of the Spanish-American War as part of the <u>Treaty of Paris, which was a document ending the War under agreed terms.</u>
   A. Treaty of Paris, which was a document ending the war.
   B. Treaty of Paris.
   C. Treaty of Paris. It was a document ending the war under agreed terms.
   D. Treaty of Paris; this document ended the war.

2. Though the twins had a lot in common, Manny was <u>more social than Ben and liked to be around other people more often.</u>
   F. more social than Ben and liked to be around other people.
   G. more social; Ben was less social than Manny.
   H. more social; Ben was less social.
   J. more social than Ben.

3. Monique's take on neo-retro art was <u>unique and could not be replicated.</u>
   A. unique.
   B. unique without replication.
   C. not replicated by her.
   D. unique to the point of not being replicated.

4. Though most people have a sense of humor, to truly become a comedian one must study the craft <u>professionally and not as an amateur.</u>
   F. professionally while not as an amateur.
   G. professionally, because being an amateur is not professional.
   H. professional.
   J. professionally.

5. The committee deemed the idea to cover all of the county's farmland with asphalt <u>both fiscally prohibitive and extremely short-sighted.</u>
   A. NO CHANGE
   B. fiscally prohibitive.
   C. extremely short-sighted.
   D. both that it would cost too much money on top of the fact that it was dumb in the long-run.

# Author's Intent

**Some of the English test questions are almost like reading comprehension questions because they require you to think about the content of the essay and make editorial decisions based on what you think the author is trying to say.**

These questions come in two formats. Here they are, with strategies for attacking them.

## 1 "GIVEN THAT ALL THE CHOICES ARE TRUE, WHICH ONE _____ "

This common question type has a really, really useful hack, which is to identify the key words within the question and focus very narrowly on them. Once you do that, it's easy to deliver a correct answer.

**🔍 For instance, take a look at this guy:**

> Given that all of the choices are true, which one provides the most detailed visual description of the team's uniforms?

The key words here are **"detailed visual description"** and **"uniforms."** Keep that in mind when you look at these answer choices

    **A.** uniforms.
    **B.** uniforms that never seemed to get fully clean in the wash.
    **C.** uniforms with the green piping and the yellow letters.
    **D.** uniforms that had been introduced in the 1970's.

**Notice how all of the answer choices are grammatically correct.** Answer **(A)** also has the advantage of being really short *(and shorter is better...most of the time)*. **Answer choice (C),** though, is the only one that **has any visual description, and that makes it the right answer.**

A summary of the strategy on these questions is **figure out what the ACT is asking you for and then make sure you deliver it.**

## "SUPPOSE THE WRITER'S GOAL HAD BEEN TO WRITE A BRIEF ESSAY THAT _____"

2

These questions require a broader focus than the previous type. You'll have to think about the essay as a whole, not just one moment within it.

Each of these questions will have **two answer choices that start with "Yes"** and **two that start with "No."**

*That's a great place to start.*

🔍 **Let's look at a sample:**

Suppose the writer's goal had been to write a brief essay that assesses the state of coral reefs in the world's oceans. Would this essay accomplish that goal?

    **A.** Yes, because it describes the demise of the Great Barrier Reef in Australia.
    **B.** Yes, because it focuses on the damage humans can do to coral reefs.
    **C.** No, because it does not share any new information about the state of coral reefs.
    **D.** No, because it focuses on one coral reef, not coral reefs around the world.

You don't have the essay to reference, so don't worry about the specific reasons why these answers might be right or wrong. Instead, look at what they're asking you to think about. These are all answers about the scope of the passage. Did the essay cover all of the coral reefs in the world? If not, the answer would be **"No."** Answer choice (**D**). is a pretty typically correct answer on this type of question. It basically says, no, because the essay is out of focus with what this question is asking.

**A nice strategy for attacking these guys is to look back at the title and the first paragraph of the essay.** Those two spots will often give away what the real focus of the essay is and whether or not the answer is **"Yes"** or **"No."**

# EXERCISE

**INSTRUCTIONS:** In each example, read the short passage and question, **underline the key word(s) or phrase(s)** in the question, and then **circle the best answer.**

Do people prefer change or stability? While we often claim to love change (we run out to buy the newest versions of our electronic gadgets, or tear down old buildings and replace them with the latest design fad), when it comes down to the big things, people prefer the comfort of the familiar.

1. Given that all of the choices are true, which of the following sentences, if added, would best illustrate "the comfort of the familiar" the author discusses in the previous sentence?
   A. For example, I am familiar with my family and friends, but I also love meeting new people.
   B. For example, some people find hammocks extremely comfortable, while others find them too unstable.
   C. For example, research shows that people sleep more soundly in their own beds than in beds in which they are less accustomed.
   D. For example, many people admit to feeling anxious when their smart phones are less than fully charged.

Space has been called the "final frontier" in the world of Star Trek as well as in our own human mythology, but what about the deep oceans? Some scientists claim that we know even less about our own planet's depths than we do about bodies like our Moon and Mars.

2. Suppose the writer's goal was to write an introduction to an essay about efforts to learn more about the Earth's deep oceans. Would this essay fulfill the writer's goal?
   F. Yes, because it introduces the idea that we do not yet know much about the deep oceans.
   G. Yes, because it references the mythology of the final frontier.
   H. No, because it focuses mostly on Star Trek and space travel.
   J. No, because it fails to mention specific details about deep ocean conditions.

The music industry has undergone a massive change since the advent of digital music technology. While only studios had the technical materials and expertise to produce truly professional recordings from the phonograph era through that of the heyday of Compact Discs in the 1990s, today's digital technology allows independent artists to record, produce, and distribute professional, innovative music to their fans all over the world.

3. Suppose the writer's goal was to convey that independent artists now find it harder to make money selling music. Would this essay fulfill the writer's goal?
   A. Yes, because it discusses how much harder it was for independent musicians to make music in the past.
   B. Yes, because it mentions the heyday of the 1990s, which implies that musicians made more money at that time.
   C. No, because it describes independent music as "innovative," and not all independent music fits this category.
   D. No, because it doesn't mention the financial status of making independent music today.

Before Sean could adjust his tie for the tenth time in so many minutes, he was on air. "Hello, and welcome to 'News as It Happens.' I'm Sean Grant," he heard himself announce as if he were a viewer watching himself on television. "Breathe," thought Sean as he stared at the camera with the look of approachable gravitas that he'd practiced with his media coach.

4. Given that all of the choices are true, which sentence should be added in order to emphasize sensory details Sean might be experiencing in this moment?
   F. If he had been watching himself on television he would have seen a handsome man of thirty-five exhibiting not even a twinge of nervousness.
   G. He thought about whether his sister and brothers were watching; surely they were.
   H. "News as It Happens," had already had a number of anchors, but Sean had been the youngest in years.
   J. He felt the heat of the bright fluorescents on his face and the stiff starchiness of his dress shirt against his chest.

One of my favorite summer activities has always been fruit picking. When I was young, my sister and I would spend entire days picking wild blackberries from the bushes near our house, eating just enough not to ruin our chances of having our mother's blackberry cobbler for dessert that evening.

5. Suppose the writer's goal had been to write a brief essay describing a particular childhood memory. Would this essay accomplish that goal?
   A. Yes, because it focuses on the writer's recollection of picking wild blackberries
   B. Yes, because it stresses the author's lifelong hobby of fruit picking.
   C. No, because it provides only a broad description of childhood.
   D. No, because it describes an activity that many people participate in every year.

# Diction

Diction means **"word choice,"** and on a typical **ACT** section you will encounter a few questions on which diction plays a role. For these questions, you will be presented with four answer choices that might seem like they mean exactly the same *(or nearly the same)* thing. Since we know there can only be one right answer to an **ACT** question, your job is to dig into the small differences between words.

### 🔍 Take this sample question:

"My sister and I were Irish, after all, and we had longed for years to hike <u>among</u> the verdant hills of our mother country."

Which of the following alternatives to the underlined portion would NOT be acceptable?
**A.** NO CHANGE
**B.** inside
**C.** through
**D.** across

The answers all describe a similar kind of movement in space, but the kind of movement indicated by the word **"inside"** is slightly different from that indicated in words like **"through," "among"** or **"across."** To hike **"inside"** the hills almost seems to suggest that the speaker and his or her sister are actually in a hill, which—unless they are on some kind of Hobbit-like journey through the Mines of Moria—doesn't make a whole lot of sense.

**Another trick of diction is that words can mean the same thing but have different applications.**

### 🔍 For example:

We use the word **"beautiful"** to describe a wide range of things, from people to paintings to sunsets to Instagrammed photos of someone's lunch *(well, maybe not that last one)*.

**"Handsome,"** however, is only used in certain contexts. It would be strange to call a painting or a sunset handsome because that's just not how that word is used.

**Some words are used to describe people but not inanimate objects; there are words that we use to describe something figuratively that we wouldn't use to describe it literally.** To answer questions like these correctly, we have to briefly leave the world of black-and-white grammar behind and step into a slightly fuzzier world...a world of connotations and relative meanings.

The good news is that we live in that world pretty much all of the time. Our language brains are programmed to notice small shades of meaning, even if we don't consciously think about it very often.

So strap in, mount up *(sorry...too many diction choices here...)* and let's do this thing!

# EXERCISE 1

**INSTRUCTIONS:** Positive vs. Negative Connotations: Each of the following word pairs means roughly the same thing, though we almost always imbue one with a positive connotation and the other a negative one. **Write a plus sign next to the positive word, and a minus sign next to the negative one.**

1. Inexpensive _____ Cheap _____

2. Childish _____ Youthful _____

3. Stubborn _____ Determined _____

4. Talkative _____ Long-winded _____

5. Elite _____ Snobbish _____

# EXERCISE 2

**INSTRUCTIONS:** Differences in Scale or Scope: Each of the following word pairs means roughly the same thing but has an important difference between them. Describe the difference between each pair of words.

1. Know v. Suppose _____

2. Halt v. Conclude _____

3. Surrender v. Forfeit _____

4. Approve v. Accept _____

5. Dislike v. Loathe _____

# EXERCISE 3

**INSTRUCTIONS:** Read the following sentences and answer the corresponding questions.

1. While they generally have poor eyesight, bats possess a sense of hearing that is particularly <u>intense.</u>

   A. NO CHANGE
   B. knowing.
   C. acute.
   D. clear.

2. To truly excel at debate, one must not only be able to <u>be argumentative for</u> one's own position but also to anticipate and rebut possible counterarguments.

   F. NO CHANGE
   G. effectively argue
   H. argue the effects of
   J. project for

3. Upon gazing for the first time at the hideous monster, the damsel <u>receded</u> in horror.

   A. NO CHANGE
   B. returned
   C. ebbed
   D. recoiled

4. Miranda was <u>granted</u> Employee of the Year because of both her innovative ideas and her consummate professionalism.

   F. NO CHANGE
   G. entitled
   H. named
   J. presented

5. To the astonishment of the university faculty, the 10-year old math prodigy <u>completed</u> the seemingly impossible problem in record time.

   A. NO CHANGE
   B. finalized
   C. ended
   D. finished off

6. One of the goals of The United States Department of Energy is to <u>reduce</u> the amount of oil we import from foreign countries.

   Which of the following alternatives to the underlined portion would NOT be acceptable?
   F. lower
   G. decrease
   H. minimize
   J. contract

# Organization and Flow

Yet another thing to think about when you read these essays **is organization.** Here are four elements of organization and flow to keep in mind:

- **ORDER** Are the ideas arranged in a sequence that makes the essay work as a whole?

- **INTRODUCTIONS** Does the opening of the essay offer a good preview of the content and tone of the essay that follows?

- **TRANSITIONS** Did the author include logical transitions between the ideas and paragraphs within the essay?

- **CONCLUSIONS** Does the conclusion bring the essay to a thoughtful end?

## ORDER

Sentences within a paragraph and paragraphs within an essay should **"preserve the logic and coherence of the essay."** In other words, the way we get from one idea to another should be a smooth journey.

*In surfing terms, you want a wave you can ride all the way in, baby. Hang ten, or whatever.*

## EXERCISE 1

**INSTRUCTIONS:** Read then reorder the sentences below so they are in the correct order.

1. Matt and Caroline, born within three months of one another, had never known a world without dual-family barbecues, summer vacations, and holiday parties.

2. By the time they were 17, though, something was clearly changing, and neither of them knew what to do about it.

3. Thus, Matt and Caroline had been best friends since before they could walk.

4. After establishing their careers, both couples even had kids at the same time.

5. Their parents had gone to college together, then all moved to another college town to pursue lives in academia.

**Correct Order:** _1_, _5_, _4_, _3_, _2_,

# EXERCISE 2

**INSTRUCTIONS:** Put the paragraphs of the essay in the correct order.

1. I was never an Olympic gymnast, but as I did compete for ten years, I can attest to the physical demands of and potential for injury in the sport. I have long-term back problems from the strenuous impact put onto my body while I was still growing. I can point to more serious injuries as well: one of my teammates actually broke her neck at the age of 15 while vaulting. The injury required multiple surgeries, and it ended not only her gymnastics career but also her chance to compete in any other sport ever again.

2. Many in the gymnastics world claim that this is the nature of the sport. They explain gender differences by pointing to the way men's and women's bodies develop as adolescence progresses into adulthood. While men's gymnastics events focus on upper body strength, which increases as an adolescent boy grows into manhood, women's events highlight speed, agility, and flexibility, which tend to decrease as a woman's center of gravity drops upon reaching late adolescence. Critics argue that the physical demands on young gymnasts are deleterious for growing bones and bodies.

3. Of course, one can argue that little girls are not forced into highly competitive gymnastics, at least in the United States. And as in any sport, it has its pros and its cons. But as the physical requirements of many of our sports are becoming more and more extreme, it may be time for society at large to reconsider how much may be too much to ask of our athletes.

4. Competitive women's gymnastics is one of the few sports in which many of the world's top competitors are legally children. Many gymnasts, both male and female, begin competing before the age of 6, but only the female athletes seem to reach the ideal physicality for all the sport entails by the age of 16.

**Correct Order:** _____, _____, _____, _____

# 📝 INTRODUCTIONS

**Introductions should introduce. Take a minute to fully absorb that brain-melter.**
Your life will forever be split into two parts: life before you read that sentence, and life after.

*You can never go back*

**OK, so an introduction has only one job, but it can accomplish that job in a few different ways.** An introductory sentence could provide the thesis of the essay, but it doesn't have to do that. It could ask an interesting question, or it could introduce an interesting detail that will be explained later. Whatever the specific nature of introductory sentence is, it needs to kick start the essay and be relevant to the central idea.

**Introductions also set the tone.** We'll talk about tone a few sections from now, but as a preview, tone is the word we use to describe how something is written. Tone can be formal, informal, analytical, personal, earnest, humorous, or anything in between. After you read the first sentence, you should be able to answer the question, **"what kind of essay am I expecting to read?"**

**Let's take a look at some sample introductory sentences.**

    **What can you tell about these essays just based on their first sentences?**

**1.** Many people associate the idea of school integration as a struggle limited to 1960s America, but there are still many places, especially in the American South, where school districts use "busing" to ensure school racial balance.
    **I can tell that Essay 1:**

    ✎ intends to be informative

    ✎ will not be either extremely positive or extremely negative

    ✎ is relatively formal

**2.** For many high school students, community service is just another thing they have to add to their already heavy loads of schoolwork, extracurricular activities, sports, and for some, part-time jobs.
    **I can tell that Essay 2:**

    ✎ intends to persuade

    ✎ will likely be negative towards required community service

    ✎ is relatively opinionated

**3.** When the sky turned green, we knew it was going to be a mean one.
    **Meanwhile in Essay 3:**

    ✎ is a piece of either memoir or fiction

    ✎ will be informal/personal

    ✎ intends to create a feeling of mystery and suspense

# EXERCISE

**INSTRUCTIONS:** Select the option that best introduces each partial-essay.

1. No. But did its scientists believe so thoroughly in the drug's possible benefits that they only saw what they wanted to see? Perhaps. However, allegations of a company-wide cover-up go too far. Investigators have uncovered a total of zero communications which link the mistakes made in the Cronifrin trials to a concerted effort on the part of Well Bridge to defraud the public in the name of financial gain.

   **A.** Did Well Bridge Inc. purposefully shred documents related to the possible dangers of the drug Cronifrin?

   **B.** Did Well Bridge Inc. purposefully bury results of the experimental drug trials that contradicted its desired results?

   **C.** Did Well Bridge Inc. purposefully expose wrong doing on the part of the pharmaceutical company involved in the Cronifrin scandal?

   **D.** Did Well Bridge Inc. gain financially because it released only positive results from the Cronifrin drug trials?

2. I went on my first cruise recently, and believe me, when they say "all inclusive," they mean it. Breakfast and lunch are basically all-day buffets. Dinner, while a more formal affair, is no less extravagant. One night I couldn't decide between the duck and the lobster tail, so the waiter asked me if he should just bring both. The kitchen threw in an extra lobster tail just for giggles! Afterward, I was surprised that I didn't have to be rolled out of the dining room like a giant medicine ball! The craziest thing is that every dinner is a three-course affair. I simply can't imagine eating a three-course dinner in my own home...every night!

   **F.** If the thought of gaining 8 lbs. in a week seems impossible, try going on a cruise!

   **G.** When I travel, I generally like to be in control of my own travel and itinerary, but I have to say there's something refreshingly simple about a cruise.

   **H.** "All-inclusive" is a term the travel industry uses to indicated that all of one's meals are included in the price of the trip.

   **J.** I detest travel; the airline always loses my luggage, my hotel can never find me a room without some loud college kids having a party next door, and any time I choose to sail, I get seasick.

3. Italian "prosecco," a slightly sweet sparkling wine, was the first to challenge the dominance of champagne, but recently Spanish "cavas" have also entered the fray. Now restaurants as well as grocery stores are starting to classify the whole lot as simply, "bubbly," without any reference to an old-school hierarchy that always favored champagne.

   **A.** A sparkling wine cannot truly be called "champagne" unless it hails from the Champagne region of France.

   **B.** Champagne has long been the drink of success and celebration, seen as both a symbol of wealth and privilege and a way to mark special occasions even for the non-millionaires among us.

   **C.** While "champagne" remains the worldwide standard for sparkling wine, other varietals have been gaining in popularity in recent years.

   **D.** Sparkling wines provide a refreshing and exciting alternative to regular wine.

# TRANSITIONS

**Metaphorically, transitions are bridges.** They help you get from one **"idea island"** to another smoothly and comfortably. The key to a transition is to acknowledge the previous idea while simultaneously introducing the next; if you don't include both a reference to what came before and what's coming up, something will be missing

*That would be like having half of a bridge to an island, and that's not much of a bridge.*

### Here's an example of a "half bridge" transition:

Politicians running for office will all tell you that "Washington is broken," but it seems that so many of them fall into the same dysfunctional traps as their predecessors. <u>These traps include being preoccupied with fundraising for re-election immediately upon taking office.</u> Congress members only serve for two years.

Notice how the underlined sentence does a good job of continuing the previous thought by starting with the phrase, **"These traps include,"** but it does nothing to introduce the idea of the length of a congressional term, which makes that next sentence seem like it's coming out of nowhere. Let's try it again with a transition that bridges both ideas.

Politicians running for office will all tell you that "Washington is broken," but it seems that so many of them fall into the same dysfunctional traps as their predecessors. <u>These traps include being preoccupied with fundraising for re-election immediately upon taking office, a reasonable concern given their short terms in office. Congress members only serve for two years.</u>

**Sometimes a writer will use a purposefully abrupt transition in order to create drama or surprise.**

### For example:

It seemed that nothing could go wrong. The day was perfect, quiet except for the sound of the birds in the trees. Quiet, that is, until an alien space ship ripped through the earth, drilling a massive hole from New York to the Philippines.

**Obviously, there is an abrupt transition there.** However, even the simple addition of the phrase **"that is"** helps to smooth the transition so that the sudden change of ideas still makes sense to the reader.

*Also, any time you ever see the phrase, "It seemed that nothing could go wrong," you can be pretty sure that something is about to go terribly, terribly wrong.*

**When the ACT asks students about transitions, it is almost always referring to transitions between paragraphs.**

To solve these questions, read the paragraphs before and after the transition sentence. Yes, the whole paragraph! Then, make sure that your answer choice creates a segue from the preceding paragraph and introduces the main idea of the next.

### ⊕ Here's an example:

Anthropologists estimate that the first evidence of the human domestication of animals occurred over 15,000 years ago with the appearance of the first domesticated dogs. Over time, human civilization expanded its dominion to include any number of mammals and birds. Reasons for domestication vary. Some animals, like goats, sheep, and pigs, were domesticated primarily for the types of commodities they provided (milk, meat, wool). Animals like horses, oxen, and dogs, on the other hand, were useful in helping with various kinds of work (hauling, hunting, protection).

**However, only one animal seems to have been tamed uniquely for the purpose of human companionship: the domestic cat.** Even though dogs were and have always been great human companions, only the domesticated cat originally dwelled indoors with humans...

The underlined sentence flows logically from the paragraph before. The phrase **"tamed uniquely for the purpose of human companionship"** draws its relevance from the idea in t he first paragraph that other animals were domesticated for reasons other than companionship, and the use of the word **"however,"** sets up the contrast that is to come in the next paragraph.

Now it's your turn!

# EXERCISE

**INSTRUCTIONS:** Read each partial essay and choose the answer choice that provides the clearest and most logical transition from one paragraph to the next.

1. Historically, when America goes to war, a host of wartime songs follow, from the homefront-focused "Tie a Yellow Ribbon" during WWII to the anti-war anthem "Fortunate Son" during the Vietnam War. So why is it that in the first decade of the 21st century, with the United States simultaneously fighting wars in Iraq and Afghanistan, was there a surprising dearth of war-related popular music to be heard on our radios and iPods?

   [1] There have been multiple films made about America's most recent wars. So why the silence in popular music? Perhaps the lack of a military draft made the war seem less relevant to the majority not in the military.

   **A.** Other art forms have not been so absent from the conversation.
   **B.** Doesn't it seem like every time you purchase a new technological gadget like an iPod, a better version comes out within a week?
   **C.** Films like "American Sniper" and "The Hurt Locker," for example, dealt with multiple aspects of the war in the middle east.
   **D.** Artists like Lady Gaga sing about serious subjects like sexuality and religion, but what about war?

2. Maggie lay awake sweating on top of the covers. The fan whirred incessantly but ineffectually; not even at top speed could it beat the sticky humidity of July in Mobile.

   [2] "That Hoke Purvis can go to hell!," shouted Mr. Phillips as he pounded a fist on the kitchen table. "Look Will," reasoned Mr. Hull, "Purvis has only presented his proposal to the council. There's no guarantee that they'll agree with him."

   **F.** Mobile, Alabama, was one of the centers in the fight for civil rights for African-Americans in the 1960s.
   **G.** At least it drowned out the sounds of the adults arguing downstairs, Maggie thought.
   **H.** Hoke Purvis was a 22-year old from a good family, but his parents for some reason had let him go to school in New York City, and he'd come home with some crazy ideas.
   **J.** Maggie thought about how dull summer was and how she longed to be back in freshly pressed fall blouses, walking to school in air that didn't feel quite so much like a soaking wet blanket.

## 4 CONCLUSIONS

**Like transitions (see how I just transitioned right there?), conclusions also need to hold down two jobs at the same time.** A good conclusion should flow logically and smoothly from the previous sentence while simultaneously **"wrapping things up."**

A good conclusion often refers to ideas mentioned in the introduction, thereby **"book-ending"** the essay, and it should at the very least be relevant to the main idea.

**A good conclusion should:**
remain **relevant to the main idea**
never undermine the main idea
of the passage

# EXERCISE

**INSTRUCTIONS:** Select the sentence that best concludes each partial-essay.

1. Many people associate the idea of school integration as a struggle limited to 1960s America, but there are still many places, especially in the American South, where school districts use "busing" to ensure school racial balance. In the '80s, when I was in elementary school in Little Rock, my parents got a letter each July informing them what school I would be attending the next year. In essence, they got a letter stating, "Rogers Elementary needs one more white girl." And I would take a bus to whatever school the letter said.

   For me, busing could be burdensome and disruptive. I sometimes had to travel hours to and from school in service of this social ideal. At the same time, busing made me who I am today. I think of my 3rd grade teacher, a black man named Mr. White, who didn't care if you were "black, white, or purple—if you keep mess on your desk, that mess is going to belong to me!"

   **A.** I still think about Mr. White to this day.
   **B.** Kids need discipline like this in this day and age when so many parents would rather be "friends" with their kids than parents.
   **C.** Mr. White grew up in the segregated South and joined the military because he felt he would be freer oversees than in his own hometown.
   **D.** I know that I benefited from experiences like these, even if the government's policies for school integration have never been perfect.

2. For many high school students, community service is just another thing they have to add to their already heavy load of schoolwork, extracurricular activities, sports, and for some, part-time jobs. Today's kids are already so over-scheduled, so overburdened, that adding a community service requirement into the mix is basically telling kids to kiss any time they thought they might still have to themselves goodbye...

   ..In conclusion, it is a bad idea to require students to complete a community service requirement to graduate because only some kids are cut out for that kind of work. Others will resent it and therefore leave high school with a bad impression.

   Still others could do more harm than good by not committing to a job that, if done with passion, could have helped people.

   **F.** With everything else high school students have to do nowadays, why force them into something that won't benefit either the students or society?
   **G.** That would be the worst possible outcome.
   **H.** And if helping people is the point of the whole thing, schools should look at other ways that students can help besides community service.
   **J.** There are so many ways you can help people today, from volunteering your time to simply texting a certain number to donate to charity on your phone!

3. When the sky turned green, we knew it was going to be a mean one. "Y'all get outta the yard now!" Mama called, already gathering the stray toys we'd left in the grass. Her "I said now!" meant she was not messing around, and my brothers and I came running through the door. We hadn't been inside more than a minute when the wind started banging against the outside of the house like a boxer with nothing to lose. In a few more minutes the screen door came unhinged and was fixing to fly away...

   ...You could tell that Mama was crying as she took stock of the damage, which I couldn't quite understand because our place had mostly been spared. But there she was, tears as big as soap bubbles rolling down her cheeks, looking as if all she could see was the rubble that could have been there. All I could think was how peaceful the world seemed afterward, like nothing had happened at all.

   **A.** But something did happen, and that thing was a tornado.
   **B.** No apologies, just a return to clear, blue skies and the smell of prairie grass.
   **C.** Captain, ever the faithful companion, put his wet nose into the folds of Mama's skirt, which made Mama laugh a little through her tears.
   **D.** I thought about Papa and how, when he was alive, he always knew just what to say to turn the scariest thing into something funny.

## Style

**Let's wrap this puppy up** *(not literally)* **with some thoughts about style.** Most people think about clothing when it comes to style. That's not a bad metaphor when it comes to thinking about writing—if the substance of what you're writing is the body, then style is the clothing you dress that body in.

*See? Style matters.* **The style you choose makes a big impact too:** picture Queen Elizabeth of England in a pastel pink wool overcoat, like she normally wears.

**Now** picture her dressed in '90s hip-hop attire.

**The essays on the ACT English section test you on style by giving you answer choices that are grammatically sound but out of style with the passage.** If an essay reads like a history textbook, you probably wouldn't want to include a sentence like, **"You don't have to tell me twice!"** because that would be WAY out of tone.

# TRY THIS EXERCISE

**INSTRUCTIONS:** Each example contains two sentences. Identify whether the two sentences have the same tone or they disagree in tone and **circle the corresponding answer**.

1. Curiosity, which is NASA's most advanced robotic rover to explore Mars, was deployed inside the Gale Crater in order to find evidence that the crater once held a massive lake. Wouldn't that be something?

   **Yes, those sentences are perfect together**

   **Uh...not so much.**

2. If I had a nickel for every time someone nearly ran me over with a shopping cart at Whole Foods, I might have enough money to shop at Whole Foods. Some grocery stores have significantly higher prices than others.

   **Two peas in a pod!**

   **I can't even read those two sentences in the same sitting.**

3. Although Thomas Edison is the first inventor to come to mind for many Americans, he is not the only prolific inventor in our history. Jerome Lemelson, for instance, held over 600 patents on devices from magnetic tape recorders to bar code scanners.

   **These sentences belong together like two lovebirds.**

   **These sentences should break up.**

4. Quick: who is the best football player in history? The answer might not be as clear as you thought.

   **Yup, that's a keeper.**

   **Horrible. Horrible.**

5. Philip Glass and Terry Riley are both composers of contemporary classical music that has been labeled as "minimal." Characteristics of this style include a steady rhythmic pulse, repetition, and gradual transformation.

   **Crank up the minimal music and let's have a party because those two sentences are great together!**

   **This simply won't do.**

6. According to an NPPGA report, farmers in North Dakota grow over 2.7 billion pounds of potatoes annually. Jumpin' Jack Flash... that's a lot of 'taters!

   **I see nothing wrong with pairing those two sentences.**

   **Really? 'Taters?**

## EXERCISE: Rhetorical Skills

Read the following essay and think about relevance, redundancy, author's intent, organization and style when answering the questions.

## TRY THIS EXERCISE

**INSTRUCTIONS:** Use all of your newfound rhetorical skills to pick the best answers on this passage.

[1]

[1] Cimicidae, more commonly known as "bed bugs," are small parasitic insects that feed solely on the blood of warm-blooded animals. [2] Throughout the WWII era and into the 1950s, the "bed bug" wreaked havoc on the citizens of most major American cities; however, by the end of the 20th century, bed bugs were thought to have been largely eradicated due to the use of pesticides. [3] Unfortunately, since the late 1990s, bed bugs have made a major resurgence. Some scientists claim that the problem has become so widespread that it may soon be officially classified as an epidemic. [1] [4] While no one can say for sure what has caused the rebirth of one of the worst nuisances on the planet, scientists suggest that the combination of increased travel (which makes it easier for bed bugs to migrate) and a shift in pest control practices (like the outlaw of certain pesticides such as DDT) has played a role.

[2]

[1] The resurgence of bed bugs in recent years has been difficult to quell. For one thing, bed bugs are natural hitch-hikers, so if someone comes in contact with them in a public space like a hotel room, it's likely that the bugs will follow him or her home, thereby infesting locations that were previously uninfested. [2] They can also hide in clothing and

1. Given that all of the following sentences are true, which one most effectively gives the reader a clear sense of the scope of the problem?
   A. NO CHANGE
   B. There have been stories in the news lately about posh hotels closing down because of bed bug problems.
   C. I am so terrified about getting bed bugs that I literally sleep with one eye open.
   D. The world is a big place, so just think of how many insects that is!

furniture, which if re-sold can infest a new home or business. [3] Additionally, since they are small and come out to feed primarily at night, bed bugs are hard to detect. 2

[4] People can sometimes go weeks or months without noticing a bed bug infestation, each day giving these critters more time to grow and multiply. 3

[3]

There's no surefire way to prevent a bed bug infestation in your home, but there are things you can do to make an infestation less likely. Bed bugs are most often found in major cities in buildings that house many occupants, like big apartment buildings and college dorms, so if you live in one of these environments, know that you are at an increased risk. 4

2. At this point the writer wants to add a sentence that would provide more information about the feeding habits of bed bugs. Should the writer make this addition?
   F. Yes, because it would allow the reader to form a more accurate picture of bed bug behavior.
   G. Yes, because this will make it easier for people to check for bed bugs in their own homes
   H. No, because this would be off-putting to the reader.
   J. No, because the paragraph is concerned with the factors that have made it difficult to eradicate bed bugs.

3. The writer is considering adding the following statement to this paragraph:
   > Personally, I don't really care why they came back; I just want to know how to keep them away from my bed!
   Should the sentence be added to this paragraph, and if so, where should it be placed?
   A. Yes, after Sentence 1.
   B. Yes, after Sentence 2.
   C. Yes, after Sentence 4.
   D. The sentence should NOT be added.

4. The writer is considering deleting the preceding sentence from the essay. If the writer were to make this deletion, the essay would primarily lose:
   F. unnecessary details that are not relevant to the focus of the essay.
   G. details about the construction of buildings in large cities and colleges.
   H. important information regarding environments in which to be particularly vigilant.
   J. a transition between a topic sentence and the details that follow.

If you are planning to travel, research any hotels in which you are planning to stay for a history of bed bug incidents. If you are not making arrangements ahead of time, check for evidence of bed bugs (dark brown or reddish spots) in hotel rooms before unpacking, and don't put your luggage on the bed. Investigate cracks and crevices of any furniture you are planning to buy before purchase, and if you buy used clothing, wash it immediately. [5]

[4]

[1] If the idea of tiny little monsters sucking your blood as you sleep doesn't creep you out enough to take action, think about this: bed bugs are expensive. [6]

5. Suppose the writer intended Paragraph 3 to introduce practical ways that people can help prevent bed bugs. Would this paragraph fulfill the writer's goal?
   A. Yes, because the essay already stated thatpeople are traveling more than they did in the World War II era.
   B. Yes, because it provides the reader with several tips to prevent an infestation.
   C. No, because most Americans don't live inlarge buildings, so the information doesn't apply to them.
   D. No, because the tone of the essay reveals thatthe author intended to entertain, not to inform.

6. At this point the writer wishes to add a personal anecdote to show how a bed bug infestation can be expensive. Given that all the statements are true, which best serves the writer's purpose?
   F. My aunt and uncle, die-hard environmentalists both finally agreed to use industrial streng,th pesticides on their infested home because they were so fed up!
   G. My friend Trisha, for example, had to move three times in a year because of bed bug infestations! The ordeal cost her several thousand dollars in moving charges and security deposits.
   H. Once on a car trip we were stopped by a blizzard. All of the hotels were full except the seediest-looking one, and we ended up sleeping on the beds with our clothes, shoes, and hats still on because we were pretty sure the room had bed bugs!
   J. If the Federal Government would just spend 1% of the money it spends funding a single fighter jet on bed bugs, I think we could eradicate this epidemic completely.

[2] So take this as a warning: have a good night, sleep tight, and...oh yeah...don't let the bed bugs bite! [7] [8]

7. For the sake of the logic and coherence of the essay, Sentence 2 should be placed:
   A. where it is now.
   B. before sentence 1 in Paragraph 1.
   C. after sentence 1 in Paragraph 2.
   D. before sentence 1 in Paragraph 4.

8. Suppose the writer had intended to provide a detailed history of how bed bugs have infested human spaces in the United States. Would this essay fulfill the writer's goal?
   F. Yes, because it discusses the bed bug problem in the middle of the 20th century as well as now.
   G. Yes, because it explains how pesticides that are now outlawed were formerly used to treat bed bug infestations.
   H. No, because a detailed history should include more scientific information about the evolution of bed bugs as a species.
   J. No, because, while the essay mentions a previous period of infestation, it deals primarily with the current bed bug problem.

**Tutor Ted.**

NOTES:

# ENGLISH: ANSWERS & SOLUTIONS

# Answers & Solutions

### Page 22 - INDEPENDENT AND DEPENDENT CLAUSES

1. The game was over, but the crowd refused to leave.
2. While I was making dinner, my dog started barking outside.
3. NO PUNCTUATION NEEDED.
4. If you are sick, you shouldn't ride the subway.
5. He followed the team for fifty years; it hardly mattered whether the team won or lost.
6. It isn't easy being tall, but it's even harder to be short.
7. Maria is my only sister; she is dutiful and decent.
8. Because Lana was so difficult to work with, the studio decided to hire another actress.
9. This Twitter feed doesn't make any sense; it reads like it is written by a computer.
10. NO PUNCTUATION NEEDED.
11. To get a ticket, you'd better buy online.
12. The famous designer decided that the town needed something really grand at its center: he proposed a rose garden flanked by cascading waterfalls. (*a semicolon, a dash, or a comma plus "so" would also be correct*)

### Page 24 - COMMA RULES

1. While the Senator made his speech on Capitol Hill, the activists organized outside.
2. After succumbing to pressure from animal rights activists, the amusement park agreed not to keep Orca whales in captivity.
3. If the chef finds even the smallest objection to the dish, he will send it back to the kitchen in anger.

### Page 24 - COMMA RULES

1. I picked up grapefruit juice, salt, and soda from the local grocery store.
2. I never had a mom, a dad, a dog, a friend, or a good night's sleep.

3. When I looked into her eyes, I saw a wild, angry animal.
4. To think clearly, to feel deeply, to love constantly: these are the objectives of an evolved human being.
5. My silent, happy sister simply nodded her head in amazement.

### Page 25 - COMMA RULES

1. My cousin Jared, who I had never met until I was an adult, plays soccer for the L.A. Galaxy.
2. I took a trip to New Orleans, the birthplace of jazz, to celebrate my graduation from music school.
3. Irving's novel, which took him twelve years to write, suffers from its long, poetic passages.

### Page 29 - APOSTROPHES & POSSESSIVES

**APOSTROPHES**
1. It's
2. its
3. It's
4. it's
5. its
6. It's

**POSSESSIVES**
1. they're/you're
2. Whose
3. Their/Your
4. You're...your/They're...their
5. Their/Your
6. who
7. They're/You're
8. whom
9. their
10. Who's/They're/You're

### Page 31 - SUBJECT-VERB AGREEMENT

1. **S:** Anne and her family, **V:** live
2. **S:** siding, **V:** has (*Remember! The phrase "on the houses" is an adjective phrase just describing the true subject, "siding."*)
3. **S:** team, **V:** hopes

4. **S:** Each, **V:** is *(Same prepositional phrase trick as in #2! "of the songs" just describes the subject "each," and "each" is always singular.)*
5. **S:** Economics, **V:** was
6. **S:** committee, **V:** is

---

## Page 33 - VERB TENSE

| | | | |
|---|---|---|---|
| 1. | C | 4. | F |
| 2. | F | 5. | D |
| 3. | D | 6. | F |

---

## Page 35 - PRONOUNS

1. **Antecedent:** Fans, **Pronoun:** their
2. **Antecedent:** model, **Pronoun:** it
3. **Antecedent:** band, **Pronoun:** its *(Collective nouns can be tricky! Yes, a band or family or team is made up of more than one person, but how many bands are they referring to? 1.)*
4. **Antecedent:** collection **Pronoun:** it
5. **Antecedent:** night **Pronoun:** it
6. **Antecedent:** city **Pronoun:** it

---

## Page 37 - OBJECT PRONOUNS

| | | | |
|---|---|---|---|
| 1. | he | 5. | him...me |
| 2. | me | 6. | whom |
| 3. | us...them | 7. | us |
| 4. | us | 8. | me |

---

## Page 38 - PUNCTUATION

1. The greatest resolution, 100 meters, is found in the upper left portion of the image.
2. When I speak of modern sculpture, I do not refer to every sculptor of our age.
3. Maybe that is so; I couldn't say.
4. The saleswoman started by describing the best television, so I quickly interrupted her to say she should begin with the cheapest offer.
5. It looked like an ordinary pot: squat and light brown with a small amount of blue glaze as trim.
6. In all fairness, I have to admit that Jesse, or someone calling himself Jesse, has done a wonderful job with the building's interior.
7. I was no longer unwilling to go north; on the contrary, the proposed journey excited me.
8. Whenever a new scholar came to our school, I used to confront him at recess to find out as much as I could about him.
9. The horse's name was Triste—which is Spanish for "sadness"—so I called her Sadie.
10. Though the experts called themselves "doctors," only one of them had ever gone to medical school.
11. For example, should a product be in excess production, its price in the market would fall, providing incentive for the public to purchase it, thus reducing the value of the stock.
12. Early in the morning before the orphans awake, Charlize plans the day's activities.
13. Mrs. Endman wore too much makeup; women always put on too much makeup when someone dies.
14. Humors Theory was first developed by the Greek physician Hippocrates, the founder of western medicine, and later expanded upon by Galen.
15. When Grandpa first decided to fly—his dream had been to fly planes—he desperately wanted to be on the front line of the air defense.
16. I'm interested in a career in nursing; I decided to try to secure a spot as a volunteer at a hospital.
17. NO PUNCTUATION NEEDED.
18. Dr. Stone wasn't insane; he was a healer.
19. Venus's atmosphere contains higher concentrations of inert or "noble" gases, especially gases like neon and argon.
20. The Army provided tents, showers, mess halls, and latrines and, waiving the age restriction, invited members as young as seventeen years old to join.

---

## Page 41 - SHORTER IS BETTER

| | |
|---|---|
| 1. | A |
| 2. | F |
| 3. | A |
| 4. | J |
| 5. | A |

## Pages 44-45 - SENTENCE LOGIC

1. C
2. F
3. B
4. G
5. B
6. F
7. A
8. G
9. A
10. J
11. B
12. G

## Page 47 - RELEVANCE EXERCISE 1

1. DELETE
2. KEEP
3. DELETE *(The highlighted portion is not TOTALLY irrelevant, but it is a bit too broad in scope, and it interrupts the flow of thoughts that is much clearer without it.)*
4. KEEP *(Conversely, this clause is not TOTALLY necessary, but it does match the paragraph's how-to tone and provides us with relevant information we would not have otherwise.)*
5. DELETE

## Pages 48-49 - RELEVANCE EXERCISE 2

**The following phrases/sentences should be DELETED:**

1. and Homare Sawa of Japan became the oldest player to score a goal.
2. Mark Zuckerberg recently settled a lawsuit with the Winklevoss twins regarding the founding of Facebook.
3. One time I found a fifty dollar bill on the street and used it to buy a new pair of skinny jeans.
4. Many Major League Baseball players come from Latin America and the Caribbean.
5. Some people don't pay their taxes, and these people are called scofflaws.
6. which was built in 1873 by a Danish farmer by the name Viktor Schmeichel
7. The term "prom" comes from the word "promenade," a dance step practiced in classic English and American social dances.
8. Divers' Ed is a mandatory class in some school districts, but others treat it as an extracurricular or private activity.
9. and casting is the process by which producers find people to be on their shows.
10. which took place on a Tuesday

## Page 50 - RELEVANCE EXERCISE 3

1. **MOVE** *(Specifically, this sentence should be moved to the beginning of the paragraph. It is clearly meant to be a "hook." The current first sentence seems to begin in the middle of a thought and would be better with a bit more leadin.)*
2. KEEP
3. DELETE

## Page 51 - REDUNDANCY EXERCISE 1

1. Redundant
2. Not redundant
3. Redundant
4. Redundant
5. Not redundant
6. Redundant
7. Redundant
8. Not redundant
9. Redundant
10. Not redundant

## Page 52 - REDUNDANCY EXERCISE 2

1. DELETE
2. KEEP
3. DELETE
4. KEEP
5. DELETE

## Page 53 - REDUNDANCY EXERCISE 3

1. B
2. J
3. A
4. J
5. A *(A sneaky one! You thought you could just pick the shortest one EVERY time. While yes, **"shorter is better"** is the rule, here these two pieces of information do tell us different things, both of which are relevant to the point being made.)*

## Pages 56-57 - AUTHOR'S INTENT

1. C
2. F *(Yes, this paragraph spends about as much time mentioning space as it does the deep ocean, but it is clear that this comparison with space is meant as an introduction to a broader discussion about the ocean or **"our own planet's depths."**)*
3. D
4. J *(What is the key phrase in the question? **"Sensory details!"**)*
5. A

80

## Page 59 - DICTION EXERCISE 1

1. +/-
2. -/+
3. -/+
4. +/-
5. +/-

## Page 59 - DICTION EXERCISE 2

1. **"Knowing"** requires a greater degree of certainty than **"supposing."**
2. To **"halt"** insinuates that a stop is both abrupt and temporary. To **"conclude"** is simply to end.
3. These are close, but the word **"surrender"** means to cease to resist an enemy or opponent, while **"forfeit"** means to lose as a result of wrongdoing.
4. The word approve is more active/positive than accept. To **"approve"** indicates you are making a direct decision to agree to or support something, while you can **"accept"** something without actually making a decision about it.
5. **"Loathe"** has a much stronger negative connotation compared to **"dislike."**

## Page 60 - DICTION EXERCISE 3

1. **C** *(Even if you don't totally know what the word **"acute,"** means, none of the rest of the options really make sense.)*
2. **G**
3. **D**
4. **H**
5. **A**
6. **J** *(Many times you can make decisions here based on the literal v. figurative usage of words. Here, the word "contract" is too literal to make sense. We use the word **"contract"** to mean that something like a lung or a balloon literally got smaller by pulling in on itself.)*

## Page 61 - ORGANIZATION & FLOW EXERCISE 1

Correct Order: 1, 5, 4, 3, 2

## Page 62 - ORGANIZATION & FLOW EXERCISE 2

Correct Order: 4, 1, 2, 3

## Page 64 - INTRODUCTIONS

1. B
2. F
3. C

## Page 67 - TRANSITIONS

1. A
2. G

## Page 69 - CONCLUSIONS

1. D
2. F
3. B

## Page 71 - STYLE

1. Uh...not so much.
2. I can't even read those two sentences in one sitting.
3. These sentences belong together like two lovebirds.
4. Yup, that's a keeper.
5. Crank up the minimal music and let's have a party because those two sentences are great together!
6. Really? 'Taters?

## Pages 72-75 - RHETORICAL SKILLS

**Question 1: (A)**
The key word is scope, meaning how big is the problem. Only one answer gives you an idea of the extent of the problem.

**Question 2: (J)**
The paragraph in question discusses why it has been difficult to get rid of the bed bugs. Their feeding habits are irrelevant.

### Questions 3: (D)

You can take your cue based on what you've read. While the tone of the passage isn't formal, it does serve to provide information about bed bugs, not personal opinion or anecdotes. This sentence would not add anything substantial to the passage.

### Question 4: (H)

Unlike the sentence in the previous question, the sentence in question here actually is valuable. Paragraph 3 discusses what you should look out for to minimize the risk of an infestation. Knowing environments where bed bugs thrive is useful information.

### Question 5: (B)

As mentioned above, the purpose of the paragraph is to provide tips to minimize the likelihood of an infestation.

### Question 6: (G)

What is the writer's purpose? The fourth paragraph starts by stating that one additional reason to stay vigilant is that dealing with bed bugs can be expensive. There's only one personal anecdote that discusses the cost of handling an infestation.

### Question 7: (A)

The sentence starts with **"So take this as a warning,"** which sounds like the author is wrapping up the passage.

### Question 8: (J)

If you glance back at the passage, you will notice that only the first paragraph provides some historical information about bed bugs; the passage as a whole does not provide a detailed history of bed bug infestations

**Tutor Ted.**

NOTES:

1_Pre-Algebra

**?**

## #HOW MANY?
**60** minutes
**60** questions

2_Elementary Algebra

That's 1 minute per question, but I'm sure you already figured that out.

The questions **start easy** and **get harder** as you go.

**3**_Intermediate Algebra

1min

# MATH

The Breakdown

## 4_Coordinate Geometry

**6 MAIN CONCEPTS:**
> Pre-Algebra
> Elementary Algebra
> Intermediate Algebra
> Coordinate Geometry
> Plane Geometry
> Trigonometry

**6**

## 5_Plane Geometry

**_trig**

**THE TAKEAWAY?**
Know your algebra, but don't sleep on Soh-Cah-Toa.

**Do...**
work **quickly & accurately.**

**Don't...**
get **stuck on 1 question** and let it **sloOOOOow** you down!

**Tutor Ted.**

NOTES:

# Introduction & Strategy

Answer 60 questions in 60 minutes: that's your task on the ACT Math section. Seems simple enough, doesn't it?

**This section really is straightforward.** Although the makers of the **ACT** tell you that it tests algebra, geometry, and trigonometry, it really tests you on these three things:

- How much math do you know?
- Do you have enough patience to get through a pile of excessively long word problems?
- Can you work quickly *(and accurately)* enough to get through all 60 questions?

**We are going to work on all three of those aspects, and here's how.** We'll start with strategies. Some strategies will show you how to take advantage of the multiple-choice nature of the test. Others will show you alternate approaches, like using your calculator, that can improve your speed and accuracy.

**After we talk about strategy, we'll move on to math content.** The **ACT** Math test covers a lot of ground—everything from 4th grade math through trigonometry and advanced algebra—so no single book can cover everything on the test. In this book, we cover the topics that give students the MOST trouble on the **ACT**, providing clear and effective strategies for tackling the bulk of the math questions you'll see on the test.

**As you work through these chapters, try out your new knowledge on the practice tests in our companion book, "Tutor Ted's ACT Practice Tests."** Practice tests are where everything on the **ACT** Math will come into play. You'll be able to assess yourself for those three factors listed above. Then, you'll know what you need to do to improve, from studying more math content to adopting some new strategies.

And then your score will go up.

And then everyone will be happy.

And we'll throw a party to celebrate.

## Sound like a plan? OK, let's get after it!

# Formulas

*Boring, but worth it!*

**The ACT provides you with none of the math formulas you will need*** so it is up to you to memorize what you need ahead of time. Lucky for you, the list isn't too extensive.

**Know each of these backwards, forwards, and upside down.** Once you know the formulas, the most important part is recognizing when you will need to use one. For that reason, even if you are awesome with formulas, it is a good idea to be familiar with what is on the list so you can quickly grab it and use it.

**If you see a problem that might involve a formula, IMMEDIATELY write the formula down on your scratch paper.** Seriously, write it down. Then, start plugging in the numbers you know and let the solution find itself.

**If you're on the real test and you can't remember a formula, you might be able to use another of our techniques from this book to solve the problem.** But, for certain types of questions, just knowing the formula will be the quickest way to lock in points.

> ***** except for the occasional inclusion of the Law of Sines or Law of Cosines formulas. If you need those guys they will give them to you on the problem.

**OK, here is the list of what you need to know.** Learn these formulas and definitions and keep them in mind when you do the practice problems in the rest of this book.

## STATS

✦ **MEAN (OR AVERAGE)** $= \dfrac{\text{sum of the terms}}{\text{number of terms}}$

✦ **MEDIAN**: the middle number in a list when items are arranged in order from small to large. When a set has an even number of items, the median is the average of the middle two terms.

✦ **MODE**: the term that occurs most frequently in a list

✦ **PROBABILITY** $= \dfrac{\text{"winning" outcomes}}{\text{total possible outcomes}}$

# COORDINATE PLANE

★ **SLOPE:** $m = \dfrac{y_1 - y_2}{x_1 - x_2}$

★ **STANDARD EQUATION OF A LINE:** $y = mx + b$, where m is slope and b is y-intercept

★ **MIDPOINT FORMULA:** midpoint of $(x_1, y_1)$ and $(x_2, y_2) = \left( \dfrac{x_1 + x_2}{2}, \dfrac{y_1 + y_2}{2} \right)$

★ **DISTANCE BETWEEN TWO POINTS** $(x_1, y_1)$ and $(x_2, y_2) = \sqrt{(x_1 - x_2)^2 + (y_1 - y_2)^2}$

★ **QUADRATIC EQUATION:** $x = \dfrac{-b \pm \sqrt{b^2 - 4ac}}{2a}$

★ **EQUATION FOR A CIRCLE WITH CENTER (H,K) AND RADIUS R:** $(x - h)^2 + (y - k)^2 = r^2$

# ALGEBRA

★ **DIFFERENCE OF SQUARES:** $(x + y)(x - y) = x^2 - y^2$

★ **EXPONENT RULES:** $(x^a)(x^b) = x^{a+b}$     $\dfrac{x^a}{x^b} = x^{a-b}$   $(x^a)^b = x^{ab}$

★ **DIRECT VARIATION:** $\dfrac{x_1}{y_1} = \dfrac{x_2}{y_2}$ or $y = kx$

★ **INDIRECT/INVERSE VARIATION:** $(x_1)(y_1) = (x_2)(y_2)$ or $y = \dfrac{k}{x}$

# SHAPE GEOMETRY

★ **AREA OF A TRIANGLE:** $A = \dfrac{1}{2}bh$ (where b is the base and h is the height)

★ **PYTHAGOREAN THEOREM:** $a^2 + b^2 = c^2$

★ **AREA OF A RECTANGLE:** $A = bh$

★ **AREA OF A TRAPEZOID:** $A = \dfrac{b_1 + b_2}{2}h$     ★ **AREA OF A PARALLELOGRAM:** $A = bh$

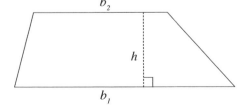

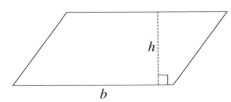

- ★ **AREA OF A CIRCLE:** $A = \pi r^2$

- ★ **CIRCUMFERENCE OF A CIRCLE:** $C = 2\pi r$ or $C = \pi d$

- ★ **VOLUME OF A CYLINDER:** $V = \pi r^2 h$

- ★ **SURFACE AREA OF A CYLINDER:** $SA = 2\pi rh + 2\pi r^2$

- ★ **VOLUME OF A RECTANGULAR SOLID (A BOX):** $V = lwh$

- ★ **SURFACE AREA OF A RECTANGULAR SOLID:** $SA = 2(lw + lh + hw)$

- ★ **NUMBER OF DEGREES IN AN $n$-SIDED POLYGON:** $(n-2)*180$

## TRIGONOMETRY

- ★ soh-cah-toa: $\text{sine} = \dfrac{\text{opposite}}{\text{hypotenuse}}$ $\quad$ $\text{cosine} = \dfrac{\text{adjacent}}{\text{hypotenuse}}$ $\quad$ $\text{tangent} = \dfrac{\text{opposite}}{\text{adjacent}}$

- ★ $\text{cosecant (csc)} = \dfrac{1}{\text{sine}}$ $\quad$ $\text{secant (sec)} = \dfrac{1}{\text{cosine}}$ $\quad$ $\text{cotangent (cot)} = \dfrac{1}{\text{tangent}}$

## SEQUENCES

- ★ **ARITHMETIC SEQUENCE:** A sequence of terms in which each term is equal to the preceding term plus (or minus) a common difference, e.g. 1, 3, 5, 7, 9 is an arithmetic sequence in which each term is 2 more than the preceding term.

- ★ **FORMULA FOR THE NTH TERM OF AN ARITHMETIC SEQUENCE:** $a_n = a_1 + (n-1)d$
  Where $a_1$ is the first term in the sequence and d is the common difference between terms.

- ★ **GEOMETRIC SEQUENCE:** A sequence of terms in which each term is equal to the preceding term multiplied by a common ratio, e.g. 2, -4, 8, -16, 32 is a geometric sequence because each term is equal to the preceding term multiplied by -2.

- ★ **FORMULA FOR THE NTH TERM OF A GEOMETRIC SEQUENCE:** $a_n = a_1 r^{(n-1)}$
  Where $a_1$ is the first term in the sequence and r is the common ratio between terms.

# Mathcabulary

Sorry to burst your bubble, but there is some vocabulary on the ACT, and oddly enough, it's on the math section. The good news is that there isn't a whole lot of it, and once you know it, you'll be able to easily work some problems that otherwise would have been nearly impossible.

*Wait...*

*I thought I didn't have to learn vocabulary for the ACT?*

## HERE'S SOME OF THAT MATH VOCAB IN ACTION:

The first two terms of a geometric sequence are 16 and 8. What is the 5th term?

A. -16
B. -8
C. 0
D. 1
E. 2

**This question is a breeze ...if you know the definition of "geometric sequence"?** Otherwise you might have to take a guess. If you're guessing, you're potentially missing out on points.

### A geometric sequence is a list of numbers
in which each term is equal to the preceding term multiplied by a constant value.

Here that multiplying constant is 1/2, because that's what you multiply by to get from 16 to 8. Multiply by 1/2 three more times to get to the fifth term and you'll find that it's 1.

**See? Know the definition—that question is easy.** Don't know the definition—you're just guessing.

So the lesson is...
study your Mathcabulary!

**You likely know a lot of these already. Make sure you know all of them by heart.**

# HERE IS WHAT YOU NEED TO KNOW:

**INTEGER:** All positive and negative whole numbers, including zero.
In other words, the set {... –3, –2, –1, 0, 1, 2, 3, ...}

**SUM:** Addition

**DIFFERENCE:** Subtraction

**PRODUCT:** Multiplication

**QUOTIENT:** Division

**MULTIPLE:** The product of two integers. Some multiples of 12 are 12, 24, and 36.

**FACTOR:** An integer which can divide evenly into another integer.
Some factors of 12 are 2, 3, and 12.

**PRIME NUMBER:** A number greater than 1 *(so, nope! 1 is not prime. I know, it's a real paradigm shifter)* that has only two factors, 1 and itself. The first few prime numbers are 2, 3, 5, 7, and 11.

**REMAINDER:** The amount "left over" after the one integer is divided into another.
For example, when we divide 17 by 5, there is a quotient of 3 and a remainder of 2.

**COEFFICIENT:** A constant number that multiplies a variable.
For instance, 3 is the coefficient in the expression 3xy.

**CONSTANT:** A number that doesn't change. Some say the only constant in the world IS change. Wrap your brain around that.

**LEAST COMMON MULTIPLE:** The smallest positive integer into which two or more integers divide evenly. For example, 24 is the LCM of 8 and 12.

**LEAST COMMON DENOMINATOR:** The smallest whole number that can be used as a denominator for two or more fractions. The least common denominator is the least common multiple of the original denominators.

**ARITHMETIC SEQUENCE:** A sequence such as 1, 5, 9, 13, 17 or 12, 7, 2, –3, –8, –13, –18 , which has a constant difference between terms. 1 + 4 = 5 ... 5 + 4 = 9 ... etc.

**GEOMETRIC SEQUENCE:** A sequence such as 2, 6, 18, 54, 162, which has a constant ratio between terms. 2 x 3 = 6 ... 6 x 3 = 18 ... etc.

**RATIONAL NUMBER:** A real number that can be expressed as a fraction such as -1/2, 0, 4/3, and 7.

**IRRATIONAL NUMBERS:** Real numbers that cannot be expressed as a fraction.
Examples include $\pi$, $\sqrt{3}$ and e.

**IMAGINARY NUMBER:** A complicated subject, but all you need to know for the **ACT** is *i*, which is equivalent to the square root of -1.

**REAL NUMBER:** Any number that isn't imaginary.

**COMPLEX NUMBER:** A number that includes both real and imaginary components, such as 3 + 5*i*.

**UNITS DIGIT:** The ones place in a number. For example 4,857.63 has a units digit of 7.

**ARC:** A portion of the circumference of a circle.

**BISECT:** To cut something into two equal halves.

**VERTEX:** One of the points where two sides of a figure meet.

**DIAGONAL:** A line segment connecting two non-adjacent vertices.

**PARALLEL:** Two lines that have the same slope and that will never intersect.

**PERPENDICULAR:** Two lines with opposite reciprocal slopes and that form a 90-degree angle where they intersect.

**ISOSCELES:** A shape with at least two congruent sides.

**EQUILATERAL:** A shape whose sides are all congruent.

**Y-INTERCEPT:** The point at which a line crosses the y-axis. The x-value of this point is zero.

**X-INTERCEPT:** The point at which a line crosses the x-axis. The y-value of this point is zero.

**DOMAIN:** All possible *x*-values within a function. The domain of $f(x) = \sqrt{x}$ is all x greater than or equal to zero, because the square root of a negative number is not a real value.

**RANGE:** All possible y values of a function. The range of the function $f(x) = x^2$ is all y values greater than or equal to zero, because the vertex of the parabola is at zero, it points upward, and the function will never produce any negative y values.

**PERFECT SQUARE:** A number that has an integer as its square root. Examples: 9, 64, 144.

**ASYMPTOTE:** A line that another curve approaches but never touches. Graph $y = \tan(x)$ on your calculator and you'll see a vertical asymptote at $x = 90°$ (or $x = \frac{\pi}{2}$ if you are in radian mode).

That is it!

**RADIANS:** A unit to measure angles. $\pi$ radians = 180°.

Of course, that is not an exhaustive list of every term across all of mathematics, but it is a collection of the most important things to know on the **ACT**.

Now here are some practice problems to help show you how valuable this knowledge is.

93

## EXERCISE

**INSTRUCTIONS:** Solve each problem and choose the correct answer.

1. Michelle is adding the following three fractions. Which of the following should she use as her least common denominator?

$$\frac{1}{11 \cdot 29 \cdot 53^2} + \frac{1}{11^2 \cdot 29} + \frac{1}{11 \cdot 29^3}$$

A. $11 \cdot 29$
B. $11 \cdot 29 \cdot 53$
C. $11 \cdot 29 \cdot 53^2$
D. $11^2 \cdot 29^3 \cdot 53^2$
E. $11^4 \cdot 29^5 \cdot 53^2$

2. When $4x + 5y = 40$ is graphed on the coordinate plane, what is the $x$-intercept?

F. 4
G. 5
H. 8
J. 10
K. 40

3. What is the smallest three-digit integer that is a multiple of 19 and has 3 as a factor?

A. 3
B. 19
C. 57
D. 114
E. 228

4. Which of the following is a rational number?

F. $\sqrt{\frac{1}{2}}$

G. $\sqrt{\frac{12}{2}}$

H. $\sqrt{\frac{33}{3}}$

J. $\sqrt{\frac{36}{3}}$

K. $\sqrt{\frac{36}{9}}$

5. What is the domain of $f(x) = \frac{2}{\sqrt{x-1}}$ for all real numbers?

A. $x > 0$
B. $x \geq 0$
C. $x > 1$
D. $x \geq 1$
E. $x > 2$

# Calculators

In school, you are probably discouraged from using a calculator, but when taking the **ACT**, you should use it as often as you can.

*Your new ACT Math best friend*

## First things first:
**Here is a list of the calculators that are NOT allowed on the ACT.**

- Texas Instruments: TI-89, TI-92, TI-Nspire CAS *(the non-CAS TI-Nspire is allowed)*
- Hewlett Packard: HP Prime, HP 48GII, HP 40G, 49G, 50G
- Casio: fx-CP400, ClassPad 300, ClassPad 330, Algebra fx 2.0, CFX-9970G *(all models)*

## Other calculator no-nos:

- You can't use the calculator on your cell phone. Or an iPad. Or a laptop.
- You can't use a calculator that uses paper tape or that makes noise.
- Your calculator can't have a QWERTY-style *(computer/typewriter)* keyboard.
- You can't use a calculator that has to be plugged in *(these really did exist—my dad had one)*.

## WHAT CAN YOU DO WITH YOUR CALCULATOR?

*Let's get to the fun part.*

**Naturally, you can use it for making calculations.** That might be the most obvious thing we include in this book, but it's important! Really! Using the calculator can save you from making arithmetic errors in your head.

**Beyond that, there are lots of great, less well-known ways to use the calculator.** We'll get into those in just a minute. In addition to using all of the awesome, built-in features of the calculator, you can use it to run programs. Shhhhhhh...don't tell anyone!

**The ACT does not allow calculators or programs with "computer algebra system functionality."** That means that you're not allowed to use a program that will solve a system of equations for you without you having to do a thing. It also doesn't allow the use of long, multi-function programs. It DOES allow for single-function programs that don't exceed 25 lines of code, and that opens up a lot of possibilities. Quadratic equations solved for you. Equations of lines given to you if you know two points on the line. Distance in 2- or 3-dimensions. There are ALL KINDS of helpful programs.

---

**You'll need a cord to connect your calculator to your computer. Find one; it will be worth it.**

**If you have a Texas Instruments TI-83+ or TI-84, check out this site:**
http://www.ticalc.org/pub/83plus/basic/math/

**For Hewlett Packard programs, visit:** http://www.hpcalc.org

**For Casio calculator programs, visit:** http://www.spiderpixel.co.uk/caspro/programsindex.html

**Programs are great, but so are the built-in functions of the calculator.** With that in mind, here is a review of some of the most useful things the calculator can do for you.
*Note: these instructions pertain to Texas Instruments calculators only.*

**Quick primer: everything written below in brackets represents a button.** For instance, to start using your calculator, you might want to think about, maybe, oh I don't know, pressing the [ON] button. If we include the [2ND] command, that means that the option you need to find is one of the blue-colored, secondary options listed ABOVE a button. An option listed in ALL CAPS after a button refers to a menu heading.

## 1 CONVERTING DECIMALS TO FRACTIONS: When a TI calculator finishes an operation, it will leave you with a decimal result.

What if the answers are expressed as fractions? Convert that bad boy on your calculator.
[MATH] --> MATH --> 1:>Frac

**Choose that option after you get a decimal answer.** Your calculator's home screen should read Ans>Frac. Press [ENTER] and you'll get the fractional version of the decimal. If the answer you got cannot be converted to a fraction, it will just give you the decimal version again.

## 2 CONVERTING FRACTIONS TO DECIMALS: Sometimes it's easier to work with decimals than fractions.

🔎 **For example:**
For the numbers below, which of the following is correct?

$$5\frac{7}{11}, 5\frac{13}{19}, 5\frac{4}{7}, 5\frac{3}{5}$$

**F.** $5\frac{7}{11} < 5\frac{13}{19} < 5\frac{4}{7} < 5\frac{3}{5}$   **J.** $5\frac{7}{11} < 5\frac{3}{5} < 5\frac{4}{7} < 5\frac{13}{19}$

**G.** $5\frac{3}{5} < 5\frac{4}{7} < 5\frac{7}{11} < 5\frac{13}{19}$   **K.** $5\frac{4}{7} < 5\frac{3}{5} < 5\frac{7}{11} < 5\frac{13}{19}$

**H.** $5\frac{4}{7} < 5\frac{3}{5} < 5\frac{13}{19} < 5\frac{7}{11}$

**Comparing this many fractions by hand would stink.** Don't do it. Use your calculator to make decimal equivalents, which are much easier to compare. Divide each of the fractional components, add 5 *(or just ignore the 5 altogether since they all include it)*, and then make your comparison.

*Now just carefully put them in order.*

$$5\frac{7}{11} \approx 5.64$$

$$5\frac{13}{19} \approx 5.68$$

*Did you get K?*

$$5\frac{4}{7} \approx 5.57$$

*Good.*

$$5\frac{3}{5} = 5.6$$

## USE THE GRAPHING FUNCTION: If a problem asks you about a visible aspect of a graph, why not just graph it and take a look? Press [Y=] in that top row of buttons just below the screen. Enter your function and press [GRAPH].

**3**

🔍 **Try it here:**
Which of the equations below, when graphed, has a vertical asymptote of 3?

**A.** $\frac{x-3}{3x+3}$

**B.** $\frac{x^2-9}{x-3}$

**C.** $\frac{3x+3}{x-3}$

**D.** $\frac{3x-3}{x+3}$

**E.** $\frac{3}{x+3}$

**If you know the vertical asymptote rules, hooray for you!** If you don't, aren't sure, or want to double check, pull out your graphing calculator and graph each equation. A vertical asymptote is a line that graph approaches but never touches. Which one of these graphs gets close to, but never touches $x=3$? Only $\frac{3x+3}{x-3}$.

## DO COMPUTATIONS USING A GRAPH: Once you've graphed an equation, you don't just have to look at it—you can let your calculator do some math for you.

**4**

🔍 **Try this:**
enter the functions $y=x^2+2$ and $y=2x+4$ in the [Y=] screen. Press [GRAPH].
Now press [2ND] [CALC]. From that menu, you can find a value on either of the graphs, a zero (or $x$-intercept), the minimum of that parabola, and the point of intersection of the two graphs.

*Holy s\*\*\*, that's handy!*

🔍 **Try the [TRACE] button as well.**
Use the left-and-right arrows to see values on a function. Press the up-and-down arrows to jump from one function to another. Type a number and press enter to find out the exact y-value at a given x-value.

Given the equation $y = 4x - 1$ over the interval $-1 \le x \le 3$, which of the following statements is (are) true?

**I.** The graph has a slope of 4
**II.** The graph has a zero at $x = -1$
**III.** The graph has a zero at $x = 0.25$

**A.** I only
**B.** III only
**C.** I and III only
**D.** II and III only
**E.** I, II, and III

*Play around with those handy tools on this question, bub.*

**This is the kind of question where you want to reflexively grab your calculator and let it do the work.** Your brain works hard enough; give it a break once in awhile. So what do you do? You punch the function into the [Y=] screen and press [GRAPH]. Now press [TRACE]. Type in -1 to see what you get as your y-value. It's not a zero, so statement II is false. Type in 0.25. It IS a zero, so statement III is true. What about statement I? Hopefully you see that 4 in front of the $x$ and can say, hey, that's my slope! That statement is true! **The answer then is (C).**

# 5 USE THE CALCULATOR TO WORK WITH IMAGINARY NUMBERS.

**The calculator can handle imaginary numbers?! It sure can.**
Press [2ND] and then the decimal button [.] and you will have *i*. Do with it whatever you please!

*Wait, whaaaaaaaaaat?*

For the imaginary number *i* and the integer *n*, which of the following is a possible value of $i^n$?

A.    -3
B.    2
C.    -1
D.    0
E.    2

**Now some of you are going to get this question in two seconds**—you know that, by definition, $i^2$ equals -1. If you know that, good on ya: choose C and move on. If you're not as fluent in *i*, just crunch some values into your calculator using that [2ND][i] button (above the decimal key) and stop once you get -1 as an answer.

These are five of literally hundreds of things your calculator can do for you. **Play around a bit.** That calculator you have is a powerful tool when you know how to use it!

# Wordy Word Problems

Have you noticed how MANY words the **ACT** uses in the math section? A ton. Too many, if you ask most students. Why is that? The **ACT's** explanation is that they are testing you on **"real world"** problems, but most of this stuff is too silly to be used by anyone on this planet.

Now featured on the math section: reading comprehension.

Awesome.

**The real answer is that they want to test your patience...** *(in addition to your knowledge, problem-solving, and meticulousness)*. It's true. They want to see if they can knock you senseless with so much text that you get overwhelmed and therefore get the question wrong.

**Here's the thing: those long, wordy problems are simple math questions in disguise.** On these questions, it's your job to simplify. If you are ready to read, translate, to note every number, and organize the given info, you'll find that the math is the EASY part.

**My advice to you is to attack wordy word problems through this four-step approach:**

- Read the problem. Pull out all the important stuff, like numbers and formulas. Write that stuff down.
- Draw, mark, and label any figures you were given or that you drew yourself.
- Read the question again to see what the **ACT** wants you to find.
- Solve that bad boy.

---

🔍 **Let's try one together to see what's up.**

The standard deviation of a set of numbers is used to quantify the spread, or dispersion, of a data set, and it is often used to understand how normal or abnormal a given data point (or set of data) is. Standard deviation of a set is calculated by finding the sum of the squares of the difference between each data point and the mean of the set. That number is then divided by the number of elements in the set, and the square root of this value is the standard deviation. What is the standard deviation of the set of numbers 3, 4, 4, 8, 11?

**A.** $\sqrt{6}$

**B.** $\sqrt{\frac{46}{5}}$

**C.** $\sqrt{14}$

**D.** $\sqrt{30}$

**E.** $\sqrt{46}$

**For starters, a problem like this would show up in the last 10 questions of the section—it's meant to be at that level of complexity/difficulty.** Second, if you were short of time AT ALL, I would skip this question, finish everything else, then come back to this bad boy. When you're ready, here is how you would solve it.

**Read the question and extract what is useful.** Do we care how or why standard deviation is used? Not while we're taking the ACT we don't. After that useless background info, we're given a verbal explanation of how to calculate standard deviation. Note that; we'll come back to it. Last, we're asked to calculate a standard deviation, and we're given a data set to use. Start there. Now go step-by-step through the explanation of the calculation.

First, we need to find the **"sum of the squares of the difference between each data point and the mean."** That's a mouthful, but let's take it apart. First, we need the mean. That's the average, which is (3+4+4+8+11)/5=6. Now we need the square of the difference between each term and the mean. That's $(3-6)^2 = 9$, $(4-6)^2 = 4$, $(4-6)^2 = 4$, $(8-6)^2 = 4$, and $(11-6)^2 = 25$. Now we need to add those: 9+4+4+4+25=46.

Getting there! Now we divide that by the number of terms (5), and take the square root. That's $\sqrt{(46/5)}$, and if you can believe it, that's the answer!
We made it!

Is that question tedious? You bet it is. Is it terribly hard? Not really. Just remember: on these wordy word problems, **the reading is the hard part.** Hang with it, follow the procedure, and you'll turn these guys into much, much simpler questions.

# Plugging In

**Do you feel sick to your stomach every time you see a problem full of variables?** Or do you think algebra problems are a breeze, but still find yourself making silly errors and losing points? Well, I have some great news for you: many problems that include variables can be made simpler and easier by replacing the variables with numbers.

*Because numbers are friendlier than variables.*

**That's right!** You are the boss of these problems because you can simply MAKE UP NUMBERS. What, you say? How could I possibly just make up numbers? Any numbers at all? The answer, basically, is yes. As long as the numbers you use follow the rules laid out by the question, you can use any numbers you want!

Even if you love algebra, check this strategy out—it might help you to work more accurately and therefore earn more points!

Remember, the **ACT** isn't school. You don't have to solve problems the way you do in the classroom. The best way to solve any **ACT** math problem is whatever way is the quickest and most accurate for you. Having multiple tools to attack a problem will help you do that.

🔎 **Let me give you a quick example to show you why algebra problems are evil and sneaky and you may be better off using real numbers. Pretend...**
you want to get some photos printed for your dad for Father's Day. The prints are 10 cents each and you order four. If you pay one dollar, how much change, in cents, do you get back?

*Not too hard, huh?*

Your answer _____

🔎 **Now let's try a similar problem, this time written in annoying ACT-speak with ugly variables.**
Alison went to the local drugstore to purchase photo prints for her dad for Father's Day. The prints cost $w$ cents each. Alison buys $x$ prints, and she pays $y$ dollars. How much change, in cents, does Alison get back?

*So much harder, right?!*

Your answer _____

99% of people get this problem wrong, even if they are really good at algebra.

**What if we ditch the algebra and toss the ugly variables out?**
We call this technique **Plugging In,** and you can use it every time
you see variables in the question and in the answer choices.
You can also sometimes use **Plugging In** in some other situations
when there are variables or unknowns.

Basically, **Plugging In** is a useful tool on any question on which the values themselves are not
important but their RELATIONSHIPS to one another are.

## PLUGGING IN STEPS:

- Replace the variables with simple numbers
  *(for example: 2, 3, 5, 10, or 100)* that fit the problem.
- Label your numbers *(for example: x=2 and y=5).* Yes, write 'em down.
- Solve the problem using your numbers.
- Write down the answer and circle it.
- Plug your numbers into the answer choices to see which one matches.

**Now let's try again:**
Alison went to the local drugstore to purchase photo prints for her dad for
Father's Day. The prints cost **w** cents each. Alison buys **x** prints, and she pays
**y** dollars. How much change, in cents, does Alison get back?

A. $wxy$

B. $y-wx$

C. $w-xy$

D. $100y-wx$

E. $100w-xy$

**Let's PLUG IN values for the variables to see if we can make this a bit simpler.**
**We start by:** picking any numbers we want for the variables.

- What if Alison buys 8 prints for 20 cents each and pays 2 dollars?
- She would then get 40 cents back in change, right?
- Solving the problem is as easy as that.
- We write down the values we started with ($w=20$, $x=8$, $y=2$), and circle
  the answer that we got: 40.

**Last step:** we replace the variables in the answer choices with the numbers we **Plugged In**
to see which one matches.

**Only answer choice (D) equals 40 when we do that, so (D) is the answer and we are done.**
No algebra necessary!

# PLUGGING IN STEPS:

**1. Use simple numbers that make the math easy.** For example, if you are working with percentages, use 100. If you are going to be dividing by 5, choose a number that is divisible by 5. Don't stress too much about finding perfect numbers. If you pick a number and it turns out to be an annoying number to work with, just start over with a fresh, new number.

**2. Always plug your numbers into all five answer choices.** Always. Even when answer choice A gives you the result that you were looking for. Even when answer choices A through D do NOT give you the result you were looking for. Why? You might have made a mistake somewhere. You might have just been unlucky and more than one answer might work with the numbers you have chosen. If more than one answer works, just plug in a new set of numbers and re-check whatever answer choices you have left. If none of the answer choices work, look back at your work and the problem to see if you can spot an error.

**3. Avoid 1, 0, and numbers that are already in the question.** Also, don't use the same value for different variables. None of these will give you the wrong answer, but if you use them, you are more likely to get more than one answer that works and then you will have to plug in a second time. No one wants to do that.

**4. Don't forget to actually write down and label the numbers you plug in.** And circle your answer choice.

**5. Pay careful attention to the wording of the problem and any restrictions on variables** *(negative/positive, even/odd, less than a certain number, etc.).* Once you have your numbers written down and labeled, it is a good idea to read the problem one more time to make sure your numbers fit and to double-check what it is that you are solving for.

---

**Ready for another question?** This one might not look quite as **Plugging In** friendly, but actually can be knocked on its butt if we Plug In numbers.

Michelle, Kelty, and Herbie took a road trip. Michelle drove the first $\frac{2}{3}$ of the way, Kelty drove $\frac{1}{5}$ of the remaining distance, and Herbie drove the rest. What is the ratio of the number of miles Michelle drove to what Kelty drove, to what Herbie drove?

A. 2:3:5
B. 10:1:4
C. 10:3:2
D. 12:2:3
E. 12:1:5

**This problem doesn't have any variables at all.** It also doesn't give us the mileage of the trip, either. Seems like we're missing something, eh? Well, let's supply it for ourselves by Plugging In. We have no idea how many miles this trip was, so let's just make up a number. We have to split the number into fifths and thirds, so 15 miles is a great number to use—it's divisible by both 3 and 5.

If the trip was 15 miles and Michelle drove 2/3 of it, then she drove 10 miles. Kelty drove 1/5 of the remaining 5, which is 1 mile, and Herbie drove the last 4. Our ratio is 10:1:4 and our answer is B.

Wasn't that easy?!

103

**Your turn to practice!** While every one of these can be solved using algebra, I recommend practicing **Plugging In** for this set. If you get this strategy down, you will have another great tool in your toolbox to attack **ACT** math.

**Hint:** If you happen to be one of those lucky people who rock algebra and have time to spare at the end of ACT math, you might think there is no reason to bother with this strategy, but unless you get a 36 every time you take a practice math section, this strategy can help you too.

**How?** Take those extra minutes you have and use them to solve algebra problems two ways—once with algebra and once with **Plugging In.** If your answers match, you can be doubly sure that you did the problem correctly. If not, you just caught an error and can fix your mistake instead of missing a question and probably a point on your score.

Plugging in:

because it's easier to imagine
3 apples and 2 bananas
than m apples and n bananas

# EXERCISE

**INSTRUCTIONS:** Solve each problem and choose the correct answer.

1. What is the area, in feet, of a circle with a diameter of $2x-5$ feet?

   A. $\left(x^2+\frac{25}{4}\right)\pi$

   B. $\left(x^2-5x+\frac{25}{4}\right)\pi$

   C. $\left(2x^2-10x+\frac{25}{2}\right)\pi$

   D. $(4x^2+25)\pi$

   E. $(4x^2-20x+25)\pi$

2. If $0<y<\frac{1}{2}$, which of the expressions below has the greatest value?

   F. $y^2$

   G. $y^3$

   H. $\frac{1}{y}$

   J. $2y$

   K. $2y^2$

3. In the figure shown below, $\angle XYW$ equals $(2a-35)°$ and $XZ$ is a straight line. What is the degree measure of $\angle WYZ$?

   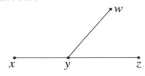

   A. $70+4a$

   B. $180-2a$

   C. $180+2a$

   D. $215-2a$

   E. $215+2a$

4. A dairy cow produces six gallons of milk in 24 hours. At this rate, how many hours will it take the cow to produce $c+2$ gallons of milk?

   F. 16

   G. 24

   H. $4c+2$

   J. $4c+8$

   K. $6c+12$

5. Circle A has a radius 5 times the length of the radius of circle B. The area of circle B is $q$ square inches and the area of circle A is $nq$ square inches. What is the value of $n$?

   A. 5

   B. 10

   C. 15

   D. 20

   E. 25

6. A developer discounts the price of her app by 40% during a flash sale. After the app becomes more popular, she increases the discounted price by 30%. The final price is what percent of the original price?

   F. 10%

   G. 70%

   H. 78%

   J. 88%

   K. 120%

7. If $\frac{a}{b}=\frac{1}{7}$ and $\frac{b}{c}=\frac{7}{9}$, then $\frac{c}{a}=$?

   A. $\frac{1}{126}$

   B. $\frac{1}{9}$

   C. $\frac{9}{49}$

   D. $\frac{49}{4}$

   E. 9

8. To get his helicopter pilots license, Andy must fly with an instructor present for a certain number of hours. During each of the first three months, Andy completes 1/7 of the required hours. On average, what fraction of his total hours must he complete during each of the remaining nine months in order to finish his requirements and get his license?

   F. $\frac{1}{7}$

   G. $\frac{1}{9}$

   H. $\frac{4}{63}$

   J. $\frac{5}{63}$

   K. $\frac{3}{7}$

# Reality Math

## Grouped problems about the "real world." I love the concept of the real world. Have you heard of "The Real World" on MTV? It was the first of the current generation of reality TV shows. If you've been paying attention, you probably know just how "real" reality shows are.

While we'd rather engage in a lively discussion of reality TV shows (which would probably force us to admit just how much we actually watch them, and that would be embarrassing), let's connect this conversation back to the **ACT**.

The **ACT** likes to ask math questions that reflect the "real world" too. You probably have already guessed that these resemble real life as much as a Kardashian family dinner party does. People writing functions to figure out how to construct a chicken coop. Some dude using trig to calculate how big to make build his triangular flower bed. That kind of stuff. Still, it's our job to handle them.

Here's the scoop: approximately twice on each **ACT** math section you will get a set of 2 to 4 math problems preceded by information that will be used to answer the questions.

**Before these problems you will see a box that looks like this:**

> Use the following information to answer questions 31-34

The math content varies widely within these problem sets, from geometry to stats to algebra—it's all fair game. The other thing is that within each set, the questions will vary. They aren't continuous, so the answer to the first question won't necessarily help you to answer the second.

**Here's how you should approach these sets:**
- Read the introductory information so you know what you're dealing with.
- Don't memorize it; often, much of the information doesn't even come into play on the questions.

**If that sounds like the Science section to you, you're right!** These questions are constructed in a similar way to the Science questions.

**Keep a flexible/open mind on these bad boys, and bring all of your math skills to the party.** The hardest thing about these problems is deciding what math strategies to employ. Once you know, the math itself should be a breeze.

# EXERCISE

**INSTRUCTIONS:** Solve each problem and choose the correct answer.

||||||||||||||||||||||||||||||||||||||||||||||||||||||||||||||||||||||||||||||||||||||||||||||||||||||||||||||||||||||||||||||||||||||||||||||||||||

> Use the following information to answer questions 1-3

Annie is building a chicken coop in her backyard, which is completely flat. The chicken coop is a rectangular solid with a triangular prism atop it, as shown in the blueprint below. The rectangular solid has a length of 16 feet, a height of 8 feet, and a width of 8 feet. The triangular ends of the prism are equilateral triangles. The four walls and the four sides of the roof will be made of wood.

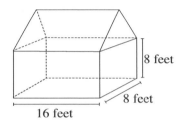

8 feet

8 feet

16 feet

1. Annie plans to cover the floor of the chicken coop with cubic bricks that are four inches on each side. What is the minimum number of bricks she will need to completely cover the entire floor?
   A. 8
   B. 32
   C. 384
   D. 512
   E. 1152

2. To the nearest foot, what is the distance from the highest part of the chicken coop to the ground in feet?
   F. 10
   G. 12
   H. 14
   J. 15
   K. 16

3. After cutting two rectangular windows of 12 feet by 2 feet and a rectangular door of 2 feet by 6 feet, the remainder of the wood must be covered with a water-proof protective coat. One jug of protective coat can cover 140 square feet. How many jugs of waterproof protective coat does Annie need to purchase to cover both the inside and the outside of all of the wood that makes up her chicken coop?
   A. 4
   B. 5
   C. 8
   D. 9
   E. 10

> Use the following information to answer questions 4-6

Figueroa Mountain Academy is printing shirts for its senior class and asked each student what size t-shirt he/she would like. All 480 senior students responded and the results are below.

| T-Shirt Size | Number of Orders |
|---|---|
| Small | 24 |
| Medium | 48 |
| Large | 96 |
| Extra Large | 120 |
| XXL | 192 |

4. Small sized t-shirts were ordered by what percent of the senior class of Figueroa Mountain Academy?
   F. 5%
   G. 10%
   H. 24%
   J. 48%
   K. 50%

5. The more t-shirts that Figueroa Mountain Academy orders at a time, the less it will have to pay per shirt. The principal considers purchasing 2000 shirts at once in order to save money. If the school would like to keep the proportion of shirt sizes the same as those in the senior year poll, how many XXL sized t-shirts should she order?

A. 192
B. 384
C. 576
D. 800
E. 1000

6. Figueroa Mountain Academy's principal puts together a pie chart of the t-shirt orders for the senior class. What is the sum of the degree measures of the central angles of the small and medium shirt sizes?

F. 15°
G. 18°
H. 36°
J. 54°
K. 72°

---

Use the following information to answer questions 7-8.

---

The Muggle Fuggle Company produces musical instrument and is deciding whether to produce either glockenspiels or euphoniums. It has collected the following information.

Investing in production equipment for glockenspiels would cost the company $3,000. The materials and labor required for each glockenspiel are $150 and Muggle Fuggle would charge $450 for each glockenspiel sold.

Investing in production equipment for euphoniums would cost the company $1,000. The materials and labor required for each euphonium are $100 and Muggle Fuggle would charge $150 for each euphonium sold.

7. If Muggle Fuggle decides to produce glockenspiels, how many glockenspiels would it have to sell in order to cover the costs of the production equipment?

A. 0
B. 7
C. 10
D. 20
E. 100

8. Muggle Fuggle projects that it will sell 30 of either instrument. Which instrument should it produce in order to make the most profit and how much profit would it make?

F. Glockenspiels at a $500 profit
G. Euphoniums at a $500 profit
H. Glockenspiels at a $6,000 profit
J. Euphoniums at a $6,000 profit
K. Euphoniums at a $6,500 profit

---

Use the following information to answer questions 9-12.

---

At Farmer Joe's Seed Stand, customers can purchase packets of flower seeds. The table below lists the type of plant, the number of seeds per packet, the regular price of a seed packet, and the current sale price of a seed packet.

Seed packets are regularly priced on weekends and are sale priced on weekdays.

| Type of plant | # of seeds per seed packet | Regular price of seed packet | Sale price of seed packet |
|---|---|---|---|
| Daisy | 10 | $1.20 | $1.00 |
| Zinnia | 60 | $5.05 | $3.75 |
| Poppy | 40 | $.80 | $.70 |
| Foxglove | 25 | $2.90 | $2.50 |
| Snapdragon | 50 | $6.00 | $5.50 |

9. What is the sale price, to the nearest cent, of each snapdragon seed?

A. $.08
B. $.09
C. $.10
D. $.11
E. $.12

10. Kate buys one packet of each of the five types of flower seeds, opens each packet and mixes them together in a bowl. Kate then picks one seed at a time and plants three in a row. If each seed is equally likely to be chosen, what is the probability that Kate will pick three poppy seeds to plant?

   F. $\frac{40}{145} \cdot \frac{39}{145} \cdot \frac{38}{145}$

   G. $\frac{40}{145} \cdot \frac{40}{145} \cdot \frac{40}{145}$

   H. $\frac{40}{185} \cdot \frac{40}{185} \cdot \frac{40}{185}$

   J. $\frac{40}{185} \cdot \frac{39}{184} \cdot \frac{38}{183}$

   K. $\frac{40}{185} \cdot \frac{39}{185} \cdot \frac{38}{185}$

11. If a customer were to buy one packet of each of the five seed types on a weekday instead of a weekend, what approximate percent less would he pay before tax?
   A. 1%
   B. 15%
   C. 16%
   D. 19%
   E. 84%

12. On a Saturday afternoon, Herbert went to Farmer Joe's Seed Stand and spent $81.60 on packets of seeds. He bought 4 times as many daisy packets as poppy packets, and 2 more snapdragon packets than poppy packets. If Herbert only purchased packets of daisies, poppies, and snapdragons, how many packets of seeds did he buy?
   F. 14
   G. 20
   H. 26
   J. 38
   K. 50

Use the following information to answer questions 13-15.

Brent created the table below that gives the population of California (to the nearest one thousand) in selected years.

| Year | Population of California (in thousands) |
|------|----------------------------------------|
| 1850 | 93 |
| 1860 | 380 |
| 1900 | 1,485 |
| 1930 | 5,677 |
| 1950 | 10,586 |
| 1970 | 19,953 |
| 1990 | 29,760 |
| 2000 | 33,872 |
| 2009 | 38,293 |

13. Between which of the following pairs of years did the population of California increase the most?
   A. 1850 to 1860
   B. 1860 to 1900
   C. 1930 to 1950
   D. 1950 to 1970
   E. 2000 to 2009

14. To the nearest whole percent, what was the percent increase in the population of California from 1900 to 2000?
   F. 2%
   G. 22%
   H. 220%
   J. 2,200%
   K. 22,000%

15. Which of the following equations best models the population of California, in millions, $x$ years after 1950?

   A. $\frac{1}{2}x + 10$

   B. $2x + 10$

   C. $10x + \frac{1}{2}$

   D. $10x + 2$

   E. $10x + 10$

# Geometry

## Problem solving strategy: How to handle geometry

**You need some math facts, formulas, and rules to solve geometry problems.** If you read, study, and memorize the geometry chapters of this book, you will have very little problem with that stuff. The **ACT** actually only tests really basic geometry: no proofs or advanced rules here.

**Still, students miss a ton of points on geometry questions.** Why? Most students lose those points because they don't approach geometry questions with the right strategy.

**The advice here might seem either A) too simple or B) too time consuming,** but if you want a higher score on the **ACT** *(no matter what level math student you are)* and are super-serious about it, do the following: **Stop thinking and start writing.**

## EVERY TIME YOU SEE A GEOMETRY PROBLEM...

- **Don't even read to the end of the problem before you start moving your pencil!** Start drawing, marking, and labeling when you read about anything that you could possibly draw, mark, or label. Write each piece of info down as you go, then look back to make sure you used every last bit.

- **Next, look at what you drew, marked, or labeled.** Is there anything else you know based on that information that you can fill it in? For instance, if two angles are on opposites sides of an intersection of two lines, you know those two angles are equal. Fill it in. Anything else? Write that too.

- **If a formula might be involved *(and you know the formula)* write it down immediately.** Take any information from the problem that could be plugged into the formula and—you guessed it—plug it in to the formula. Even simple formulas like the area of a triangle or the circumference of a circle: write them down and fill in any info you know.

- **Now that you've done those three things, you will have everything you need to solve.** Do nothing in your head and everything on your paper or in your calculator. End result? Your scores go up, and you are happy.

*So happy.*

**Quick hint:** When working with π, you rarely need to use the decimal value of 3.1415... Most of the time you should just leave π as a symbol.
If the radius of a circle is 8, think of the area as 64π, not 201.061929...etc.

🔍 **Let's demonstrate this approach to geometry problems in action.**
A circle has a diameter of $\frac{10}{\pi}$ feet. In square feet, what is its area?

    **A.** 25

    **B.** 100

    **C.** $\frac{25}{\pi}$

    **D.** $\frac{100}{\pi}$

    **E.** $\frac{100}{\pi^2}$

## Notice how this is testing a very simple concept – the area of a circle – but it is super confusing because why the $@*% is there a π on the bottom of a fraction?

**Don't panic; just draw and label.**

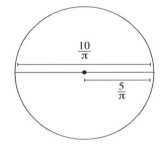

**Now that we've drawn it out, the steps become clearer.**
The diameter is $10/\pi$, which means the radius is $5/\pi$. The circle area formula is $a=\pi r^2$, so our area here is $a= \pi \times (5/\pi)^2$.

**Show ALL of your steps** *(be careful to square that whole fraction, top and bottom)* and we wind up with $25/\pi$, the right answer.

🔍 **Let's do another one.**
Denise is building a rectangular park that is 70 by 120 meters. Completely inside the park will be a perfectly circular duck pond. What is the maximum possible area of the surface of the pond in square meters?

    **F.** 1,225π

    **G.** 3,600π

    **H.** 4,900π

    **J.** 9,000π

    **K.** 14,000π

scary looking problem: not so scary anymore!

Don't scrunch up your face, stare at the celling, and hope the answer will be somewhere up there if you just look hard enough. Instead—draw! And write the formula for the area of a circle!

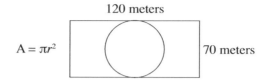

$$A = \pi r^2$$

Now that we have a drawing, we can tell what the limiting factor of the pond is. The 70 meter side is the same as the length of the diameter of the circle, so the radius is 35 meters and we can plug that straight into our formula.

$A = \pi r^2$

$A = \pi 35^2$

$A = 1225\pi$ or answer choice (F)

⊕ **Last one! Now we're going three-dimensional.**

A rectangle measuring 3 feet by 4 feet is rotated around its longest leg to form a cylinder. What is the volume of the cylinder in cubic feet?

**A.** $12\pi$

**B.** $16\pi$

**C.** $36\pi$

**D.** $48\pi$

**E.** $144\pi$

## 3-D problems cause ALL kinds of stress to students.

Guess what the secret to solving them is? **Draw, mark, and label.**

So we start by drawing the rectangle, labeling the lengths. Next, we do our best to show what it would look like when we rotate it around the long side of 4. Last, we write the formula for volume of cylinder: $V = \pi r^2 h$.

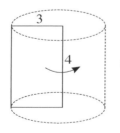

$V = \pi r^2 h$

Without a picture, this problem would be nearly impossible, but with the visual, most of the problem is already done. We can see that the radius is 3, and the height is 4. Those numbers can go right into our formula and turn this thing into a snap.

$V = \pi r^2 h$

$V = (\pi)(3^2)(4)$

$V = 36\pi$

**Take this lesson from this section:** geometry questions aren't just about knowing a bunch of formulas and they're DEFINITELY not about "being really good at geometry." They're about drawing, marking, and labeling.

If you do those three things, you will be golden!

**Plan A:** You know all of the content on the math section and can solve each question the way it was meant to be solved, or using a calculator, or by plugging in numbers, or by using any of the other awesome strategies designed to get you the right answer quickly.

*Let's talk about Plan A and Plan B.*

**Plan B:** You're not sure what to do and you're kinda freaking out. You KNOW that there is a way to solve this question, but you're not sure what it is. You turn to Plan B: an alternate way to get to the right answer *(or really close to the right answer)*. You choose a really good answer and move onto the next question.

**If Plan A sounds like the best approach in an ideal world... it is.** You may have noticed, however, that we do not live in an ideal world. We live in a world featuring stolen cell phones, parking tickets, and Justin Bieber.

> When the best approach in an ideal world does not pop into your brain, it pays to have backup strategies. We call the first one, **"Eyeballing It."**

**A great way to get rid of wrong answers is to use your eyes to make an estimate.** See a figure? Eyeball it! No figure is given but one is described? Draw a figure and eyeball it!

**This is a terrific technique, especially on geometry questions.** It's also great for anyone who has forgotten their geometry, never liked geometry, or doesn't have enough time to do every **ACT** math problem.

# When can you eyeball it?

|||||||||||||||||||||||||||||||||||||||||||||||||||||||||||||||||||||||||||||||||||||||||||||||||

## WHEN THE QUESTION INCLUDES A PICTURE.

If you see a shape, line, or figure in the question, you can probably estimate lengths and then eliminate several answer choices. Sometimes you can get the correct answer without doing any geometry! While the **ACT** math instructions tell us that "illustrative figures are NOT necessarily drawn to scale," they are actually drawn so accurately that you can often get rid of several incorrect answers without doing much math.

In the square below, diagonal $\overline{BD}$ is 12 feet in length. What is the length, to the nearest foot, of $\overline{AB}$?

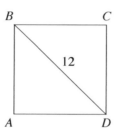

**A.** 4.0
**B.** 5.7
**C.** 6
**D.** 8.5
**E.** 10.4

**If you know how to solve this the "right" way, great!** You can and should use that approach. If you do NOT know how to solve this, answer a little question for us: How long does AB LOOK to you? Use your fingers, your pencil, or your eyeballs, and compare the line lengths.

**Write down how long you think line AB is:** _____
AB is shorter that BD, but more than half of it. You might have guessed somewhere between 7 and 10.

**If you did guess a number in that range, what would you choose as your answer?** 8.5? Well, guess what? That's the right answer.

# WHEN IT IS POSSIBLE FOR YOU TO DRAW A SHAPE OR PICTURE.

What if the **ACT** doesn't GIVE you a figure? You can make your own!

🔍 **Watch:**

An equilateral triangle and a square have sides of equal length. What is the ratio of the area of the triangle to the area of the square?

**F.** $\sqrt{2}:1$
**G.** $\sqrt{3}:\sqrt{2}$
**H.** $\sqrt{3}:2$
**J.** $1:1$
**K.** $1:2$

*Bleargh.*

## The question sounds time consuming and the answer choices look scary. Let's draw a picture and try using our eyeballs. First, we sketch.

 *Good enough!*

**Now, let's estimate.** Even though my drawing isn't perfect, I can still get close. The triangle is smaller than the square, but still more than half as big. So maybe the triangle is ¾ as big as the square? If that is our estimate, then the ratio of the areas would be 3:4.

Now what do I do with these terrible answer choices?

**Tip:** if the question or answer choices have square roots, trigonometry, or π in them, grab your calculator and turn them into regular ol' decimal value numbers.
**This step will make eyeballing infinitely easier.**

When we do that on this problem, we end up with these values:

**A.** 1.41
**B.** 1.22
**C.** .87
**D.** 1
**E.** 0.5

Which one is closest to our estimate of 3:4 *(which, expressed as a decimal is 0.75)*?
Answer choice (C), right? Well, we once again have found the correct answer just by eyeballing it.

**Eyeballing it will not always get you down to just one answer choice.** Even if it gets you down to two or three choices, your probability of getting that question has gone way up. **So when Plan A doesn't work out, don't be shy about "eyeballing it" as your Plan B.**

# Play Around

**Here's another Plan B strategy for solving math questions when you don't have a Plan A: Do something. Anything.** Take one step, then another, and then another. You might just find the path to the answer. We call this approach **"playing around."** It really works.

**Here are some ways you can play around:** draw a figure. Add a line to a figure. Simplify something using algebra. Write down the information from the problem. Test a value to see if it works. Just do something.

🔎 **Here's an example that's definitely a good "playing around" type of question.**
A cardboard circle has eight identical sectors, each of which is painted a different color. Starting on the yellow sector, Ray works clockwise around the circle, placing plastic discs on every *n*th sector. He continues to place discs on every *n*th sector, working clockwise, until all of the sectors have exactly one plastic disc placed on top. Which of the following could be the value of *n*?
**A.** 2
**B.** 3
**C.** 4
**D.** 6
**E.** 8

## You might ask yourself: what, exactly, is Ray hoping to accomplish?
**That question is impossible to answer, so let's get to the strategy.** We're not sure where this thing is going, so we're going to play around. First, let's draw a picture. Then, let's start placing disks. Now you just let the pencil and paper do the work.

> The question asks for *n*. We have answer choices to plug in for *n*. What if *n* is 2? Re-read the question with 2 as your *n*, and notice that means that Ray is going to place a plastic disc on every 2nd sector. So, draw some tokens, son! Did it work? Hopefully you saw that, once you get to the 5th token, you end up on the same sector where you started. If he puts a token on every 2nd sector, Ray is just going to keep putting tokens on the same four sectors forever. That might be an acceptable situation for Ray, but it's not for us. Moving on to the next answer choice.

> Erase the first tokens you wrote down for *n*=2, and let's try *n*=3. Round and round we go!

> **What happened?** If you did it carefully, you drew exactly one token in each of the sectors. That means *n*=3 is the right answer.

**This problem masquerades as a serious math problem** with all of its "*n*th disc" business, and there really is math here...we just don't need to use it. This problem, like many others on the **ACT**, is just checking to see if you are reading carefully and whether you can follow a long-ass string of directions.

The point is, don't be intimidated and don't expect to know what exactly to do the first time you read a problem. Just do anything you know how to do and see if you can roll with it from there. Drawing, re-reading, and trying the answers are all good ways to get started.

Sometimes when you play around, a pattern will emerge. In fact, **playing around** is one of the best ways to discover a pattern!

**Try this problem:** write some numbers down and see if you notice any sort of pattern. To decorate her bedroom, Caroline decides to stencil the fraction $\frac{1}{7}$ in decimal form around the top of her walls. She writes a zero, then a decimal point, and then has room for exactly 100 more characters. She continues writing the decimal until she runs out of room. What digit will appear in the 100th space?

**F.** 1
**G.** 2
**H.** 4
**J.** 7
**K.** 8

**First off, Caroline and Ray should date. Second, start writing and see what happens!**
1/7 is a repeating decimal and goes on forever. One way to find the answer is to just write out 100 digits. Is that the best, fastest, most accurate way? No.

Another way is to start writing out the sequence to find a pattern you can use. **Hint: there is always a pattern.** 1/7=0.14285714285.......

Notice that after the decimal point, the same six digits (142857) repeat over and over. That means we can count based on groups of 6. The nearest multiple of 6 below 100 is 96. After that we would have exactly four more characters. What's the fourth character in the sequence? 8!

Boo-ya.

**Important hint:** writing out the terms is a good idea, but not if it exceeds 10 or 15 terms. Playing around is great, but if you spend five minutes carefully writing out 100 terms, it is no longer serving you well as a strategy!

# using the Answer Choices

Our last Plan B strategy is based on one very basic, exciting fact: the answer to every problem is right in front of you.

That thing you're trying to find? It's already there! One of those five little answer choices is right. If Plan A *(knowing the material and solving the question the "right" way)* doesn't work, you can work backwards from the answer choices instead. Sometimes that will even be faster than using the "right" way to solve it.

This Plan B strategy bears the descriptive title **Using The Answer Choices.** It is a powerful tool in your **ACT** math strategy arsenal. It will keep you from falling into traps. It will boost your score.

⊕ **Let us show you how it works.**
A gym teacher is sorting athletic equipment into bins and notices that she has twice as many baseballs as footballs, 19 more basketballs than baseballs, and one less volleyball than basketballs. She counts exactly 100 balls and has only four types of balls. How many footballs does she have?
**A.** 9
**B.** 10
**C.** 25
**D.** 26
**E.** 31

**On a complicated algebra problem like this one, most students will jump right in and start writing a bunch of equations.** Then they will get confused and cross a bunch of stuff out and start over. Finally, they will get an answer that matches an answer choice and circle it. Huurah! But the answer is usually wrong. **Don't be most students.**

## Be an ACT ninja.

**Fun fact:** the **ACT** only cares whether you filled in the bubble that corresponds to the right answer. They do not care how you got there. Think about the way the **ACT** designs this exam. They write a problem. Then they figure out every possible way a student can screw it up. Then they surround the correct answer with four plausible "trap" answers. Then they laugh. They laugh and laugh and laugh.

**How does a ninja do this problem?** A ninja tries the answer choices. Notice that the question is asking for just one thing: footballs. That means that one of the five answer choices IS the number of footballs.

**Let's just start with one of the answer choices and see what happens.** If 25 is the number of footballs, what else do I know? Go back to the problem and find out (don't just read this explanation—actually go back and check it out for yourself). There are twice as many baseballs, so there must be 50 of those. There are 19 more basketballs than baseballs, which means 69 basketballs and then minus one for 68 volleyballs. The total number of balls is 212. Way too high.

**But wait! You are a ninja.** You are doing NONE of this in your head and ALL of it on scratch paper to stay organized.

Since 212 was too high, let's try a small number of basketballs. How about 9? Use the scratch paper and information you have already set up. Nine footballs works and we celebrate!

The process looks like a time-waster at first, but I promise you, if you practice **Using The Answer Choices**, it will soon be one of your new math best friends.

How do you recognize a **Using The Answer Choices** problem? If you see these two things you can start with the answer choices:

- ✎ The question asks for the value of one and only one thing.
- ✎ The answer choices are composed of numbers *(and no variables)*

🔎 **Look at this next problem and see if you can recognize the two hints that this problem could be solved with Using The Answer Choices.**
The height of a triangle is 4 feet longer than its base and its area is 70 square feet. What is the length, in feet, of its base?
- **F.** 4
- **G.** 7
- **H.** 10
- **J.** 14
- **K.** 28

yay!
Let's
try 'em!

**Now there is certainly a way to do this problem algebraically by setting up an equation using *x* for the length of the base and *x+4* for the height.** However, I notice that the question asks for one and only one thing – the length of the base. And I see that the answer choices are numbers.

**The question asks for base length.** Cool. Let's grab 10 and assign it as the base length. Then go back to the problem to see what you know if the base length is 10. Well, the height is 4 more, so the height is 14. Back to the problem and what else do we know? The area is 70. Does a triangle with a base of 10 and a height of 14 have an area of 70? Don't do it in your head. Instead, draw the triangle, label everything, write the formula, and carefully solve it step by step.

**In school you get partial credit if you do most steps right and then just make one tiny mistake.** On the **ACT**, you get zero credit if you make any mistakes. This is a test of meticulousness, so it pays to work carefully.

## USING THE ANSWER CHOICES STEPS:

▣ Recognize that you can use the answer choices. If the question asks for one thing and the answer choices are numbers, you can.

▣ Underline the one thing that the question is asking for and draw an arrow to your choices.

▣ Assign the value of the middle answer choice to the one unknown thing.

▣ Work backwards from that piece of information to unravel the rest of the problem. Anything you find, label.

▣ When one answer choice fits every part of the problem you are done.

🔍 **This next problem looks a bit different, but we can still use the answer choices.**
Which of the following represents the complete solution set of $225x = 36x^3$?

**A.** $x = 0$

**B.** $x = \pm\frac{2}{5}$

**C.** $x = \pm\frac{5}{2}$

**D.** $x = \pm\frac{2}{5}, x = 0$

**E.** $x = \pm\frac{5}{2}, x = 0$

**The question asks for one thing: solutions.** The answers ask for numbers and don't include unknown variables. Time to **Use The Answer Choices**.

**You can do the algebra on this one, but you don't have to: this is a multiple choice test and you have options.** Even if you are the top algebra student in your school, you can **Use The Answer Choices** to double-check your answers. Almost everyone gets this problem wrong when they do the algebra. Don't believe us? Do it by hand before reading the next part. Our psychic abilities tell us you will choose answer choice (C). Were we right? If so, you fell into an **ACT** trap *(you may have forgotten that x could equal zero)*.

**Toss algebra out the window, start with the answer choices, and you will be less likely to make a mistake.** Toss 0 in for *x* in the equation and it works! Try 2/5 for *x* and it fails. Try 5/2 for *x* and it works. The only answer choice that holds up is E. Your paper should show your results as you find them. **Don't do anything in your head. Do as much as possible in your calculator and then write it down.**

## HERE IS A SET OF PROBLEMS THAT CAN BE SOLVED BY **USING THE ANSWER CHOICES**.

# EXERCISE

**INSTRUCTIONS:** First, look at each one and recognize what makes starting with the answer choices possible (*and awesome*) in these selected questions. If you aren't sure, re-read the chapter.

Next, use the answer choices to solve EVERY SINGLE question in this set. You have been using algebra, geometry, and regular school math for years. If you already have a 36 on ACT math – cool – keep doing what you are doing. If not, lock down the strategy of **Using The Answer Choices** by making yourself try it on each of these.

1. What is the value of $r$ if $3\frac{1}{4} = \frac{27}{r} - 1/8$ ?
   A. 3
   B. 5
   C. 8
   D. 8.63
   E. 91.125

2. For what value of $x$ is $y = \frac{x^2 + 3x - 40}{x^2 - 10x + 25}$ undefined?
   F. -5
   G. -1
   H. 0
   J. 1
   K. 5

3. The equation $-3(x+7) + 4x = 8(-2)$ is true for what value of $x$?
   A. -23
   B. -5
   C. 2
   D. 5
   E. 37

4. Rohan is purchasing a $70,000 car on a payment plan. He makes a $7,000 down payment and then is required to make 6 annual payments, each of which will be double the amount of the preceding year's payment. How much will his first car payment be?
   F. $500
   G. $1,000
   H. $2,000
   J. $8,000
   K. $9,000

5. Which of the following is one possible solution of $3x^2 + 36 = 21x$ ?
   A. -4
   B. -3
   C. 0
   D. 1
   E. 4

6. In the equation $x^2 + bx + 24 = 0$ , what is one possible value of $b$ that yields no rational solutions for $x$?
   F. -10
   G. 11
   H. 14
   J. 17
   K. 25

7. To alleviate the stress of finals week, Brian and Joanne go to Rent-a-Pug where people can rent pug dogs to cuddle for $20 per hour. Joanne gives Brian half of the money in her wallet to pay for pug cuddling and doggy treats. She spends $4 to buy a pug hat and then has just enough cash left to rent herself a pug for an hour. How much money did Joanne begin with?
   A. $40
   B. $44
   C. $48
   D. $52
   E. $56

8. What is the smallest integer that is divisible by every integer between 1.5 and 9.5?
   F. 2,520
   G. 10,080
   H. 60,480
   J. 181,440
   K. 362,880

9. Twice the sum of the numbers $x$ and $y$ is 22 and the value of $y$ is one more than four times the value of number $x$. What is the value of number $x$?
   A. 2
   B. 7
   C. 9
   D. 11
   E. 13

**10.** A contestant on a game show gets 3 points for every correct problem in the regular round and 5 points for every correct answer in the lightning round. If Jim scored 136 points and got 4 times as many regular round questions correct as he did lightening round questions, how many lightning round questions did he answer correctly?

- **F.** 8
- **G.** 12
- **H.** 15
- **J.** 18
- **K.** 24

**11.** For what value of $n$ will $4^n$ have a value between $8^3$ and $8^4$?

- **A.** 3.5
- **B.** 5.5
- **C.** 7
- **D.** 8
- **E.** 9.5

**12.** During an art sale, John reduces his original asking price of $3000 by 60%. He then reduces the sales price by another 60%. He continues to reduce the price by 60% until the painting sells. If the painting sells as soon as the price falls under $200, how many times did John have to reduce the price by 60%?

- **F.** 2
- **G.** 3
- **H.** 4
- **J.** 5
- **K.** 6

**13.** Anne is grocery shopping for a party buys frozen pizzas and 2-liter bottles of soda. The store sells frozen pizzas for $4.25 each and 2-liter bottles of soda for $1.50 each. If Annie buys only those two items, purchases 18 items in total, and spends $54.50 before tax, how many frozen pizzas did she purchase?

- **A.** 7
- **B.** 8
- **C.** 9
- **D.** 10
- **E.** 11

NOTES:

# Circles

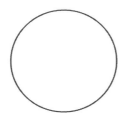

**This is a circle.**

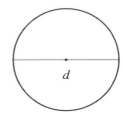

**Radius, r,** is the distance from the center of the circle to any point lying on the circle. Think **"spokes of a bicycle tire."**

**Diameter, d,** is the distance from one point on the circle, passing through the center, to an alternate point on the circle.

*Proud to be round!*

The area of a circle is the amount of stuff inside the circle. We calculate area using this formula: **Area of a circle = $\pi r^2$**

Just to make sure we're on the same page, **which circle has a greater area?**:

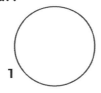

1

2

**Hint:** If you picked #2, it might be time for the ol' **"college isn't for everyone"** speech.

**The circumference or perimeter** *(same thing: these words can be used interchangeably)* is the distance around the circle. Circumference/perimeter is determined using the equation **$C=2\pi r$ or $C=\pi d$**

$C=2\pi r$

**Radius fun fact:** all of the radii in a circle are the exact same length. That is actually what makes a circle so...circular. If the **ACT** ever includes another figure *(like a triangle)* that overlaps with a circle, **make sure to note whether the side lengths are radii of the circle. If they are, then they are the same length.**

## Which has a greater circumference: a unicycle wheel or a wheel on your luggage?

If you said **"unicycle wheel,"** you're correct. If you said **"luggage wheel,"** reread the definition of circumference. If you said **"it depends on the size of the luggage"** then you're a wisecrackin' smartass who's thinking way too much and you should know that your creative thinking will get you nowhere on the **ACT**.

**Here's a key concept: when a wheel spins once, it travels the length of its circumference.** Keep that in mind on a problem in which a wheel is turning or a ball is rolling—the distance it travels is the same as its circumference.

*Not so bad so far, right? OK, next...*

## Circles have 360 degrees.

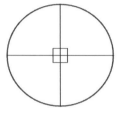

**Think four right angles.**

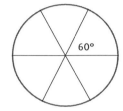

**Or six 60° angles.**

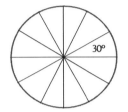

**Or twelve 30° angles.**

## And that brings us to sectors. Sectors are parts of a circle. They look
like slices of pizza. Just like a slice of delicious pizza, a sector is part of a circle. That is the key concept with sectors. You still use the two basic circle formulas—circumference and area—then you use the angle measure of the sector to figure out how much of the circle you have. This particular sector has a central angle of 40°. How much of a circle is that? A whole circle is 360°, so this is 40°/360° of a circle, or 1/9th. **To find the area of this sector, you'd find the area of a whole circle. Then find 1/9th of that.**

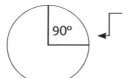

**Next up are arcs.** If sectors are slices of pizza, then arcs are the crust—they are part of the circumference. Just like sectors, they represent a proportion of the whole circle. If you want to find the length of an arc, just multiply the total circumference by the fraction of the circle that belongs to the arc.

**This arc intercepts 90°, which is ¼ of the circle. Thus, the arc length is ¼ of 2πr.** If a problem asks for the degree measure of an arc, it is asking for the measure of the central angle it intercepts. For example, both the central angle and the arc measure in this circle are 90°.

**With both sectors and arcs, you always want to think about how much of the circle you have, and the way to do that is to compare the central angle of the arc or sector to 360°.** A nifty formula that relates degrees, sectors, and arcs is this: degrees/360=(arc length)/2πr=(area of sector)/(πr²).

Last thing: you may need to know the equation of a circle graphed on the coordinate plane. **Here's the equation: $(x-h)^2+(y-k)^2=r^2$**

**And here's what you need to know: (h,k) are the coordinates of the center of the circle, and r is the radius of the circle.**

**That's it!** If you want to express your love for circles, why not lie down on the floor and roll around like you're a circle? **Please do this after I'm gone.**

One last piece of advice: When you see an ACT word problem mentioning tires, it's a circle problem.
Bicycle tires with spokes: it's a circle problem with the spokes as radii. Beach ball: circle problem.
Rubber ball: circle problem. Rims on a tricked-out ride?
Yeah dawg: it's a circle problem.

# EXERCISE

**INSTRUCTIONS:** Solve each problem and choose the correct answer.

1. If a circle has a circumference of $8\pi$ meters, what is the area of the circle, in square meters?
   - **A.** $4\pi$
   - **B.** $8\pi$
   - **C.** $16\pi$
   - **D.** $40\pi$
   - **E.** $64\pi$

2. Over a certain 24-hour period, Rob spent 7 hours sleeping, 8 hours studying, 3 hours eating, 2 hours cleaning, and 4 hours with friends. If this information was put into a pie chart, how many degrees would the central angle of the sleep section be?
   - **F.** 70
   - **G.** 72
   - **H.** 90
   - **J.** 105
   - **K.** 180

3. If a circle is graphed on the standard $(x,y)$ coordinate plane, has a center at the origin, and has $y$-intercepts of 6 and -6, what is the equation of the circle?
   - **A.** $(x+y)^2 = 6$
   - **B.** $(x+y)^2 = 36$
   - **C.** $x^2 + y^2 = 6$
   - **D.** $x^2 + y^2 = 36$
   - **E.** $x^2 + y^2 = 144$

4. What is the diameter of a circle that has an area of $121\pi$ meters?
   - **F.** 11
   - **G.** 22
   - **H.** 44
   - **J.** 60.5
   - **K.** 121

5. A wireless internet transmitter is powerful enough to give people internet access as long as they are no more than 45 feet away from it in any direction. What is the approximate area, in square feet, that this transmitter covers?
   - **A.** 141
   - **B.** 543
   - **C.** 2,025
   - **D.** 6,362
   - **E.** 8,100

6. A circle has its center at point $R$, located at (-5,-5). Point $Q$, which is (0,-17), is on the circle. What is the equation of the circle?
   - **F.** $(x+5)^2 + (y+5)^2 = 25$
   - **G.** $(x-5)^2 + (y-5)^2 = 169$
   - **H.** $(x+5)^2 + (y+5)^2 = 169$
   - **J.** $(x-5)^2 + (y-5)^2 = 289$
   - **K.** $(x+5)^2 + (y+5)^2 = 289$

7. The equation $x^2 + (y-7)^2 - 28 = 0$ is graphed on the standard $(x,y)$ coordinate plane. What are the coordinates of the center and what is the radius of the resulting circle?
   - **A.** Center of (0,7) and radius of $\sqrt{28}$
   - **B.** Center of (0,7) and radius of 14
   - **C.** Center of (0,7) and radius of 28
   - **D.** Center of (0,-7) and radius of $\sqrt{28}$
   - **E.** Center of (0,-7) and radius of 14

8. In the figure below, a sector is shaded in a circle of radius $9\sqrt{2}$ If the area of the sector is $18\pi$, what is the measure of the central angle of the shaded sector?
   - **F.** 36°
   - **G.** 40°
   - **H.** 45°
   - **J.** 54°
   - **K.** 60°

**9.** In the circle shown below, diameters $QT$ and $RS$ cross at the center $O$. If arc $\overset{\frown}{QS}$ is $12\pi$ and arc $\overset{\frown}{ST}$ is $4\pi$, then what is the length of $QT$?

A. 8
B. 12
C. 16
D. 32
E. 64

**10.** If the area of a circle is $\frac{\pi}{4}$, then what is the circumference of the circle?

F. $\frac{\pi}{4}$

G. $\frac{\pi}{2}$

H. $\pi$

J. $2\pi$

K. $4\pi$

**11.** If the length of an arc within a circle is equal to $\frac{7\pi}{18}$ of the circle's diameter, what is the central angle of the arc?

A. 70
B. 100
C. 140
D. 180
E. 240

**12.** A superhero, Circle Woman, has a perfectly round face and the center of her mask, $Z$ is in the exact center of her face. If her mask is made up of straight lines $VW$, $XY$, $WY$, and $VX$, and $\angle WVZ$ is 70 degrees, what is $\angle XZY$?

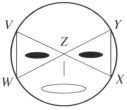

F. 30°
G. 40°
H. 50°
J. 60°
K. 70°

NOTES:

# Let's start with the basics of triangles.

The total measure of the interior angles of a triangle is 180 degrees.

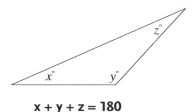

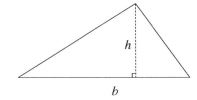

**x + y + z = 180**

*I want to talk to you about sails, roofs, and ladders leaning against houses.*

If you don't have this one down cold and aren't looking for it on every problem that gives you an angle measure, **you might as well be taking the test in ancient Sanskrit while performing a handstand.**

The area of a triangle is 1/2*bh*, where *b* is the length of the base and *h* is the height.

**This is pretty basic, right?** Finding a triangle's area is as simple as knowing the base and height. The height has to be perpendicular to the base. Perpendicular means **"at a right angle."** You knew that.

*Next*

# The Pythagorean Theorem: $a^2 + b^2 = c^2$

That means one little side squared plus the other little side squared equals the big side (*hypotenuse*) squared. The hypotenuse is always opposite the right angle. Not too hard.

**There is a very good chance you will see the Pythagorean Theorem on the ACT.** As my mom once said, if you get to the end of the ACT and you haven't used the Pythagorean Theorem, you didn't do it right. She's a math teacher, so she should know.

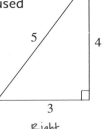

Right

**Isosceles triangles have two equal sides and two equal angles.**

Whenever the test makers tell you that two sides of a triangle are equal, they are really trying to tell you that the angles opposite those two sides are equal. The reverse of that statement is true too.

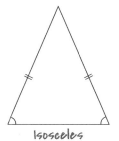

Isosceles

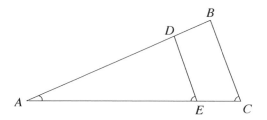

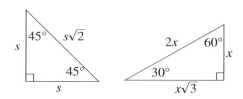

## Similar triangles:

- ✸ Have angle measures that are the same and side lengths that are proportional.

- ✸ As soon as you know that two angles of two triangles are the same, you have similar triangles.

- ✸ When you have similar triangles, you can set up proportions to solve for any missing side lengths.

- ✸ Frequently, the test makers will draw similar triangles that overlap, like the ones in the drawing above.

## 45-45-90 and 30-60-90 "special" right triangles:

These special lil' guys are just about every math student's least favorite triangles. They have these unique relationships between their side lengths, and you've got to memorize them. Do it. Memorize them.

# EXERCISE

**INSTRUCTIONS:** Solve each problem and choose the correct answer.

1. The sum of two angles in a triangle is 94°. What is the degree measure of the third angle?

   **A.** 32
   **B.** 86
   **C.** 90
   **D.** 94
   **E.** 106

2. Triangle $RTU$, as shown below, is isosceles and $\angle TQS \cong \angle TRU \cong \angle TUR$. $TU = 9$, $SQ = 4$, and $QT = 6$. What is the length of $RU$?

   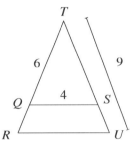

   **F.** 4
   **G.** 5
   **H.** 6
   **J.** 7
   **K.** 9

3. Which of the following is equivalent to the length of one leg of a right triangle, in inches, if the other leg is $r$ inches and the hypotenuse is 5 inches?

   **A.** $\sqrt{5+r^2}$

   **B.** $\sqrt{25-r^2}$

   **C.** $\sqrt{r^2-25}$

   **D.** $\sqrt{r^2-5}$

   **E.** $5+r^2$

4. In the triangle $QRS$ shown below, what is the sum of the angle measures $a, b, c, d, e, f, g,$ and $h$?

   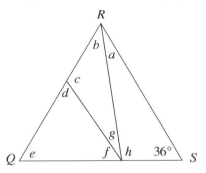

   **F.** 180
   **G.** 324
   **H.** 360
   **J.** 504
   **K.** 576

5. For triangle $SRQ$ below, $\angle RQS$ is a right angle and $RQ$ is 20 meters. What is the length, in meters, of $QS$?

   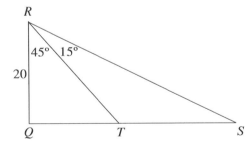

   **A.** 20

   **B.** $20\sqrt{2}$

   **C.** $20\sqrt{3}$

   **D.** $\dfrac{20}{\sqrt{2}}$

   **E.** $\dfrac{20}{\sqrt{3}}$

**6.** A right triangle has one leg that is 27 inches, and a hypotenuse that is 45 inches. What is the length, in inches, of the other leg?

    **F.** $\sqrt{72}$

    **G.** 17

    **H.** 36

    **J.** 72

    **K.** $\sqrt{2{,}754}$

**7.** In the triangle shown below, side *XY* is 7.9 feet and side *YZ* is 8.1 feet. Which of the following CANNOT be true?

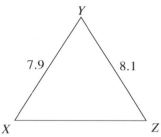

    **A.** $\angle XYZ > \angle XZY$

    **B.** $\angle XZY > \angle XYZ$

    **C.** $\angle YXZ > \angle YZX$

    **D.** $\angle YZX > \angle YXZ$

    **E.** $\angle ZYX > \angle ZXY$

**8.** As shown in the figure below, *PQS* is a triangle and point *R* is located on *QS*. $\angle PRQ$ is 70 degrees, and *PQ* is congruent to *PR* is congruent to *RS*. What is the degree measure of $\angle QPS$?

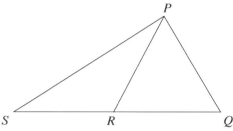

    **F.** 35

    **G.** 40

    **H.** 70

    **J.** 75

    **K.** 110

**9.** The base of a ladder that is 20 feet long sits exactly 12 feet away from the base of a wall. How high up the wall will the ladder extend?

    **A.** 10 feet

    **B.** 12 feet

    **C.** 14 feet

    **D.** 16 feet

    **E.** 18 feet

These four rules will give you percentage problem error immunity. *100% Awesome.*
**0% wrong, 100% right.**

# WHEN COMPUTING WITH PERCENTAGE, YOU HAVE TO MOVE THE DECIMAL PLACE TWO POSITIONS TO THE LEFT. YOU HAVE TO CONVERT IT BEFORE YOU CAN USE IT.

- 10% = .1
- 150% = 1.5
- 200% = 2.0

Another way to think about this same concept is that you're dividing the percent value by 100 *(which is literally what "percent" means... "per" means divide, and "cent" means 100)* to attain the decimal version. That way of thinking comes in handy when you're dealing with something like *n* percent. Turn that into *n*/100 and you'll be on the right path.

# PERCENTAGE PROBLEMS ARE OFTEN AN EXERCISE IN TRANSLATING WORDS INTO A MATH EQUATION.

🔍 **Oh heck yeah!! Watch:**

After it has played 20 games, a baseball team has won 40% of its games. What percent of the remaining 40 games must the team win in order to finish with a win percentage of 60%?

**The secret here is to turn these words into math.**
Assign a variable to the value you're trying to find—here, we'll use *x* to represent the percent of the remaining 40 games that they win.

**Here's the equation then:** $0.40 \cdot 20 + \frac{x}{100} \cdot 40 = 0.60 \cdot 60$

**Here's what is happening in that equation:**
First, you're taking 40% of the first 20 games to see how many games they've won so far. To that you're adding x percent of the next 40 games. The goal is to win 60% of the 60 total games, so that goes on the other side of the equation. When you solve for x, you'll get 70, and you'll be right.

**Here are some helpful translation tips for these wordy word problems:**
- If the problem says **"n percent,"** write **"n/100."**
- Whenever the problem says **"of,"** multiply.
- When a problem says **"is,"** that means =

If the problem hints at an unknown value by saying something like **"what"** or **"a number,"** then use a variable in that spot.

## 3 YOU HAVE TO MEMORIZE THE *(very simple)* FORMULA FOR PERCENTAGE CHANGE.

$$\text{percent change} = \frac{\text{amount of change}}{\text{original amount}} \cdot 100$$

Got it? Great.

If you know the formula, these problems are crazy easy. **If you don't know the formula, you will be sad. :-(**

**The most important thing is knowing that you divide the amount of change by the original amount—whichever value was your starting value.** If the stock market went from 17,500 to 18,000, then 17,500 is the original amount. If a flower grew from 10cm to 12cm, then 10cm is the original amount.

## 4 ON DIFFICULT PERCENTAGE PROBLEMS, YOU WILL OFTEN HAVE TO FIND TWO *(or more)* SEPARATE PERCENT CHANGES.

The tricky thing is that you have to calculate the second percent change based on an intermediate value, not the value you started with.

**Here's a sample problem:**
The price of a television is increased by 10 percent, and then that new price is decreased by 40 percent. The final price is what percent of the original price?

**The tempting (but wrong! very wrong!) thing to do on this problem would be to add those two changes together and call it a day.** It went up by 10 percent, down by 40 percent, so the final price must be a reduction of 30 percent. Sorry homie; it doesn't work that way.

**You have to apply each change separately.** The easiest and best number to plug in on a percent problem is 100, and you'll know why in a second. Watch what happens when we set the original price at $100. A 10% increase brings the new price to 100 + (0.10 x 100) = $110. **Here's where Rule #4 comes into play.**

At this point, that new price of $110 goes down by 40%. To find that, we have to use $110 as the starting point. 110 — (0.40 x 110) = $66. Now, what percent of $100 is $66? 66%. Boom. That's why it's handy to plug in 100 on percent problems.

You ready to practice?

# EXERCISE

**INSTRUCTIONS:** Solve each problem and choose the correct answer.

1. If 135% of a number is 270, then 80% of the number is what?
   A. 108.0
   B. 160.0
   C. 200.0
   D. 216.0
   E. 291.6

2. Crowdfunding website GoFundMe's profits in 2012 were 20% higher than their profits in 2011. In 2013, profits increased by 30% over 2012. By what percent were 2013's profits greater than 2011's profits?
   F. 10%
   G. 25%
   H. 30%
   J. 50%
   K. 56%

3. A used car was originally priced at $9,000, but its price was reduced 10%. Later, the discounted price was reduced by an additional 15%. The final price was what percent of the original price?
   A. 12.5
   B. 23.5
   C. 25.0
   D. 75.0
   E. 76.5

4. James grew from 130 pounds to 169 pounds between age 14 and 18. By approximately what percent did his weight increase during this time period?
   F. 22
   G. 23
   H. 28
   J. 30
   K. 70

5. The length of a certain caterpillar at noon on Monday was 10 inches. On Tuesday is was 20% longer than it was on Monday, and on Wednesday it was 20% longer than it was on Tuesday. If this pattern continues, approximately how long, in inches, will the caterpillar be on Friday?
   A. 17.3
   B. 18.0
   C. 20.0
   D. 20.7
   E. 24.9

6. What is $\frac{1}{8}$ of 48% of $9,000?
   F. $54
   G. $450
   H. $540
   J. $2,344
   K. $34,560

7. A cancer foundation hopes to raise $800,000 for new research. It has a list of 24,300 names of people who have previously donated. If 10% of the people on the list each donate $100 and 30% each donate $50, by approximately what percent will the cancer foundation be short of its goal?
   A. 20%
   B. 24%
   C. 50%
   D. 76%
   E. 80%

8. A stuffed bear was $35 and then was put on sale for $28. By what percent was the price of the bear decreased?
   F. 7
   G. 20
   H. 25
   J. 30
   K. 35

9. Nate bought 200 sodas for a party. After the first hour, 40% of the sodas were gone. After the second hour, 30% of the remaining sodas were gone. How many sodas were left after 2 hours?
   A. 24
   B. 60
   C. 80
   D. 84
   E. 140

10. What number is 130% of 680?
    F. 523
    G. 810
    H. 884
    J. 5,230
    K. 8,840

11. 25 is what percent of 5?
    A. 5%
    B. 20%
    C. 25%
    D. 400%
    E. 500%

12. On Fridays, Foodie Foods discounts its personalized cakes 30% from the usual price of $20. Fei orders one personalized cake on Friday with extra frosting, which costs additional 10% on top of the sale price. How much, excluding tax, does Fei pay for her cake?
    F. $12.00
    G. $12.60
    H. $14.00
    J. $15.40
    K. $16.00

13. At Eggstacular, all fresh eggs are the same price, but if a customer buys 11 eggs, she gets the 12th egg free. If Shelby pays for 11 eggs and gets one free, approximately what percent less does she pay than if she had to pay the full price for all 12 eggs?
    A. 7%
    B. 8%
    C. 10%
    D. 90%
    E. 92%

NOTES:

# Proportions and Ratios

Ratios are one of these fundamental math topics that you learn about in elementary school then never deal with again until you get to the **ACT**. Because it may have been awhile since you dealt with these guys, they're worth refreshing.

*Ratios: not just for 4th grade extra credit anymore.*

**At the most basic level, a ratio is a comparison between parts of a group.** If you have two red marbles and three green marbles, the ratio of red-to-green marbles is 2:3. If you have four red marbles and six green marbles, the ratio of red-to-green is 4:6, which you can simplify to 2:3. In both cases, the ratio tells you that, in that very important sack of marbles that you carry with you everywhere you go, you always keep 2 red marbles for every 3 green marbles.

What we want to do with ratios when they show up on the **ACT** is to make them more useful to us. The way we do that is by turning them into proportions.

**A ratio compares part of something to another part** *(like red marbles to green marbles)*.
A proportion compares part of something to the total *(i.e. red marbles to total marbles)*.

**Finding the total is as simple as adding all of the parts of the ratio. It's just that easy!** I encourage my students to start every ratio problem that way: add up all of the parts so that you have a number that represents the total number of elements in the group.

🔎 **Let's look at a sample problem:**
In a class of 28 students, the ratio of boys to girls is 3:4. How many students in the class are girls?

Like we said, to solve a ratio problem, the first step is to add the parts of the ratio together. Here's that's 3 + 4 = 7. Obviously. That 7 number represents all of the kids in the class, both boys and girls. What that means is that of every 7 students, 3 will be girls. Now we can set up a proportion and solve for the number of girls.

$$\frac{4 \text{ girls}}{7 \text{ students}} = \frac{x \text{ girls}}{28 \text{ students}}$$

Cross-multiply and simplify and you'll get that x = 16.

**One other ratio technique that some students prefer—add an "x" after each term in the ratio.** If the ratio of the water to flour to yeast in the dough is 4:5:1, think of them at 4x, 5x, and 1x. You can use those values to solve for x (the value that the ratio will be multiplied by to find what you're looking for). If there are 80 pounds of dough, set up the equation 4x + 5x + 1x = 80. x = 8. Once you know that, you can use it to find the amount of water (4x=4(8)=32), flour (5x=5(8)=40), or yeast (1x=8).

*Simple as that. Let's practice.*

# EXERCISE

**INSTRUCTIONS:** Solve each problem and choose the correct answer.

1. The ratio of the heights of a daughter to her father is $5:9$. If the father's height is 180 cm, how tall is the daughter?
   A. 64 cm
   B. 70 cm
   C. 93 cm
   D. 96 cm
   E. 100 cm

2. Two rectangles are similar and have side lengths in a ratio of $2:7$. If the smaller rectangle is 5 inches by 8 inches, what is the area, in inches of the larger rectangle?
   F. 40
   G. 117
   H. 360
   J. 490
   K. 560

3. To make his famous secret spice blend, Andy mixes 4 parts salt, 3 parts pepper, and 1 part garlic powder, by volume, in a container. If the container holds 24 tablespoons, and Andy plans to fill it to the top, how many tablespoons of salt should Andy include?
   A. 6
   B. 8
   C. 12
   D. 16
   E. 24

4. The amount of ground coffee needed to brew a pot of coffee is in direct proportion to the number of cups of coffee in the pot. If 150 grams of coffee are needed to brew 10 cups of coffee, how many grams of coffee are needed to brew 9 cups of coffee?
   F. 100
   G. 125
   H. 135
   J. 145
   K. 165

5. Jen, a landscape architect, is drawing up plans for a triangular park. On her drawing, the park has side lengths of 2, 6, and 7 inches. If the drawing is to scale and the longest side of the park will be 679 feet, how long will the shortest side be?
   A. 45
   B. 97
   C. 113
   D. 194
   E. 582

6. Square $X$ has sides that are twice as long as those of square $Y$. Square $Y$ has sides that are twice as long as those of square $Z$. What is the ratio of the area of square $Z$ to the area of square $X$?
   F. $1:16$
   G. $1:4$
   H. $1:2$
   I. $4:1$
   J. $16:1$

7. The regulation dimensions for a high school football field are 160 feet by 360 feet. If Jeremy is to make a perfect 1/80 scale model of a football field, what will be the dimensions, in feet, of the model?
   A. 0125' x .0125'
   B. 2' x 2'
   C. 2' x 4'
   D. 2' x 4.5'
   E. 2' x 5'

8. A pet shelter currently has cats, dogs, and pigs for adoption in a ratio of $5:6:7$ and no other types of animals. If this shelter has 18 dogs, how many total animals are available for adoption?
   F. 18
   G. 21
   H. 42
   J. 54
   K. 210

9. A right triangle has a ratio of $3 : 5$ for its two perpendicular legs. If the area of the triangle is 120 square feet, what is the length of the longer of the two legs?

   A. 10
   B. 12
   C. 15
   D. 20
   E. 24

10. Suppose a triangle has measures of angles in a ratio of $2 : 3 : 4$. How many degrees is the smallest angle?

    F. 2
    G. 9
    H. 20
    J. 40
    K. 60

11. The width and length of a rectangle are in the ratio $1 : 3$. If the rectangle's perimeter is 64, what is the width of the rectangle?

    A. 8
    B. 12
    C. 20
    D. 24
    E. 40

12. The ratio of red to blue to white cars in a certain car lot is $4 : 3 : 7$, and no cars of any other color are present. Which of the following statements must be true?

    I.   If there are 28 total cars, then 3 cars are blue.
    II.  If there are 48 red cars, then there are 84 white cars.
    III. There are more blue cars than red cars.

    F. I only
    G. II only
    H. I and II
    J. II and III
    K. I, II, and III

13. In an isosceles right triangle, what is the ratio of the leg to the hypotenuse?

    A. $1 : 1$
    B. $1 : \sqrt{2}$
    C. $1 : \sqrt{3}$
    D. $1 : 2$
    E. $1 : 3$

14. Jake buys two books for $42. If the ratio of the prices of the books was $3 : 4$, what was the price of the more expensive book?

    F. $10.50
    G. $14.00
    H. $21.00
    J. $24.00
    K. $28.00

# Distance and Midpoint

How many things can you do with two little points? A few things, actually. This chapter deals with two, distance and midpoint. On the **ACT**, you need to be able to find the distance between two points.

## DISTANCE

The formula for the distance between two points $(x_1, y_1)$ and $(x_2, y_2)$ is

$$\sqrt{(x_1 - x_2)^2 + (y_1 - y_2)^2}$$

**It is great to know, but there are also a couple of pretty fun workarounds.** The first is to make a Pythagorean triangle on the coordinate grid, and solve for the distance using $a^2 + b^2 = c^2$.

Let's say we want to find the distance between (-3, 6) and (3, -2). You can make a quick sketch and draw a right triangle with legs parallel to the x and y axes.

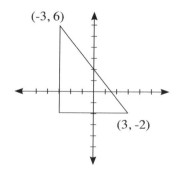

(-3, 6)

(3, -2)

*Isn't that fun? Not really, but it is a little interesting, right?*

How long is the up-and-down leg? It's 8. And the side-to-side leg? 6.

**Do the Pythagorean theorem on these bad boys and you will get a hypotenuse/distance of 10.** In fact, the distance formula is really just the Pythagorean formula solved for the hypotenuse.

*No? Geez, someone's in a grumpy mood.*

The other way to find distance between two points is to use a distance program in your calculator. We've studied ACT's calculator policy, and that is a totally legal program to use on the test. Check out the calculator chapter for more on how to get programs like that onto your calculator.

||||||||||||||||||||||||||||||||||||||||||||||||||||||||||||||||||||||||||||||||||||

## MIDPOINTS

If you want, you can memorize the formula, which is

$$\text{midpoint} = \left( \frac{x_1 + x_2}{2}, \frac{y_1 + y_2}{2} \right)$$

**Notice how this formula is simply the average of two x coordinates and the average of two y coordinates.** That's really all a midpoint is—the average of two other points.

Some **ACT** midpoint questions give you the midpoint and one endpoint and ask you to find the other endpoint.

**Two ways to solve: first, use the formula.** Plug in everything you know and solve for what you don't.

**Second, use a bit of logic.** Suppose a problem gave you the endpoint (7, −1) and the midpoint (4, −3) and asked you to find the other endpoint. Think of one coordinate at a time, starting with the x. If the other endpoint is 7 and the midpoint is 4, then those two values are 3 apart. The other endpoint has to be another 3 units away from 4, so it is 1. The y coordinates go from −1 to −3. What would be the next equally spaced value? −5. Our other endpoint is going to be (1,−5).

Oh, and there's a program for finding midpoints too.
Check out that calculator chapter to learn more!

## EXERCISE
**INSTRUCTIONS:** Solve each problem and choose the correct answer.

1. Point $R$ is located at $(8,-2)$ in the standard coordinate plane and is exactly halfway between point $Q$ at $(12,6)$ and point $S$. What are the coordinates of point $S$?
   A. $(2, -8)$
   B. $(4, -10)$
   C. $(4, 8)$
   D. $(10, 2)$
   E. $(20, 4)$

2. The midpoint of $Q$ and $S$ is at $(6,7)$. If $Q$ is located at $(0,5)$ and point $S$ at $(r,t)$, what is the value of $r-t$?
   F. 2
   G. 3
   H. 4
   J. 5
   K. 6

3. A line segment graphed on the standard $(x,y)$ coordinate plane has its endpoints at $(-4,6)$ and $(8,8)$. What is the midpoint of the graph of the line segment?
   A. $(-6,7)$
   B. $(2,1)$
   C. $(2,7)$
   D. $(6,7)$
   E. $(12,14)$

4. In the $(x,y)$ coordinate plane, what is the distance between points $(4,8)$ and $(-44,-12)$?
   F. 40
   G. 44
   H. 48
   J. 52
   K. 68

5. What is the $y$ coordinate of the midpoint of line $AB$ if point $A$ is located at $(-4,-8)$ and $B$ is located at $(4, 28)$?
   A. 0
   B. 1
   C. 10
   D. 20
   E. 36

6. A circle is graphed on the standard coordinate plane and a diameter of the circle is drawn. If the diameter has endpoints of $(-28, 15)$ and $(-4,5)$, what is the length of the radius of the circle?
   F. 10
   G. 12
   H. 13
   J. 24
   K. 26

7. If a line segment has endpoints of $(-2, 7)$ and $(4, -1)$, what is the straight line distance between them?
   A. 4
   B. 6
   C. 8
   D. 10
   E. 14

8. A town consists of square city blocks that measure $\frac{1}{8}$ off a mile on a side. Corey's home is 8 blocks south and 10 blocks east of the high school and Rachel's home is 16 blocks north and 4 blocks west of the same high school. What is the approximate straight-line distance, in miles, between Corey and Rebecca's homes?
   F. 1.3
   G. 3.5
   H. 4.8
   J. 5.0
   K. 12.0

# MATH — Slope

If you're over age 30 and still know how to find the slope of a line you're probably a math teacher. Alas, **ACT** Inc., in coordination with a shadowy international conspiracy, has decided that knowing how to calculate a slope will determine whether or not you're qualified for college.

*Here's the brutal truth: you'll never graph the equation of a line after high school.*

**The slope of a line equals the change in the y-coordinates over the change in the x-coordinates.** Some people call it rise-over-run. The formula to find slope looks like this:

$$\text{Slope, or } m = \frac{y_2 - y_1}{x_2 - x_1}$$

**What are these mysterious x and y coordinates?** Why, any two points on the line you're dealing with. Say we have the points (-3, -1) and (5, 3). What's the slope of that line?

$$m = \frac{3 - (\text{-}1)}{5 - (\text{-}3)}$$

$$m = \frac{4}{8}$$

$$m = \frac{1}{2}$$

**Basically, you need to know two points in order to find slope.** On a harder question you may be given the slope and not given all of the coordinate information. Whatever the situation, use the slope formula, plug in all the information you know, and solve for the information you don't know.

**Slope is also a useful of describing the visual relationship between y and x.** A line has a positive slope if, as the x-values increase, the y-values increase. **Basically, it goes up and to the right.**

A line with a negative slope goes down and to the right, because as the *x*-values increase, the *y*-values decrease.

**Once you know slope, you can plug it into the equation for a line.** A lot of lines come in the form y = mx+b, where m is the slope you just found, and b is the y-intercept... the point where the line touches the y-axis.

**Match these descriptions to their corresponding graphs:**
A line with a positive slope and positive y-intercept
A line with a negative slope and negative y-intercept
A line with a negative slope and positive y-intercept
A line with a positive slope and negative y-intercept

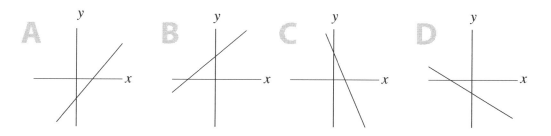

Slope is also a useful way of looking at parallel and perpendicular lines. Parallel lines have the same slope. What about perpendicular lines? What's the relationship of these slopes? Perpendicular lines have opposite reciprocal slopes.

**If you graph two lines, there are three things that can happen.** *(Keep in mind when you're reading this that a solution is a point that is on both lines—basically a point of intersection.)*

- **If two lines are parallel and have different y-intercepts,** they have NO solutions since the lines will never cross.

- **If the lines are parallel and have the same y-intercept,** they have INFINITE solutions since the lines lie on top of one another.

- **If the lines have different slopes,** they have ONE solution since the lines will always cross exactly once.

The slope of a horizontal line = 0
Vertical lines have a slope that is undefined.

**Remember that you can find slope if you have any 2 points on a line.** Sometimes, the **ACT** will give you a point...without really giving it to you.

**For example,** if a question says that a line passes through the origin, we actually know that it passes through the point (0,0). Likewise, if you're given an x- or a y-intercept, you know half of the coordinate pair, since the y-coordinate of the x-intercept is 0, and the x-coordinate of the y-intercept is 0.

# EXERCISE

**INSTRUCTIONS:** Solve each problem and choose the correct answer.

1. What is the slope of the graph of the line $2 = 5y + 3x$?

   A. $-\frac{5}{22}$

   B. $-\frac{5}{3}$

   C. $-\frac{3}{5}$

   D. $\frac{3}{5}$

   E. $\frac{5}{2}$

2. Which of the following is the slope of the line that contains points $(1,5)$ and $(-3,7)$?

   F. $-2$

   G. $-\frac{1}{2}$

   H. $\frac{1}{2}$

   J. $1$

   K. $2$

3. A line is defined by any two points in the standard coordinate plane. What is the slope-intercept form of the equation that defines the line formed by $(4, 2)$ and $(-5,0)$?

   A. $y = \frac{2}{9}x + \frac{10}{9}$

   B. $y = -\frac{2}{9}x + \frac{10}{9}$

   C. $y = \frac{2}{9}x - 5$

   D. $y = \frac{9}{2}x - 16$

   E. $y = -\frac{9}{2}x + \frac{10}{9}$

4. Which of the following is an equivalent equation to $5 - y = 8x$?

   F. $y = -8x - 5$

   G. $y = -8x + 5$

   H. $y = 5x - 8$

   J. $y = 8x + 5$

   K. $y = 8x - 5$

5. The line $3x = -4y$ is graphed on the coordinate plane. A line with which of the following slopes would intersect this line in such a way as to create four right angles?

   A. $-\frac{4}{3}$

   B. $-\frac{3}{4}$

   C. $\frac{3}{4}$

   D. $\frac{4}{3}$

   E. $3$

6. The equation $y - 4x = 5q^3$ is graphed on the coordinate plane. The point $(-7, 12)$ is on the line and $q$ is a constant. What is the $y$-intercept of the line?

   F. $-4$

   G. $2$

   H. $4$

   J. $12$

   K. $40$

7. Two equations, $y = ax+b$ and $y = cx+d$ are graphed on the coordinate plane and $a, b, c,$ and $d$ are constants. If this system of equations has one solution, what must be true?

   A. $a \neq b$

   B. $c \neq d$

   C. $a \neq c$

   D. $b \neq d$

   E. $a \neq d$

8.  What is the value of $m$ if $y = mx + b$ and $3x + 9y = 1$ are parallel?

    F.  $-\frac{1}{3}$

    G.  $-3$

    H.  $\frac{1}{3}$

    J.  $3$

    K.  $9$

9.  Which of the following linear equations is perpendicular to the equation $4y + 3x = 5$ when graphed on the coordinate plane?

    A.  $y = -\frac{3}{4}x + 5$

    B.  $y = -\frac{4}{3}x - 3$

    C.  $y = \frac{3}{4}x + 5$

    D.  $y = \frac{4}{3}x - 4$

    E.  $y = \frac{5}{3}x - 4$

NOTES:

# Tutor Ted.

NOTES:

# Foiling, Factoring, and Quadratics

*When is okay to drop an F bomb? Right FACTORING now, mothaFOILERS!*

What should you do if you have an equation that looks like (8x+5)(4x+1), or (x+4)²? **FOIL it, baby!** FOIL, an acronym that stands for **"First, Outer, Inner, Last,"** reminds you how to distribute when you multiply one binomial by another.

🔍 **Let's do one together: (8x+5)(4x+1)**

First terms $8x \cdot 4x = 32x^2$

Inner terms $5 \cdot 4x = 20x$

Outer terms $8x \cdot 1 = 8x$

Last terms $5 \cdot 1 = 5$

Then add 'em up: $32x^2 + 20x + 8x + 5 = 32x^2 + 28x + 5$

**One of the most common careless errors students make when dealing with algebraic equations is seeing something that looks like $(x+7)^2$ and simply squaring the $x$ and then the 7 and calling it $x^2 + 49$. DO NOT DO THIS.** Instead, remember that squaring means that you multiply something by itself. Write out the two things that must be multiplied—in this case $(x+7)$ times $(x+7)$—and you will be more likely to remember to FOIL.

🔍 **Try a few:**

$(x+4)(x-2) =$ _____

$(x-1)(x+5) =$ _____

$(3x+5)(2x+1) =$ _____

$(x+4)^2 =$ _____

$(a+b)^2 =$ _____

‖‖‖‖‖‖‖‖‖‖‖‖‖‖‖‖‖‖‖‖‖‖‖‖‖‖‖‖‖‖‖‖‖‖‖‖‖‖‖‖‖‖‖‖‖‖‖‖‖‖‖‖‖‖‖‖‖‖‖‖‖‖‖‖‖‖‖‖‖‖‖‖‖‖‖‖‖‖‖‖‖‖‖‖

## THE REVERSE OF FOILING IS FACTORING.

Factoring is helpful on problems that look something like this $x^2 + x - 6 = 0$. You may recognize that as a quadratic equation. Factoring is classic Algebra I; you probably spent months working on it back then. We'll review some of the key techniques here.

Take the sample equation $x^2 - 7x + 12 = 0$.

**We're going to factor that into two separate binomials.** Both will start with an $x$ so that when we FOIL the first terms we get an $x^2$.

Now, what comes next? The two other values in those parentheses have to multiply to +12 and add together to make –7. Think through the factors of 12 to find two that add to –7. Here, those are –4 and –3.

$$(x-4)(x-3)=0$$

That is our factored version of the equation.

🔎 **Practice up on these bad boys:**

$x^2 - x - 6 = 0$ _____

$x^2 - 10x + 25 = 0$ _____

$2x^2 - x - 3 = 0$ _____

# THE **ACT** MIGHT GIVE YOU THE ROOTS *(or solutions)* TO A QUADRATIC AND THEN ASK YOU TO FIND THE EQUATION.

**What do you do in that case?** Suppose the problem tells you that a quadratic equation has roots of 2 and 7. What you do is create factors that would generate those roots/solutions. Here, those factors would be $(x-2)(x-7)=0$. Voila! You have a quadratic with roots of 2 and 7.

🔎 **What is the factored form of each of the following?**

A quadratic equation that has roots of -4 and -5 _____

A quadratic equation that has roots of 1 and 2 _____

A quadratic equation that has only one root which is 13 _____

**Quadratic equations can involve quite a bit of complexity.** If you're feeling like this is a place where you need more substantial review, grab an Algebra I textbook and review these guys there. We'll give you one more pointer for how to handle these things on the **ACT**, though: use your calculator. You can graph quadratic equations to find their vertices and their roots. You can run a quadratic program. What makes taking the **ACT** easier for you? Do it that way.

149

## EXERCISE

**Instructions:** Solve each problem and choose the correct answer.

1. Which of the following is equivalent to $(3x-2y)^2$?
   A. $(xy)^2$
   B. $9x-8y$
   C. $9x^2-4y^2$
   D. $9x^2+4y^2$
   E. $9x^2-12xy+4y^2$

2. What is $(5a-3b)(3a+b)$ equivalent to?
   F. $15a^2-3b^2$
   G. $15a^2-14ab-3b^2$
   H. $15a^2-14ab+3b^2$
   J. $15a^2-4ab-3b^2$
   K. $15a^2-4ab+3b^2$

3. $(x-3)^3=?$
   A. $x^3-27$
   B. $x^3+27$
   C. $x^3-9x^2-9x-27$
   D. $x^3-9x^2+27x-27$
   E. $x^3-27x^2+27x-27$

4. When $x+5+x^2=25$, what is one possible solution of $x$?
   F. -2
   G. -5
   H. -6
   J. 5
   K. 30

5. If $x>0$ then the expression $\dfrac{3x}{x^2+8x+16}+\dfrac{3x}{x+4}$ is equivalent to what?

   A. $\dfrac{3x^2+15x}{x^2+8x+16}$

   B. $\dfrac{3x^2+3x+12}{x^2+8x+16}$

   C. $\dfrac{3x^2+12x}{x^2+8x+16}$

   D. $\dfrac{6x}{x^2+8x+16}$

   E. $\dfrac{6x}{x+4}$

6. What is one of the factors of the equation $x^2+9x+18=0$?
   F. $x-3$
   G. $x-6$
   H. $x+6$
   J. $x+9$
   K. $x+18$

7. The expression $(2x-4)(x+1)$ is equivalent to which of the following expressions?
   A. $-2x+1$
   B. $2x^2-4$
   C. $2x^2-2x-4$
   D. $2x^2+2x-4$
   E. $2x^2+6x-4$

8. Which of the following expressions is equivalent to $\dfrac{(4x+6)^2}{4}$
   F. $x^2+\dfrac{3}{2}$
   G. $x^2+12x+\dfrac{3}{2}$
   H. $x^2+12x+9$
   J. $4x^2+6x+9$
   K. $4x^2+12x+9$

9. What is true about the solutions of $x$ for $4^{x^2-1}=1$?
   A. $x$ has two real solutions.
   B. $x$ has one real solution.
   C. $x$ has one real and one imaginary solution.
   D. $x$ has two imaginary solutions.
   E. $x$ has one imaginary solution.

**10.** For the graph on the coordinate plane shown below, what is true about the zeros of the function?

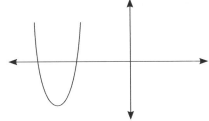

**F.** The function has no real zeros.
**G.** The function has two negative real zeros.
**H.** The function has two positive real zeros.
**J.** The function has one positive and one negative real zero.
**K.** The function has one negative real zero.

**11.** If $x^2 + dx + 21$ has two negative real solutions and $d$ is an integer constant, which of the following could be the value of $d$?
**A.** $-10$
**B.** $-4$
**C.** $4$
**D.** $10$
**E.** $21$

**12.** Constants $q$ and $r$ are integers in the equation $x^2 + qx + r = 0$. If $-4$ is the only solution for $x$, then what is the value of $q$?
**F.** $-4$
**G.** $4$
**H.** $8$
**J.** $-8$
**K.** $16$

# Inequalities =-) > =-(

There are two ways to handle inequality problems:

- 🔖 Do algebra
- 🔖 Plug in numbers

We're pretty partial to **plugging in**, but if you want to be TOTALLY sure that you're right, we recommend that you use both methods to double check for any mistakes.

## ALGEBRA AND INEQUALITIES

**Inequalities on the ACT only involve one variable, so they can usually be solved simply using algebra.** Do what you normally do, which is get the variable alone on the left and all the other stuff on the right.

**There are just two very important rules to remember:**
Whenever you multiply or divide both sides by a negative number, you must flip the inequality sign. ¡Muy importante!

    🔎 **For example:** $-x < 3$ becomes $x > -3$ because you divided both sides by -1 to isolate $x$.

**If an absolute value is involved, be careful as extraneous solutions may appear. ALWAYS plug in numbers to check your answer on these types of problems.**

    🔎 **For example,** if an absolute value is less than a negative number, there will be NO solutions. In the inequality $|x+8| < -7$, there are NO solutions for $x$, because absolute values turn out positive values. You can do the algebra, get a solution, but that solution will be WRONG. :-|

## PLUGGING IN AND INEQUALITIES

**Here's the alternative to algebra. Plugging in** is a super easy, highly accurate way to handle inequality problems, especially when absolute value signs or anything weirder is involved.

Pick numbers to plug-in for the variables in the problem. Choose your numbers based on the answer choices. For example, imagine you had these answer choices:

    **A.** $x < -7$
    **B.** $-7 < x < -4$
    **C.** $-4 < x < 0$
    **D.** $0 < x < 4$
    **E.** $x > 4$

**You can get away with trying just a few values to see which one is correct.** The numbers you would try are -8, -6, -2, 2, and 6. The number that works tells you that answer choice is right. That approach might seem like a blunt instrument (*"Caveman smash math problem with rock!!!"*) but it works! Remember, this test rewards you for the right answer, not the most elegant way of getting there.

# EXERCISE

**Instructions:** Solve each problem and choose the correct answer.

1. Which of the following has equivalent solutions to those on the graph shown below?

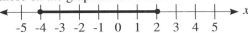

   **A.** $x \le 2$ and $x \ge -4$
   **B.** $x \le 2$ or $x \ge -4$
   **C.** $x \ge 2$ and $x \le -4$
   **D.** $x \ge 2$ or $x \le -4$
   **E.** $x = 2$ and $x = -4$

2. Which of the following inequalities is equivalent to $8(3x+2) > 6(7x-3)$?

   **F.** $x < -\frac{17}{9}$

   **G.** $x < -\frac{5}{18}$

   **H.** $x < 1$

   **J.** $x < \frac{5}{18}$

   **K.** $x < \frac{17}{9}$

3. Which of the number lines below shows the solution set of $18 - 4x \le 10$?

   **A.**

   **B.**

   **C.**

   **D.**

   **E.**

4. Which of the following inequalities is equivalent to $5(x-6) \ge 6(x-7)$?

   **F.** $x \le 1$
   **G.** $x \ge 1$
   **H.** $x \ge 6$
   **J.** $x \le 12$
   **K.** $x \ge 12$

5. When simplified, $-\frac{7}{5}x + 2 \le 16$ is equivalent to which of the following?

   **A.** $x \le -\frac{98}{5}$

   **B.** $x \ge -\frac{40}{7}$

   **C.** $x \ge -10$

   **D.** $x \le -10$

   **E.** $x \ge 10$

6. If $5x - 3 > 11$ and $-3x > -18$, which graph shows the complete solution set for $x$?

   **F.**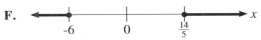

   **G.**

   **H.**

   **J.**

   **K.** (empty set)

7. Which of the inequalities below has the same solution set as $\frac{6+4x}{3} - 4 > 0$ ?

   **A.** $x > 0$

   **B.** $x > \frac{1}{2}$

   **C.** $x > 1$

   **D.** $x > \frac{3}{2}$

   **E.** $x > 12$

8. Which of the following is equivalent to $|-6x+2| > 4$?

   **F.** $x < -\frac{1}{3}$

   **G.** $-\frac{1}{3} < x$ and $x < \frac{1}{3}$

   **H.** $-\frac{1}{3} > x$ or $x > \frac{1}{3}$

   **J.** $x < -\frac{1}{3}$ or $x > 1$

   **K.** $x < -\frac{1}{3}$ and $x > 1$

# Absolute Value

**You should feel positive.** Absolute values are a breeze, right? Everything inside the absolute value bars turns positive and that's it. Right?

**Careful, though.** This is a standardized test and the test writers only put problems on the test that they think you will make a mistake on. And they know EXACTLY what mistakes you are likely to make. The good news is that so do we.

Absolute value problems will be easy if you learn the exact rules, know the pitfalls, and watch out for traps.
**Read this section carefully,** work the problems, and you will know everything you need to know to get every absolute value problem absolutely, positively correct.

🔍 **Try a few easy ones:**

$|3| = $ _____

$|-3| = $ _____

The answer to both questions is 3 because absolute value bars turn whatever is inside them positive. **Hey, way to go.**

🔍 **Now try these:**

$|4-7| = $ _____

$|-7+4| = $ _____

The answer to both of these is also 3. If you got 11 for either, you are making the first common absolute value mistake that costs delightful students such as you points off your score. The rule you need to know is that you must do everything inside the absolute value bars FIRST, and THEN make the result positive.

🔍 **Let's add a variable into the mix:**

$|x| = 3. \quad x = $ _____

**Answers: ±3.** This time we can't turn whatever inside positive first because we don't know what $x$ is. If there is an unknown inside absolute value bars, we must set that stuff equal to both the positive and negative value of whatever it equals.

$$|x| = 3$$
$$x=3 \quad \text{or} \quad x=-3$$

**Why is this true?** Try each of our solutions and you will see that since what goes in for $x$ becomes positive, both -3 and 3 turn into 3 after they are processed by the absolute value bars.

🔍 **Let's try another:**
$|x-4|=6$. What does $x$ equal? _____

$$|x-4|=6$$

$$x-4=6 \quad \text{or} \quad x-4=-6$$
$$x=10 \qquad\qquad x=-2$$

🔍 **And another:**
$2|7-x| = 5+6$. What does $x$ equal? _____

$$2|7-x|=5+6$$
$$2|7-x|=11$$
$$|7-x|=5.5$$

$$7-x=-5.5 \quad \text{or} \quad 7-x=5.5$$
$$-x=12.5 \qquad\qquad -x=-1.5$$
$$x=12.5 \qquad\qquad x=1.5$$

**This brings us to another terrific piece of absolute value advice:** if there is a variable inside the absolute value bars, move everything that is not inside the bars to the opposite side and simplify that stuff as much as possible. Then set the items in absolute value bars equal to ± the other stuff

Now, what if you see a problem that involves multiple absolute value signs, an inequality sign, or *(worst case scenario)* BOTH of those bad boys?

$$|x-3| < |x+5|$$

**Another piece of advice: don't be a hero. In fact, don't even bother doing these by hand.** If you see more than one absolute value sign and/or an inequality, there is a good chance that your algebra will produce answers that DON'T ACTUALLY WORK. **They're called extraneous solutions.**

**So, If you see a problem with multiple absolute values, an inequality, or ANYTHING else that is generally ugly, work backwards from the answer choices to see what works.** Doing it that way will prevent you from falling into the extraneous answer trap. Do it. Trust us.

You have learned so much.

Try some practice problems.

Make us proud!

155

## EXERCISE

**Instructions:** Solve each problem and choose the correct answer.

1. $|-12|-|4-37| =$
   A. $-45$
   B. $-21$
   C. $21$
   D. $45$
   E. $53$

2. What is the value of $6-7|-3+9-4|$?
   F. $-16$
   G. $-8$
   H. $-2$
   J. $8$
   K. $16$

3. Which of the following is the value of $(-4)|-9+5|$ ?
   A. $-56$
   B. $-16$
   C. $0$
   D. $16$
   E. $56$

4. $|(5)(-8)+(7)(3)|$
   F. $-61$
   G. $-21$
   H. $-19$
   J. $19$
   K. $61$

5. What is the value of $x$ when $x+36 = |-12|$?
   A. $-48$
   B. $-24$
   C. $18$
   D. $24$
   E. $48$

6. What are all values for $x$ that would make $|2.5+x| = 9$ true?
   F. $x=-11.5$ and $x=6.5$
   G. $x=-6.5$ and $x=6.5$
   H. $x=-6.5$ and $x=11.5$
   J. $x=-2.5$ and $x=2.5$
   K. $x=6.5$ and $x=11.5$

7. For $|r|-3 = r+4$, what is the value of $r$?
   A. $-1$
   B. $-3.5$
   C. $0.5$
   D. $1$
   E. $3.5$

8. Which of the following is equivalent to $|x| \le 6$?
   F. $-6 \le x \le 6$
   G. $-6 \le x$
   H. $x \le 6$
   J. $6 = x$
   K. $6 \le x$

9. If $-10 = 3|x|-|x|^2$, what are the real solutions of $x$?
   A. $\pm 2$
   B. $\pm 5$
   C. $2$ and $-5$
   D. $-2$ and $5$
   E. $\pm 2$ and $\pm 5$

10. What are the solutions of $|x-7| < 6$ ?
    F. $x > -1$ and $x < -13$
    G. $x > -1$ or $x < -13$
    H. $x < 1$ and $x > 13$
    J. $x > 1$ and $x < 13$
    K. $x > 1$ or $x < 13$

11. Which of the following is equivalent to the statement below?
    "$x$ can be any real number that is 7 units or less away from -4"
    A. $|x+4| \le 7$
    B. $|x-4| \le -7$
    C. $|x-7| \le 4$
    D. $|x+4| \ge 7$
    E. $|-x-7| \ge 4$

12. Which of the following contains the complete solution set for $x$ if $|-.0625x| = -\frac{x}{16}$ ?
    F. $x < 0$
    G. $x > 0$
    H. $x \leq 0$
    J. $x = 0$
    K. The empty set (no solutions)

13. Todd's pet snake typically eats $x$ calories per day, but sometimes it eats as many as $y$ more calories or as few as $y$ fewer calories. What inequality could Todd write that would give all possible values of $d$, if $d$ represents his pet snake's total caloric intake each day?
    A. $|d-x| \leq y$
    B. $|d+x| \leq y$
    C. $|d+y| \leq x$
    D. $|d-y| \leq x$
    E. $|dy| \leq x$

14. What must be true if the absolute value of $q$ is always equal to $-q$?
    F. $q$ is negative or zero.
    G. $q$ is positive or zero.
    H. $q$ is zero.
    J. $q$ is any real number.
    K. $q$ has no real solutions.

15. Which of the following is an expression equivalent to $|x-y|$ where $x$ is an even integer that is less than $y$?
    A. $2x$
    B. $2y$
    C. $y-x$
    D. $x-y$
    E. $x+y$

NOTES:

# Trigonometry

## Soh-Cah-Toa: is there a more lasting, more widely used, yet almost completely random mnemonic device?

Of the 60 math problems on the **ACT**, four will be trigonometry problems, and half of those will test nothing more than your basic, run-of-the-mill trig ratios, known by students everywhere by the acronym Soh-Cah-Toa. What that means is that even if you have never done a trig problem in your life, you can get the points for these questions if you learn this simple acronym. So that's what we're going to do. Right now!

## How do I recognize a trigonometry problem?

**Now what the **** is Soh-Cah-Toa?**

**If you see sin, cos, or tan in any problem or in the answer choices, you KNOW you are dealing with a trigonometry problem.** In addition, if a problem has an object that casts a shadow, or a ladder leaning up against a wall, or someone looking up at an angle, that problem is ALMOST CERTAINLY a Soh-Cah-Toa problem. Once you know that, you should IMMEDIATELY write Soh-Cah-Toa on your scratch paper because Soh-Cah-Toa is going to help you solve that problem.

## SOH-CAH-TOA

Let's use this triangle as the basis for everything Soh-Cah-Toa.

**Most basic trig involves right triangles.** Notice that in this triangle we marked one angle as (that's called 'theta' if you haven't seen it before). The sides of the triangle are labeled based on their location relative to that angle. The leg next to the angle is called the adjacent side, the leg across from the angle is called the opposite side, and the side across from the right angle is called the hypotenuse.

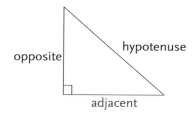

The capital letters in Soh-Cah-Toa stand for sin, cos, and tan. The small letters *(o, a, and h)* represent o for **"opposite,"** a for **"adjacent,"** and h for **"hypotenuse."**

**Historical footnote:** Soh-Cah-Toa is named after a Native American princess who was clever and somewhat brave. She once successfully measured the height of a teepee by measuring the length of its shadow and its angle of incidence, and thus we have the trig ratios that honor her legacy. *Footnote to the above historical footnote: this footnote is not true.

**When a question asks for sin, your job is to think about the "Soh" part of Soh-Cah-Toa.**
"Soh" means "sine = opposite / hypotenuse."
You'll create a little fraction with the opposite side on top and the hypotenuse on the bottom.

### 🔎 Here are the three trig ratios

$\sin \theta \longrightarrow$ "Soh" $\longrightarrow \dfrac{\text{opposite}}{\text{hypotenuse}}$

$\cos \theta \longrightarrow$ "Cah" $\longrightarrow \dfrac{\text{adjacent}}{\text{hypotenuse}}$

$\tan \theta \longrightarrow$ "Toa" $\longrightarrow \dfrac{\text{opposite}}{\text{adjacent}}$

### 🔎 And here is an example triangle with real, actual numbers on it.

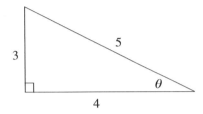

In this triangle, the side of length 4 is adjacent to, the side of length 3 is opposite, and 5 is the hypotenuse. Thus, when we use Soh-Cah-Toa we get:

$$\sin \theta = \frac{3}{5}$$
$$\cos \theta = \frac{4}{5}$$
$$\tan \theta = \frac{3}{4}$$

*Not that hard, is it?*

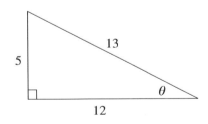

### 🔎 Now you try it with this triangle:

$\sin \theta = $ _____

$\cos \theta = $ _____

$\tan \theta = $ _____

That's it! Those are the basics of Soh-Cah-Toa trig.
**Next,** try it out on some **ACT** problems.

## EXERCISE

**Instructions:** Solve each problem and choose the correct answer.

1. In the figure triangle below, $RQ$ is 120 feet, $PR$ is perpendicular to $RQ$, and $\angle PQR$ is 42°. Which of the following expressions, in feet, is equivalent to the length of $PR$?

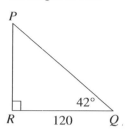

    **A.** $\dfrac{120}{\sin 42°}$

    **B.** $\dfrac{120}{\tan 42°}$

    **C.** 120 sin 42°
    **D.** 120 cos 42°
    **E.** 120 tan 42°

2. An incomplete map of Kirin's home, school, and gym is pictured below. Which expression is equivalent to the distance between Kirin's home and Kirin's gym?

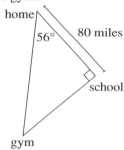

    **F.** 80 tan 56°
    **G.** 80 cos 56°
    **H.** 80 sin 56°

    **J.** $\dfrac{80}{\cos 56°}$

    **K.** $\dfrac{80}{\tan 56°}$

3. The right triangle shown below has side lengths of $q, r,$ and $s$, in feet. What is the value of $\cos \theta$?

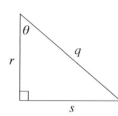

    **A.** $\dfrac{r}{q}$

    **B.** $\dfrac{s}{q}$

    **C.** $\dfrac{q}{r}$

    **D.** $\dfrac{q}{s}$

    **E.** $\dfrac{r}{s}$

4. The top of a tree is 80 feet away from a flower and the angle of elevation from the flower to the top of the tree is 42° as shown below. In feet, approximately how tall is the tree? (Note: sin 42°≈.670, cos 42°≈.743, tan 42°≈.900)

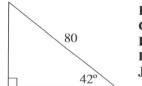

    **F.** 54
    **G.** 59
    **H.** 72
    **I.** 89
    **J.** 120

5. A 33 foot wire is stretched between the top of a flagpole and the ground and the wire makes a 32° angle with the ground, as shown below. Which of the following is an equivalent expression for the height of the flagpole?

    **A.** 33 sin 32°
    **B.** 33 cos 32°
    **C.** 33 tan 32°
    **D.** 33 cot 32°
    **E.** 33 sec 32°

**6.** In $\triangle QRS$ shown below, $RQ$ is 3 meters, $QS$ is 8 meters, and $\angle Q$ is a right angle. What is the sine of $\angle R$?

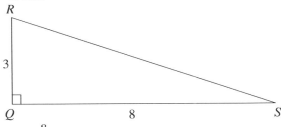

**F.** $\frac{8}{\sqrt{73}}$

**G.** $\frac{3}{\sqrt{73}}$

**H.** $\frac{\sqrt{73}}{8}$

**J.** $\frac{3}{8}$

**K.** $\frac{8}{3}$

**7.** In rectangle $ABCD$ shown below, $AB$ is 20 meters and $\tan \angle CAB$ is 1.05. What is the length of $AC$ in meters?

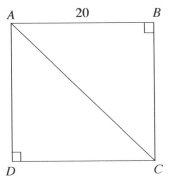

**A.** 21
**B.** 28
**C.** 29
**D.** 30
**E.** 31

**8.** In the right triangle shown below, $q$ and $r$ are lengths of the legs and $s$ is the length of the hypotenuse. Which of the following equations must be true?

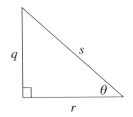

**F.** $\cos \theta = \frac{q}{s}$

**G.** $\cos \theta = \frac{s}{q}$

**H.** $\sin \theta = \frac{q}{s}$

**J.** $\tan \theta = \frac{r}{s}$

**K.** $\tan \theta = \frac{q}{s}$

**9.** Cody is designing a skateboard ramp with a right triangular cross-section as shown in the sketch below. He wants the elevated portion of the ramp to be 9 feet long and the angle between the ramp and the ground to be 25°. Which equation would give Cody the height, in feet, that he should build his ramp?

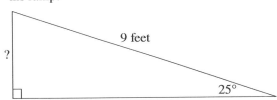

**A.** $\dfrac{9}{\sin 25°}$

**B.** $\dfrac{\sin 25°}{9}$

**C.** $\dfrac{1}{9\sin 25°}$

**D.** $9\sin 25°$

**E.** $25\sin 9°$

**10.** Triangle ABC is shown below and ∠B=90°. What is the tan ∠C?

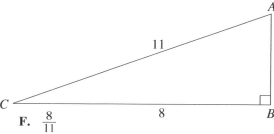

**F.** $\frac{8}{11}$

**G.** $\frac{11}{8}$

**H.** $\frac{\sqrt{57}}{11}$

**J.** $\frac{11}{\sqrt{57}}$

**K.** $\frac{\sqrt{57}}{8}$

**11.** In $\triangle PQR$ shown below, $\sin P = \frac{5}{8}$ and $R$ is a right angle. What is $\cos P$?

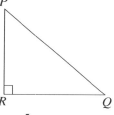

**A.** $\frac{5}{8}$

**B.** $\frac{8}{5}$

**C.** $\frac{\sqrt{39}}{8}$

**D.** $\frac{\sqrt{130}}{8}$

**E.** $\frac{8}{\sqrt{39}}$

NOTES:

# Lines and Angles

Let's do a 180° on your understanding of this stuff. Unless you already understand it completely, in which case, just keep on going straight.

**Lines: they're so serious!** Take a look at this guy ----> :| Lighten up, solemn straight-face guy!

**Here are the things you need to know about lines:**

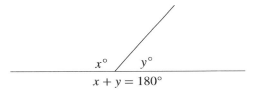

The sum of the angles on one side of a line is 180°.

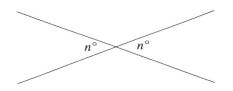

The angles opposite each other when two lines cross are equal to each other. They're called **vertical angles.**

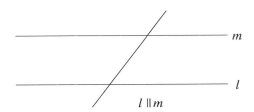

**Parallel lines cut by a transversal form a gazillion equal and supplementary angles.**
We said that two parallel lines cut by a transversal form a bunch of equal and supplementary angles. But which ones? When you were in Geometry class, you learned a bunch of names for angle pairs like **"alternate interior"** and **"same side exterior."**

We're going to skip that naming thing and use a little shortcut we call **number-all-the-angles-around-each-point-in-a-clockwise-fashion.**

**Here's how you do it: you number all the angles around each point in a clockwise fashion.**

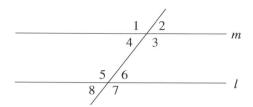

**Important thing: Make sure you start in the same place at both points of intersection.** Here we started at the top-left angle. This will tell you everything you need to know.

- ✦ All the angles marked with an odd number are equal to each other.

- ✦ All of the angles marked with an even number are equal to each other.

- ✦ Any odd angle and even angle are supplementary— which means they add up to 180 degrees.

All that knowledge is enough to put a smile on your face, isn't it, solemn straight-face guy? :| _Guess not._

- ✦ We mentioned that supplementary angles add up to 180°.

- ✦ One more definition: two angles are complementary if their sum is 90°.

If you can keep these angle rules and definitions in mind,
you can answer basically every question about angles on the **ACT.**

_Let's practice..._

# EXERCISE

**Instructions:** Solve each problem and choose the correct answer.

1. Line segments $AB$ and $CD$ cross at their respective midpoints to form four angles. If the degree measure of one of the four angles is five times the degree measure of another one of the four angles, what is the sum of the two larger angles?
   A. 40°
   B. 150°
   C. 180°
   D. 240°
   E. 300°

2. As shown in the figure below, $\angle ABD$ is 130° and $\angle DFE$ is 85°. If $CB$ is congruent to $BD$, then what is the measure of $\angle DEF$?

   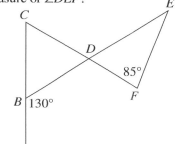

   F. 30°
   G. 50°
   H. 65°
   J. 95°
   K. 150°

3. In the figure below, line $AB$ is parallel to $CD$ and line $EF$ is parallel to $GH$. Line $AB$ intersects line $EF$ at point $I$. If $\angle AIE$ is known, how many other angles in this diagram can be found with certainty?

   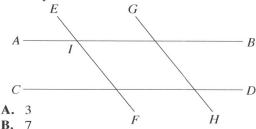

   A. 3
   B. 7
   C. 8
   D. 15
   E. 16

4. In the figure below, $AB$ and $CD$ are perpendicular and $\angle CDF$ is 35 °. What is the measure of $\angle GFB$?

   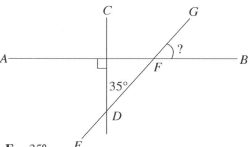

   F. 35°
   G. 45°
   H. 55°
   J. 65°
   K. 75°

5. In the figure below, points $A, C, E, G, J,$ and $L$ are collinear and line segment $AL$ is intersected by four other lines. $\overline{FH}$ and $\overline{IK}$ are parallel, $\angle BCE$ measures 130°, $CE$ and $ED$ are congruent, and $EF$, $GH$ and $FG$ are congruent. What is the measure of $\angle IJL$?

   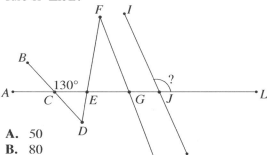

   A. 50
   B. 80
   C. 100
   D. 130
   E. 150

6. Two lines, $LM$ and $NP$ intersect in a plane at point $O$, which is the midpoint of each line. If the measure of $\angle LON$ is 82°, what is the measure of $\angle NOM$?
   F. 8°
   G. 41°
   H. 82°
   J. 98°
   K. 278°

# Mean, Median, Mode

**The "M" Words**

Here's a great way to get mean, median, and mode questions wrong: have an ambiguous knowledge of the definition of the terms. Let's fix that potential pitfall by learning those terms so that you know them inside and out. After that, we'll show you a couple of traps the test makers use to make these problems a little bit harder.

## MEAN

**Definition:** The mean *(also known as the average)* is the sum of items in a set divided by the number of items.

$$\text{Average} = \frac{\text{sum of the terms}}{\text{\# of terms}}$$

🔍 **Easy problem:**
What is the mean of 7, 8, 6, 6, 1, 9, 6, and 7?

To find the mean, we add the list and divide by 8. $\frac{7+8+6+6+1+9+6+7}{8} = 6.25$

**Trap:** A straightforward question will give you numbers in the set and ask for the average. The **ACT** may instead give you the average and leave out some other piece of information. **Ooooooooooooooooooooooooh, tricky!** The way to handle a problem like that is really simple: **write the formula down and plug in what you know.**

**Average/mean problem often require multiple steps.** That makes writing everything out even more important. **Heads-up: The data may be presented to you as a chart or graph.** Extract the data from the table or graph then use the average formula as prescribed.

*Don't be over-whelmed.*

### 🔍 Trickier problem:

The average age of a group of 8 students is 11. When one student leaves the group, the average decreases to 10. How old was the student who left the group?

**How do we solve this bad boy? By using the average formula.**

$$\text{average} = \frac{\text{sum}}{\text{\# of students}}$$

$$11 = \frac{\text{sum}}{8}$$

$$88 = \text{sum}$$

**That sum of 88 represents the ages of the students all added together. We can use that number to figure out the age of the one student who left.**

$$\text{average} = \frac{\text{sum}}{\text{\# of students}}$$

$$10 = \frac{88 - x}{7}$$

$$70 = 88 - x$$

$$x = 18$$

**In this case, the student who left the class was 18** *(and he probably left because he realized he was a senior hanging out with 5th graders).*

## MEDIAN

**Definition:** The median is the middle value in a list of items arranged from least to greatest—it's the middle one. When there are an odd number of terms, one of those terms is the median. If there are an even number of items, you take the average of the two middle terms to find the median.

Here's a trick: you know that grassy area that runs down the middle of the road?  That's called a median. Why?  Because it's in the middle.

### 🔍 Easy problem:

What is the median of 7, 8, 6, 6, 1, 9, 6, and 7?

**To find the median, we first have to arrange the list from least to greatest. Because we have an even number of terms, we take the average of the middle two terms to find the median.**

$$1, 6, 6, 6, 7, 7, 8, 9$$

$$\frac{6 + 7}{2} = 6.5$$

**Trap:** The **ACT** may give you the set of numbers in a non-standard way and/or in a chart or graph that makes figuring out which number is the middle or occurs the most much harder. How to avoid that? **Always, always, always re-write the list of terms and write them in order of small to large.**

**What if the test could give you a long list of terms *(say, more than 30)* and asks you to find the median?** Scratching off the smallest, then the largest, then the next smallest, etc., might not be practical: it would take too much time and potentially be error prone.
**Instead, figure out where the middle term is going to fall and find it directly.**

🔎 **Here's how:**
When you have an even number of terms, divide the number of terms in half. If there are 44 terms, then we must have 22 smaller terms and 22 larger ones. The median will be the average of the 22nd (the biggest of the smaller half) and the 23rd (the smallest of the larger half).

When you have an odd number of terms, subtract one from the total—that's the median that you're subtracting out—divide what is left in half. If you start with 23 terms, subtract one then divide by 2, you get 11. That will tell you that you have 11 smaller terms, 11 larger terms, and 1 median. The median will be the 12th term in sequence, whether you're counting from the bottom or from the top.

## MODE

**Definition:** The mode is the term that occurs most often. Think of the simple similarity between those two words to help you remember that definition: <u>MO</u>DE is the one that occurs the <u>MOST</u>.

🔎 **Easy problem:**
What is the mode of 7, 8, 6, 6, 1, 9, 6, and 7?

**To find the mode, we simply check to see which number occurs the most often.**
**1, 6, 6, 6, 7, 7, 8, 9**

**6 is the mode because there are more 6s than there are of any other term.**

**Trap: There can be more than one mode.** Suppose a set of numbers has three 6s AND three 2s as well. **In that case, you've got two modes, bro.**

OK, you know the definitions and traps.
Let's play ball.

# EXERCISE

**Instructions:** Solve each problem and choose the correct answer.

1. What is the mean of 10, 7, 5, 7, 9, and 16 ?
   A. 6
   B. 7
   C. 8
   D. 9
   E. 10

2. What is the median of
   16, 18, 9, 12, 24, 19, 18, 6, 14, 4?
   F. 14
   G. 15
   H. 19
   J. 22.5
   K. 26

3. At a produce stand, avocados cost $1.40 each. When you buy 11, you receive the 12th avocado free. What is the average price of 24 avocados, rounded to the nearest cent?
   A. $1.10
   B. $1.20
   C. $1.28
   D. $1.34
   E. $1.40

4. In his first three seasons, a baseball player hit 6, 18, and 23 home runs, respectively. How many home runs would the player need to hit in his 4th season in order to average 20 home runs hit over all four seasons?
   F. 16
   G. 18
   H. 20
   J. 23
   K. 33

5. What was Jonny's average quiz score on six quizzes if he scored a 94 on both of the first two and a 97 on each of the last four?
   A. 95
   B. 95.5
   C. 96
   D. 96.5
   E. 97

6. Standardized Test Prep High has 300 students, 120 of whom are juniors, and the remainder of whom are seniors. During a food drive, the average junior brought in 14 pounds of nonperishable food items while the average senior brought in 15 pounds. What is the average weight in pounds of nonperishable food items brought in per student during the food drive?
   F. 14
   G. 14.4
   H. 14.5
   J. 14.6
   K. 14.75

7. Denise's average test score on six tests is 8. When her lowest test score is omitted, her average rises to 9. What was her lowest test score?
   A. 3
   B. 4
   C. 5
   D. 6
   E. 7

8. The average of 6 integers is 25. After the integer 20 is removed from the list, what is the average of the remaining integers?
   F. 20
   G. 22.5
   H. 25
   J. 26
   K. 30

Use the following information to answer the next two questions

The chart below shows the results of a survey that Rob took in his neighborhood. He asked 26 families the number of pets they own and then tallied his results.

| Number of pets | Number of families |
|----------------|--------------------|
| 1 | 1 |
| 2 | 3 |
| 3 | 5 |
| 4 | 4 |
| 5 | 8 |
| 6 | 4 |
| 7 | 1 |
| 8 | 0 |

9. What is the average number of pets owned by the families in Rob's survey, rounded to the nearest tenth?
   A. 3.7
   B. 4.0
   C. 4.2
   D. 4.5
   E. 7.0

10. What is the product of the mode and the median of the number of pets Rob's neighbors own?
   F. 1.5
   G. 9.5
   H. 22.5
   J. 24
   K. 40

NOTES:

Probability: the topic that your math class studies for the last half of the last class period before spring break. By then, everyone's brain has gone to Cancun—your teacher's included. Lucky for you, the level of probability on the ACT isn't too advanced... so don't sweat it if your mind was in Mexico too.

## THE IMPORTANT THINGS YOU NEED TO KNOW:

★ $\text{Probability} = \dfrac{\text{\# you want (aka the ``winners'')}}{\text{\# of total items you have}}$

★ Probability is always a decimal or fraction between zero and one.

★ If the probability of something happening is p, then the probability of it NOT happening is $1 - p$.

★ The probability that multiple things will ALL happen is the product of the probabilities of each thing happening individually.

## Let's say you roll a normal die and want a 5 to show up on top.

**What is the probability of that happening?**
It's $\frac{1}{6}$, since dice have six sides and we have one "winner," the 5.

**What is the probability of an even number showing up on top?** That would be $\frac{3}{6}$. We still have six possible outcomes, and three of them (2, 4, and 6) are winners. We can reduce that fraction to $\frac{1}{2}$.

**What's the probability of rolling a 5 on one die and an even number on a second die?**
We use the answers to the previous two questions to answer that one. Your probability of getting a 5 is $\frac{1}{6}$, and your probability of getting an even is $\frac{1}{2}$. If BOTH of those things have to happen for us to "win," then the probability is the product of those two individual outcomes. $\frac{1}{6} \times \frac{1}{2} = \frac{1}{12}$.

*Seer, not too bad.*

Now, press 'pause' on those Mexican daydreams while we do some practice problems.

## EXERCISE

**Instructions:** Solve each problem and choose the correct answer.

1. A jury has 12 voting members and 3 alternates listening to arguments. If one member of the jury is selected at random, what is the probability that that person was an alternate?

   A. $\frac{1}{3}$

   B. $\frac{1}{4}$

   C. $\frac{1}{5}$

   D. $\frac{1}{12}$

   E. $\frac{1}{15}$

2. A laundry basket contains 150 socks, 4% of which are black. What is the probability that you will NOT choose a black sock if you randomly grab one sock from the laundry basket?

   F. $\frac{1}{60}$

   G. $\frac{1}{125}$

   H. $\frac{2}{75}$

   J. $\frac{24}{25}$

   K. $\frac{59}{60}$

3. In a standard playing card deck there are 12 face cards, 4 aces, and 36 numbered cards. Poker players are dealt cards clockwise. The first 6 players are all dealt a numbered card. What is the probability that the 7th player will also be dealt a numbered card?

   A. $\frac{7}{52}$

   B. $\frac{7}{36}$

   C. $\frac{15}{23}$

   D. $\frac{5}{6}$

   E. $\frac{6}{7}$

4. A jar of gummy bears holds only 7 cinnamon bears, 5 lemon bears, 9 orange bears, and 16 pineapple bears. How many cinnamon bears must you add to the jar in order to make the probability of drawing a cinnamon bear exactly $\frac{2}{7}$?

   F. 5

   G. 7

   H. 12

   J. 14

   K. 30

5. A high school has 36 freshmen, 45 sophomores, 23 juniors, and $n$ seniors. If a student is randomly selected to serve as Ambassador of the Day, what is the probability that the selected student will be a freshman?

   A. $\frac{1}{36}$

   B. $\frac{1}{104}$

   C. $\frac{36}{104}$

   D. $\frac{36+n}{104+n}$

   E. $\frac{36}{104+n}$

||||||||||||||||||||||||||||||||||||||||||||||||||||||||||||||||||||||||||

**6.** A six-sided die is rolled three times. What is the probability that an even number lands face up all three times?

    **F.** $\frac{1}{2}$

    **G.** $\frac{1}{3}$

    **H.** $\frac{1}{4}$

    **J.** $\frac{1}{8}$

    **K.** $\frac{1}{16}$

**7.** Matsumoto's shave ice is served in three flavors: lime, grape, and pineapple. Of the 50 shave ices served yesterday, 21 were lime, 14 were grape, and 15 were pineapple. If two shave ices are selected from what was served yesterday, what is the probability that both of the shave ices were grape?

    **A.** $\frac{14}{50} + \frac{14}{50}$

    **B.** $\frac{14}{50} \times \frac{14}{50}$

    **C.** $\frac{14}{50} \times \frac{13}{50}$

    **D.** $\frac{14}{50} \times \frac{14}{49}$

    **E.** $\frac{14}{50} \times \frac{13}{49}$

NOTES:

# Functions

*Functions are fun, son!* Not dance party fun or anything, but fun enough to be tolerable on the ACT. Luckily most of the function problems are rather straightforward on the ACT.

🔍 **The majority of function questions look like this:**
When $f(x) = 9x^2 + 5x - 3$, what is the value of $f(-4)$?

A. -142
B. -52
C. 11
D. 121
E. 1,273

## THERE ARE THREE MAIN THINGS TO REMEMBER:

**The letter f here is not a variable.** Instead it denotes a function. Functions on the **ACT** are typically f(x), g(x), and h(x). The letters themselves mean nothing—they're just the ways we've come up with to **"name"** functions. I like to think of them as Fiona, Greg, and Hakim. Thanks for nothin' Fiona, Greg, and Hakim!

**Whatever is in parentheses is the input**, or the "x" and thus gets inserted into the equation for all x's. On the **ACT**, the x-value is often negative or a fraction, so be mindful of that when it comes to squaring and distributing that x value.

In the problem above, we want f(-4). All we have to do is plug in -4 for every x in the equation.
f(-4) = 9(-4)2 + 5(-4) – 3 = 121

🔍 **Sometimes the ACT will offer up a double function question.**
If $f(x) = 3x^2 - x$, then $f(f(-2)) =$

F. -22
G. 14
H. 38
J. 574
K. 4,294

**All we need to do here is use the function twice.** We do that by working from the inside out: start inside the parentheses to find f(-2), then find f of the value we got when we did that.

🔍 **Watch:**
$f(x) = 3x^2 - x$
$f(-2) = 3(-2)^2 - (-2) = 14$

**We found that f(-2) = 14. Now we just plug 14 into the function.**
$f(14) = 3(14)2 - (14) = 574$

**Sometimes the ACT wakes up in a REALLY bad mood and decides to give you a function with two input variables.** Don't panic. Just plug the first number in for the first variable and the second number in for the second variable.

> $f(a,b)$ is a function of two variables and $f(a,b) = a^b - (a + b)$.
> Which of the following is the value of $f(3,2)$ ?
> A. 0
> B. 1
> C. 4
> D. 5
> E. 8

**In this problem, a=3 and b=2. So f(a,b) = f(3,2) = 3² – (3+2) = 4**

If the **ACT** is fed after midnight, it turns into an evil gremlin who is likely to include a problem like this one: a function in disguise.

> A new operation ‡ is defined as $h \ddagger g = h^2 + g^3$. What is the value of $7 \ddagger 2$?
> F. 9
> G. 14
> H. 20
> J. 25
> K. 57

You may be thinking, oh no, what is ‡ ? Did I sleep through that day of class? Is this from Algebra 5 when I'm only in Algebra 2?

**This problem may look strange or unfamiliar, but it's just another function question...in disguise.** If you see bizarre symbols and the words "defined as," you are probably just facing a function problem. h ‡ g works just the same as f(h, g). So, in this case 7 goes in for all the h's and 2 goes in for all the g's. **Check it out—we'll write the "new operation" (aka the function) on top, and the version with the numbers below.**

$h \ddagger g = h^2 + g^3$
↑   ↑
$7 \ddagger 2 = 7^2 + 2^3 = 57$

Simple as that, homeslice.

OK, time to practice your new dance moves.

175

# EXERCISE

**INSTRUCTIONS:** Solve each problem and choose the correct answer.

1. Consider the function $g(x) = 3x^2 - 5x$. What is the value of $g(-2)$?
   A. -1
   B. 2
   C. 4
   D. 22
   E. 46

2. What is the value of $h(-6)$ when $h(t) = -t^2 + 4t - 4$?
   F. -64
   G. -22
   H. -6
   J. 8
   K. 16

3. Given the function $g(x, y) = x^y - xy$, what is the value of $(3,4)$?
   A. 27
   B. 42
   C. 69
   D. 74
   E. 81

4. A function $f$ of the variable $t$ is defined as $f(t) = -16t^2 + 40t + 18$. What is the value of $f(0.25)$?
   F. 27
   G. 42
   H. 44
   J. 74
   K. 86

5. What is the value of $f(-5)$ when $f(x) = -4x^2$?
   A. -100
   B. -1
   C. 1
   D. 20
   E. 100

6. Given the function $h(x) = |3 - x|^3 - 1$, what is the value of $h(1)$?
   F. 1
   G. 4
   H. 5
   J. 7
   K. 64

7. For the function $g(x) = \dfrac{-2x^2 - 16x - 30}{16x + 48}$, what is the value of $g(-4)$?
   A. $-\dfrac{111}{2}$
   B. $-\dfrac{15}{56}$
   C. $-\dfrac{9}{8}$
   D. $-\dfrac{3}{4}$
   E. $-\dfrac{1}{8}$

8. What is the value of $f(f(2))$ when the value of $f(x)$ are as shown below?

   | $x$ | $f(x)$ |
   |-----|--------|
   | 2   | 4      |
   | 4   | 8      |
   | 6   | 2      |
   | 8   | 10     |
   | 10  | 6      |

   F. 2
   G. 4
   H. 6
   J. 8
   K. 10

9. A new operation, ▪, is defined on pairs of ordered integers as follows: $(x, y) \; ▪ \; (a, b) = \dfrac{xa + yb}{xa}$. What is the value of $(3, 4) \; ▪ \; (-5, 1)$?
   A. -60
   B. -5
   C. $\dfrac{7}{12}$
   D. $\dfrac{11}{15}$
   E. 3

10. Let $a \; ● \; b \; ● \; c = a^b - c^a$ for all real numbers. What is the value of $2 ● 3 ● 5$?
    F. -24
    G. -17
    H. 10
    J. 30
    K. 33

# Exponents and Scientific Notation

**It's math, and there are rules.** When it comes to exponents, the rules are especially important, as pretty much all of the ACT's exponent questions are based on them. Once you memorize these rules, you will show exponent problems who's the boss. Who's the boss?! In the 1980's, maybe it was Tony Danza. Today? You are.

*Teeny tiny, floating numbers: the gnats of mathematics*

## RULES:

- $x^a x^b = x^{a+b}$    **If the same base is multiplied, ADD the exponents.**
- $\dfrac{x^a}{x^b} = x^{a-b}$    **If you divide one base by the same base, SUBTRACT the exponents.**
- $(x^a)^b = x^{ab}$    **When you raise a base to another power, MULTIPLY the exponents.**
- $\sqrt[b]{x^a} = x^{\frac{a}{b}}$    **Whenever you take the ROOT of a base, DIVIDE the exponents.**

   **Try these:**

$(x^8)(x^2) =$ _____

$\dfrac{x^8}{x^2} =$ _____

$(x^8)^2 =$ _____

**Muy importante: you can only use these rules when the BASES ARE THE SAME.**

## MORE RULES:

- **Anything raised to the 0 power equals 1**      --->    $x^0 = 1$
- **Anything raised to the power of 1 equals the base.**   --->   $4^1 = 4$

**Sneaky question: What power is the variable x raised to?** Seems like a trick question, right? But it isn't, and the **ACT** will test you on it.

Anything without a power is secretly (*shhhhh!*) raised to the power of one.

## NEGATIVE EXPONENT RULE:

NEGATIVE exponents are RECIPROCALS. When a negative exponent is in the numerator, you flip it into the denominator and make the exponent positive. Vice versa: if you have a negative exponent in the denominator, flip it up into the numerator and make the exponent positive.

$$x^{-a} = \frac{1}{x^a}$$

## FRACTIONAL EXPONENT RULES

**FRACTIONAL exponents create ROOTS.** The top of the fraction remains as a normal exponent and the bottom goes outside to the root. The bottom one is weird, annoying, and strange, so it gets kicked out of the root's house.

$$x^{\frac{a}{b}} = \sqrt[b]{x^a}$$

Heads-up! An easy and important one to memorize is the $\frac{1}{2}$ power. That power is just another name for a regular ol' square root.

⊕ **Try simplifying a few of these guys:**

$x^{-\frac{1}{2}} = $ _____

$x^{\frac{2}{5}} = $ _____

$x^{-\frac{4}{3}} = $ _____

## EVEN- AND ODD-POWER RULES

The ACT will test you on the fact that a negative base raised to an even exponent creates a positive number and a negative base raised to an odd exponent yields a negative number.

⊕ **For example**
$(-2)^2 = 4$, while $(-2)^3 = -8$.

Keep this in mind and *(most importantly)* keep an eye on your parentheses when raising something to a power.

⊕ **For example**
$(-2)^2 = 4$ but $-2^2 = -4$.

Without the parentheses, the second equation is 2 squared then multiplied by -1, and as such it equals -4.

## SCIENTIFIC NOTATION RULE.

**Scientific notation uses exponents as well. In scientific notation, the number 7,392,800 is written as 7.3928 × 10$^6$.**

The rule is that the decimal point goes after the leftmost digit, any numbers following *(except for ending zeros)* get listed after the decimal, and then that number is multiplied by whatever power of 10 you need. Finding the correct power is easy: just count how many places you moved the decimal! In this case we moved the decimal 6 places.

**To decide whether you want a negative or positive power, think about whether you want your decimal place sliding to the right (positive) or to the left (negative).**
Big numbers get positive exponents, really small numbers get negative ones.

*Ok, last exponent rule!*

🔎 **For example**
How would .000487 be written in scientific notation?
As 4.87*(10$^{-4}$)

🔎 **Practice by putting a few numbers into scientific notation:**

98,570,000,000 = _____
.00000083 = _____
40 = _____
-.890 = _____

🔎 **...and now by putting numbers in scientific notation format into regular ol' normal numbers:**

3.76 × 10$^6$ = _____
5 × 10$^{-3}$ = _____
-2.2222 × 10$^2$ = _____
1.234 × 10$^{-7}$ = _____

## What a really great set of rules, huh?

Next, some practice problems that will probably be **the single most fun thing** you ever do to the power of 10.

# EXERCISE

**INSTRUCTIONS:** Solve each problem and choose the correct answer.

1. The expression $(5a^3)(7a^3)$ is equal to:
   A. $12a^6$
   B. $12a^9$
   C. $35a^3$
   D. $35a^6$
   E. $35a^9$

2. $(x^4)^{20}$ is equivalent to:
   F. $80x$
   G. $24x$
   H. $x^5$
   J. $x^{24}$
   K. $x^{80}$

3. For all $w \neq 0$, which of the following is equivalent to $(w^{-4})^{-2}$ ?
   A. $\dfrac{1}{w^8}$
   B. $\dfrac{1}{w^2}$
   C. $w^6$
   D. $w^8$
   E. $w^{16}$

4. The product of 9,856 and 10 raised to which of the following powers is equivalent to 0.00009856?
   F. -8
   G. -7
   H. -6
   J. -5
   K. -4

5. If $r > q > 0$, then $\dfrac{-18r^8q^4}{9r^2q}$ is equivalent to:
   A. $-2r^6q^3$
   B. $-2r^4q^4$
   C. $-2rq$
   D. $-9r^6q^3$
   E. $-9r^4q^4$

6. What is the value of $k$ if $(x^3x^2)^4(x) = x^k$ ?
   F. 9
   G. 10
   H. 20
   J. 21
   K. 24

7. $(a^6)(a^{-2})(a)$ is equivalent to:
   A. $a^{-12}$
   B. $a^{-2}$
   C. $a^{-1}$
   D. $a^4$
   E. $a^5$

8. Which of the following is equivalent to $[(x^4)^2x^2]^4$ ?
   F. $x^8$
   G. $x^{12}$
   H. $x^{16}$
   J. $x^{40}$
   K. $x^{64}$

9. For which of the following values of $x$ is $64(2^x) = (4^0)^2$ ?
   A. $x = -6$
   B. $x = -4$
   C. $x = 0$
   D. $x = 4$
   E. $x = 6$

10. $-6x^2(4x^5 - 5x^3)$ is equivalent to:

    F. $-24x^7 + 30x^5$

    G. $-24x^7 - 30x^5$

    H. $-24x^{10} + 30x^6$

    J. $-24x^{10} - 30x^6$

    K. $-24x^{10} + 30x^{10}$

11. What is the value of $(3)(3^n)$ if $2^n = 16$?

    A. 4

    B. 9

    C. 16

    D. 81

    E. 243

12. $(8)(6^{\frac{1}{3}})$ is equivalent to:

    F. $-16$

    G. $\dfrac{8}{6^3}$

    H. $\dfrac{8}{\sqrt[3]{6}}$

    J. $8\sqrt[3]{6}$

    K. $16$

13. Approximately how many times the speed of sound ($7.61 \times 10^2$ miles per hour) is the speed of light ($6.71 \times 10^8$ miles per hour)?

    A. $1 \times 10^4$

    B. $1 \times 10^6$

    C. $9 \times 10^4$

    D. $9 \times 10^5$

    E. $13 \times 10^4$

14. What is the value of 9% of $6.75 \times 10^4$?

    F. 60,750,000

    G. 6,075,000

    H. 607,500

    J. 60,750

    K. 6,075

15. When $x \neq y \neq 0$, what is the value of $\dfrac{0.00001x}{10^{-6}x} \times \dfrac{10^{-4}y}{0.001y}$ ?

    A. $10^{-2}$

    B. $10^{-1}$

    C. 1

    D. 10

    E. $10^2$

16. Which of the following *must* be less than 0 if $(x^4)(y)(z^2) < -1$ and $x$, $y$, and $z$ are all integers?

    F. $x(z^4)$

    G. $xz$

    H. $xy$

    J. $(x^2)y$

    K. $(x^4)(z^2)$

# Imaginary and Complex Numbers

When most of us think about imaginary things we think of fun stuff. Flying dogs. Candy palaces. Imaginary numbers are a little different.

*The most self-absorbed of all the numbers. It's always about i, i, i !*

**An imaginary number is one that includes the value i.** It is defined this way: $i^2 = -1$. That essentially makes i equal to the square root of -1. What that does is allow us to continue working on a problem even when a negative value shows up underneath a square root. What you do is factor it out from the radical. Like so:

$$\sqrt{-49} = \sqrt{-1} \cdot \sqrt{49} = 7i$$

**A real number is a number with no imaginary parts.** Examples of real numbers are 8, $\frac{1}{3}$, .05, $\pi$, and -5. Pick a number, any number: it's probably a real number.

A **complex number** is a sum or difference of a real number and an imaginary number. $2 + i$ and $7 - 8i$, for instance.

🔍 **Tell us whether each of the following is imaginary, real, or complex.**

$\frac{1}{4}$ _____

$\frac{1}{4}i$ _____

$34 - \sqrt{-3}$ _____

-0.00000007 _____

$78\pi$ _____

$\sqrt{-\pi}$ _____

$i$ _____

$70 + i$ _____

Earlier we pointed out that $i^2$ is -1. What about $i^3$? Well, based on exponent rules, it would be the same as $(i)(i^2)$. That equals $(i)(-1)$ or $-i$.

OK, how about $i^4$? That one is the same as $(i^2)(i^2)$, which is $(-1)(-1)$, which equals 1.
And $i^5$? That would be equivalent to $(i^4)(i)$ or just i. Notice that $i^5$ is the same as $i^1$. A pattern is forming! Every set of four powers of i repeats in the same pattern.

🔍 **Check it out:**

| | | |
|---|---|---|
| $i = i$ | $i^5 = i$ | $i^9 = i$ |
| $i^2 = -1$ | $i^6 = -1$ | $i^{10} = -1$ |
| $i^3 = -i$ | $i^7 = -i$ | |
| $i^4 = 1$ | $i^8 = 1$ | *etc.* |

How does all of this affect your life? You may have to multiply two complex numbers or a complex number by a real number. Start by FOILing or distributing as you normally would.

🔍 **For example:**
$6(5+i)=30+6i$

**Once you do that, some terms might show up that you can simplify further.**
**Take a look at this one:**
$(8+i)^2 = (8+i)(8+i) = 64 + 8i + 8i + i^2 = 64 + 16i + i^2 = 64 + 16i + (-1) = 63 + 16i$

🔍 **You try a few:**

$4(2+i)=$ _____

$i(3+7i)=$ _____

$(2+3i)(3+5i)=$ _____

$(1+4i)^2$ _____

$(5+6i)(5-6i)=$ _____

$(1+2i)(1-2i)=$ _____

**Notice that something magical happened in that last two: the imaginary part disappeared!**
A pair of complex numbers that have a real product are called complex conjugates *(let's call them "best buds" for simplicity)*. These are always in the form of $(a+bi)(a-bi)$ Hold up! That's just the difference of squares! Sure is. Just switch the sign between the two best buds (from minus to plus, or vice versa), and your imaginary terms will magically disappear...

🔍 **Below, find each number's best bud and the product of the two.**

$(5+i) \times$ _____ = _____

$(2-2i) \times$ _____ = _____

$(2-6i) \times$ _____ = _____

# One final thing... that you'll probably wonder why we didn't mention first:

**Your fancy graphing calculator can handle all kinds of operations with i for you.** On the TI-83+/TI-84 family of calculators, $i$ is located as the 2nd function above your decimal key. Try it out. Punch in $(6+3i)(4-i)$. Press enter. Gasp in wonderment at how easy that was. More on how to work with imaginary numbers on your calculator in the Calculator chapter.

Ok. With all that knowledge and that amazing calculator trick, you should be ready for some **ACT**-style complex and imaginary number problems!

## EXERCISE

**INSTRUCTIONS:** Solve each problem and choose the correct answer.

1. Which of the following is equivalent to $\frac{2+i}{2+i} \times \frac{2}{i-2}$ ?

    A. $i-2$

    B. $2+i$

    C. $2-i$

    D. $\frac{-4-2i}{5}$

    E. $\frac{4+2i}{5}$

2. What is the product of $3i+4$ and $5i-2$?

    F. $2+8i$

    G. $-23+14i$

    H. $-8+15i$

    J. $70$

    K. $120$

3. What is the value of $i^6+i^{10}$?

    A. $-16$

    B. $-2$

    C. $0$

    D. $2$

    E. $16$

4. The complex number $i$ is equal to $\sqrt{-1}$ . What is the value of $(6+i)^2$?

    F. $35$

    G. $36$

    H. $37$

    J. $35+6i$

    K. $35+12i$

5. The imaginary number $i$ is defined such that $i^2 = -1$. What does $i + i^2 + i^3 + ... + i^{83}$ equal?

    A. $i$

    B. $-i$

    C. $i-1$

    D. $1-i$

    E. $-1$

6. When the complex number $(2+i)$ is multiplied by $n$, the result is 5. What is the value of $n$?

    F. $1-i$

    G. $5+i$

    H. $2-i$

    J. $\frac{2}{3}+\frac{i}{3}$

    K. $\frac{3}{2}+\frac{3}{i}$

7. Which of the following complex numbers, when multiplied by $4i+5$, produces a real number?

    A. $4i + 5$

    B. $4i - 5$

    C. $5i + 4$

    D. $5i - 4$

    E. $9i$

# Math in Three Dimensions

On the **ACT**, most formulas for three-dimensional shapes will be given to you within a problem, but here are some that are good to know. If you understand how they work, you will remember them better and be able to handle any tricky 3-D problems.

*The fourth dimension, of course, is time.*

*And time, of course, is an illusion.*

## VOLUME OF A RECTANGULAR SOLID *(OR A BOX)* =
**length × width × height**

## SURFACE AREA OF A RECTANGULAR SOLID = 2(lw + lh + hw)

**What is a rectangular solid?** A box. Why can't they just call it a box? We wish we knew. Anyway, you can memorize the surface area formula, or you can understand how it works, which is more fun and easier to remember.

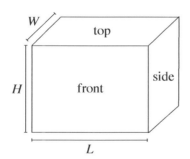

**Think of surface area as exactly how much paper you would need to wrap a box, with no excess.** As you can see below, you would need enough for the top, the front, and the side. Then you'd need twice that amount, because the top is the same as the bottom, the front is the same as the back, and the right side is the same as the left side. That is why the formula makes sense: it's the area of each of the three different sides added up, then doubled to find the area of all six faces of the box.

## VOLUME OF A CYLINDER = $\pi r^2 h$

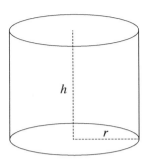

Beware overly complicated terminology: sometimes a cylinder will be called a "right circular cylinder." What is a right circular cylinder? It's a can. Just a regular ol' can. To find the volume of one of these bad boys, we find the area of the circular base and multiply it by the height of the cylinder.

## SURFACE AREA OF A CYLINDER = $2\pi r^2 + 2\pi rh$

**This formula looks super-complicated,** but really, you could figure this one out on your own if you tried. If we were going to wrap this in wrapping paper we would need two circles, one for the top and one for the bottom. Then would need to cover the middle part with a rectangle that wraps around the middle.. The rectangle's two dimensions are the height of the can and the circumference of the base. Add up the area of that part plus the two bases and you have surface area of a cylinder.

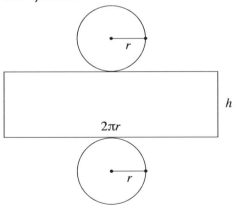

**Here's what you should keep in mind on these 3-D questions:** even though they always show up in the range of the difficult questions on the test *(usually between #51-60)*, they are always simpler than they sound, and you're usually given the formulas you need. **Just think: these things are just cans and boxes.**

# EXERCISE

**INSTRUCTIONS:** Solve each problem and choose the correct answer.

1. If a rectangular solid is 4 inches high, 6 inches wide, and 5 inches long, what is its surface area in square inches?
   - **A.** 15
   - **B.** 30
   - **C.** 74
   - **D.** 120
   - **E.** 148

2. A fish tank is 18 inches long, 6 inches wide, and 9 inches tall and is filled with nothing but water. The volume of the water is 648 cubic inches. What is the current depth of the water in inches?
   - **F.** 6
   - **G.** 9
   - **H.** 18
   - **J.** 54
   - **K.** 148

3. The formula for the volume of a right cylinder is $V=\pi r^2 h$. If one right cylinder has a radius three times as long and a height three times as tall as a smaller right cylinder, how many times the volume of the smaller cylinder is the larger cylinder?
   - **A.** 3
   - **B.** 9
   - **C.** 27
   - **D.** 81
   - **E.** 243

4. The formula for the volume of a cone is $V=\frac{1}{3}\pi r^2 h$ in which $h$ is the height and $r$ is the radius. Cone $A$ has a volume of $9\pi$ cubic inches and its height and radius are equal. In cubic inches, what is the volume of Cone $B$, which has the same height and a radius that is 4 inches longer than that of Cone $A$?
   - **F.** $13\pi$
   - **G.** $16\pi$
   - **H.** $36\pi$
   - **J.** $49\pi$
   - **K.** $169\pi$

5. A right circular cylinder is shown in the figure below, with dimensions given in inches. What is the total surface area of this cylinder, in square inches? (Note: The total surface area of a cylinder is given by $2\pi r^2 + 2\pi rh$ where $r$ is the radius and $h$ is the height.)

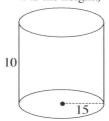

   - **A.** $100\pi$
   - **B.** $150\pi$
   - **C.** $500\pi$
   - **D.** $750\pi$
   - **E.** $2250\pi$

6. What is the surface area of the triangular prism, shown below, in square meters, if the length is 15 meters and the triangular portions are equilateral with sides 5 meters in length?

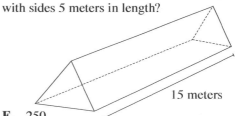

15 meters

   - **F.** 250
   - **G.** 275
   - **H.** $225+\frac{25}{2}\sqrt{3}$
   - **J.** $225+25\sqrt{3}$
   - **K.** 625

7. A silo is formed by placing half of a sphere on top of a right circular cylinder, as shown below. If the height of the silo is 18 feet and the diameter is 6 feet, what is the approximate volume of the entire silo, in cubic feet?
   (Note: The volume of a sphere is $\frac{4}{3}\pi r^3$, where $r$ is the radius, and the volume of a cylinder is $\pi r^2 h$ where $r$ is the radius and $h$ is the height.)

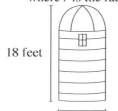

18 feet

6 feet

   - **A.** 339
   - **B.** 396
   - **C.** 452
   - **D.** 481
   - **E.** 565

# Advanced Trigonometry

**Trig for Fancy Pantses**

**Advanced Trigonometry** Ready for the harder stuff? Hang on. First, make sure you understand everything in the Soh-Cah-Toa chapter before tackling this one. All of it. **OK, ready now?**

**Trigonometry problems beyond Soh-Cah-Toa include inverse functions, the unit circle, graphing, identities, radians, and other tricky topics.** If you haven't learned trig in school, hate this stuff, aren't aiming for a 28+ on math and/or don't usually have time to do all the math problems, just ignore this section and move on: nothing to see here. But if you are hardcore and ready to learn the trig stuff that shows up on the hardest questions, let's go.

**On easier questions, the ACT measures angles in degrees, but on advanced trigonometry problems you will likely see some angles measured in radians.** Luckily, radian and degree conversion is easy. Use this formula, or just know that every 180 degrees is equivalent to $\pi$ radians.

$$\frac{degrees}{180} = \frac{radians}{\pi}$$

⊕ **Try converting a few yourself:**

What is $540°$ in radians? _____

What is $45°$ in radians? _____

What is $8\pi$ radians in degrees? _____

What is $\frac{\pi}{3}$ radians in degrees? _____

## OTHER FUNCTIONS YOU SHOULD KNOW:

**Besides sine, cosine, and tangent,** there are a few other trig functions that you should know.

**Each of the three trig rations has a little buddy: its reciprocal.** Memorize which little buddy goes with which function.

| | | |
|---|---|---|
| ✱ | cosecant (or csc) | $\csc \theta = \frac{1}{\sin \theta}$ |
| ✱ | secant (or sec) | $\sec \theta = \frac{1}{\cos \theta}$ |
| ✱ | cotangent (or cot) | $\cot \theta = \frac{1}{\tan \theta}$ |

🔍 **Your turn:**

If $\sin \theta = \frac{1}{2}$, what is $\csc \theta$? _____

If $\cot \theta = 4$, what is $\tan \theta$? _____

If $\cos \theta = -.2$, what is $\sec \theta$? _____

||||||||||||||||||||||||||||||||||||||||||||||||||||||||||||||||||||||||||||||||||||||||

## QUADRANTS:

**Trig ratio problems also include questions about quadrants:** in those cases, you must figure out whether the answer will be positive or negative. Do you know the acronym All Students Take Calculus? The first letter of each of those words corresponds with which functions are positive in which quadrants, starting in quadrant I and working counterclockwise.

🔍 **Use the chart below as a refresher to remember which functions are positive where.**

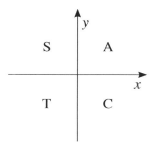

📓 **In quadrant I** *(between 0 and 90 degrees)*, all trig functions are positive.

📓 **In quadrant II** *(between 90 and 180 degrees)*, only sine and its reciprocal, cosecant are positive, while cos, tan, sec, and cot are negative.

📓 **In quadrant III** *(between 180 and 270 degrees)*, only tangent and its reciprocal cotangent are positive, while sin, cos, csc, and sec are negative.

📓 **In quadrant IV** *(between 270 and 360 degrees)*, only cosine and its reciprocal secant are positive, while sin, tan, csc, and cot are negative.

*Make sense?*

🔍 **Let's find out.**

In which quadrant is tan positive, but sin negative? _____

In which quadrant is cos positive, but tan negative? _____

In which two quadrants is sin negative? _____

In which two quadrants is cos positive? _____

Another trig topic you are likely to see on the **ACT** is **inverse functions.**
These are not bad if you know how to handle them.

🔍 **An inverse trig function looks like this:**

$\tan^{-1}(.5) = ?$

**In these cases, what looks like an exponent isn't an exponent.** Anytime you see a trigonometry function with a tiny -1 above it, you've got an inverse trig function, not an exponent. This is one of those instances in math where a symbol that has multiple meanings. Thanks a lot, Inventors of Math!

**The inverse function does the opposite of what the regular function does.** When we have something like tan-1(1.5), the 1.5 is not an angle measure—it's the value of the tangent ratio. When you solve this on your calculator, you'll get the measure of the angle that has that particular tangent.

**That is awesome news for anyone who has a calculator.** Find the inverse trig function (on TI-83 and TI-84 calculators, it's the [2nd] function above the normal [TAN] key), type in the function, and you have your answer. Anytime you know the value of a trig ratio but not the angle measure, your calculator can give you the answer using those inverse buttons.

One last thing on inverse trig functions: the **ACT** will get fancy at times and put the letters **"arc"** in front of each function instead. If you see arcsin, arccos or arctan, don't panic—those mean exactly the same thing as sin-1, cos-1, and tan-1.

🔍 **Want to try? Sure you do.**

If $\cos 0° = 1$, what is the value of arccos 1 and $\cos^{-1} 1$ ? _____

If $\cos 60° = \frac{1}{2}$, what is the value of arccos $\frac{1}{2}$ and $\cos^{-1} \frac{1}{2}$ ? _____

If $\tan 180° = 0$, what is the value of arctan 0 and $\tan^{-1} 0$ ? _____

**Sometimes the ACT will have a question about graphing a trig function.** If you have a graphing calculator it can help, but there are two trig vocab words/concepts that you should know in addition to using that calculator.

**Amplitude** is $\frac{1}{2}$ the total height of the graph of the function from its lowest point to its highest. The normal amplitude of a basic y = sin(x) or y = cos(x) graph is 1. Why? Because the range of those functions is -1 to 1, a difference of 2, and amplitude is half of that value. When you start to mess around with the functions, like by adding a value in front of the sin or cos, the amplitude changes. In y = a sin(x), a is equal to the amplitude.

**Period is the length of one cycle of the graph of the function in the x-direction.** The normal period for sin and cos is $2\pi$, and for tan the normal period is $\pi$. Those period values change when you add a coefficient in front of the x value. **In y = sin(bx), b changes the period.** To find your new period, take the normal period and divide it by b. For sin and cos, the period is $2\pi/b$, and for tan and cot, the period is $\pi/b$.

⊕ **Let's look at an example.**

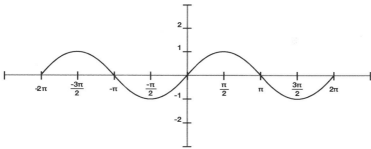

⊕ **This is the graph of y=sin(x).** It ranges from y=-1 to y=1, so its height is 2 and its amplitude is 1 (1/2 of 2). It completes one full cycle between -π and π, so its period is 2π.

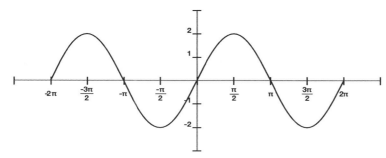

⊕ **Now, This is the graph of y=2sin(x).** Notice that this wavy line is taller and has an amplitude of 2. But it still has a period of 2π since it still completes one full cycle between -π and π.

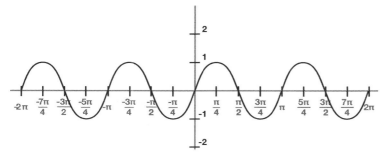

⊕ **This is the graph of y=sin(2x).** This one cycles twice as fast, so its period is π (notice how it repeats once between 0 and π). Its height is the same as the first graph, so it still has an amplitude of 1.

**OK, quick rundown of trigonometric identities.** This is a topic that we could spend 30 pages discussing, but on the **ACT**, you really only need to know one thing.
That is: $\sin^2\theta + \cos^2\theta = 1$

**That's true for ANY angle.** Here is how this identity might come into play on an **ACT** question, You'd get something like this...

$$\tan^2\theta\cos^2\theta + \cot^2\theta\sin^2\theta$$

...and be asked what it could equal. You want to simplify based on your newfound trig expertise. $\tan^2\theta = \frac{\sin^2\theta}{\cos^2\theta}$ and $\cot^2\theta = \frac{\cos^2\theta}{\sin^2\theta}$. When you make those two changes in the expression and you simplify, you're left with $\sin^2\theta + \cos^2\theta$. And what does that equal? 1.

## OK, last thing, I swear!

You need to know the Law of Sines and Law of Cosines....but only kinda. Why only kinda? On most problems that use one of those two formulas, the problem will give you the formula. The reason that these are worth studying is that it's helpful to know roughly how they work before you get to those problems.

These two Laws (pretty serious that they're called laws...better not mess around with these guys) are used to find missing information within non-right triangles.

## Here are the two formulas:

LAW OF SINES: $\dfrac{\sin A}{a} = \dfrac{\sin B}{b} = \dfrac{\sin C}{c}$

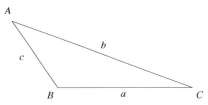

LAW OF COSINES: $c^2 = a^2 + b^2 - 2ab\cos C$

**Now that one is pretty ugly.** The **ACT** will almost certainly provide this formula on any problem that would require it, so memorization is probably unnecessary. Knowing how (and why) you use it is a good idea, though. The Law of Cosines helps you solve for the third side of a triangle when you know the other two sides and the angle included between them. When you know that stuff, you just punch it into the formula and solve for what you don't know.

**OK, let's give these trig practice problems a shot.**

Whew! That's a lot of learnin'!

# EXERCISE

**INSTRUCTIONS:** Solve each problem and choose the correct answer.

1. What is $\cot\theta$ when $\tan\theta = 1$ and $\cos\theta = \frac{-\sqrt{2}}{2}$ ?

   A. -1

   B. $\frac{-\sqrt{2}}{2}$

   C. $\frac{\sqrt{2}}{2}$

   D. 1

   E. 2

2. When $\tan\theta = -\frac{3}{4}$ and $180° < \theta < 360°$, what is $\sin\theta$ ?

   F. $-\frac{5}{4}$

   G. $-\frac{3}{5}$

   H. $\frac{3}{5}$

   J. $\frac{4}{5}$

   K. $\frac{5}{4}$

3. If the lines $\frac{y}{x} = -1$ and $y = 0$ are graphed on the standard coordiante plane, what is the cosine of the angle that is formed between the two lines in the second quadrant?

   A. $\frac{-\sqrt{3}}{3}$

   B. $\frac{-\sqrt{2}}{2}$

   C. $\frac{\sqrt{3}}{3}$

   D. $\frac{\sqrt{2}}{2}$

   E. 1

4. If $\cos\theta = -1$, what is the value of $\sin\theta$?

   F. -1

   G. $-\frac{1}{2}$

   H. 0

   J. $\frac{1}{2}$

   K. 1

5. A portion of the graph of $y = \sin(2x)$ is show below. What is the period of $y = \sin(2x)$?

   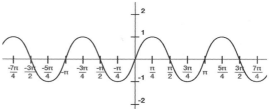

   A. 1

   B. 2

   C. $\frac{\pi}{2}$

   D. $\pi$

   E. $2\pi$

6. What is the radian equivalent of 720 degrees?

   F. $\pi$

   G. $2\pi$

   H. $3\pi$

   J. $4\pi$

   K. $5\pi$

7. When $180° < \theta < 270°$ and $\tan\theta$ is $\frac{3}{4}$, what is $\cos\theta$?

   A. $\frac{5}{4}$

   B. $\frac{4}{5}$

   C. $\frac{3}{4}$

   D. $-\frac{3}{5}$

   E. $-\frac{4}{5}$

8. What is the hypotenuse of a right triangle with legs of lengths $\frac{4}{\csc\theta}$ and $\frac{4}{\sec\theta}$ if $0 < \theta < \frac{\pi}{2}$

   F. 1

   G. 2

   H. 4

   J. 16

   K. 64

9. What is the amplitude of the function
$f(x) = 4\sin(3x + 2) - 1$?
A. 0
B. 1
C. 2
D. 3
E. 4

10. How many values of θ are there such that
$\sin\theta = -\frac{\sqrt{3}}{3}$ between 0 and $2\pi$?
F. 0
G. 1
H. 2
J. 3
K. 4

11. Rebecca is sitting in class with her friends Scott and Pepe. She knows that the desks of Scott and Pepe are 30 feet apart. Rebecca calculates the angles between her and her friends, and those angle measures are marked in the diagram below. Assuming Rebecca has made her calculations correctly, what is the distance in feet between Rebecca and Pepe? (Note: The law of sines states that in every triangle, the ratio of a side's length to the sine of the angle opposite that side is equal for all three sides.)

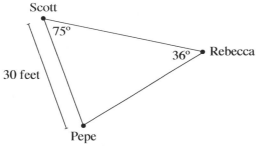

A. $\dfrac{30\sin 75°}{\sin 69°}$

B. $\dfrac{30\sin 36°}{\sin 75°}$

C. $\dfrac{30\sin 75°}{\sin 36°}$

D. $\dfrac{30\sin 69°}{\sin 75°}$

E. $\dfrac{\sin 75°}{30\sin 36°}$

NOTES:

# MATH Logic

There are ACT math problems that give you no numbers, no variables, no shapes, no nothing...just a bunch of bizarre statements that about people and things. **These are logic questions.**

*It may be illogical that these are considered math problems... but you still have to do them*

Although they might seem more like Reading questions, logic does fall under the math umbrella.

## METHOD #1: KNOW YOUR CONTRAPOSITIVE

Speaking of umbrellas, Cindy, Ross, and Kristin go walking in the rain. If they have umbrellas, they will not get wet. After the walk, Ross is as wet as a dishrag.

**What can we conclude?**
Hopefully you said, **"that dingbat Ross didn't have an umbrella!"** Well, how do we know that? Here's how it works in terms of logic:

If you have an umbrella, you don't get wet. Think of that statement as, **"If A, then B."** Ross **got wet. That's "not B."**

When an **"If A, then B"** statement is true, one other statement is true: **"If not B, then not A."**

**"If not B, then not A"** is called the contrapositive. It's essentially the double-reverse of the original statement: you switch the order of the statements AND you put a **"not"** in front of them. If Ross got wet, then he did not have an umbrella.

Knowing the contrapositive is method #1 to becoming a logic master.

## METHOD #2: DRAW A DIAGRAM

Good news for all the doodlers out there: you can draw a diagram to help with logic problems. You can draw an Euler diagram and use it to help figure out how different groups overlap or don't overlap.

🔍 **Watch:**

*OK, go!*

On any **ACT** logic question, those two techniques should carry you: look for the contrapositive ("If not B, then not A"), and draw a diagram when necessary.

## EXERCISE

**INSTRUCTIONS:** Solve each problem and choose the correct answer.

1. What must be true if the following statement is true?

> If a fish has exactly three eyes, then it has had radiation poisoning.

A. If a fish has exactly two eyes, then it does not have radiation poisoning.
B. If a fish has exactly two eyes, then it does not have radiation poisoning.
C. A fish has not had radiation poisoning if and only if it has exactly three eyes.
D. If a fish has exactly one eye, then is has had radiation poisoning.
E. If a fish has not had radiation poisoning, then is does not have exactly three eyes.

2. If the statements below are true, what else can be concluded as also true?

> Every vampire is a pirate.
> Every zombie is a pirate.
> Every demon is a vampire.

F. No zombies are vampires.
G. No zombies are demons.
H. Every demon is a pirate.
J. Every zombie is a vampire.
K. Every vampire is a zombie.

3. Evan's bedroom has the same exact dimensions as Owen's bedroom. The length, width, and height of Evan's room are directly proportional to the length, width, and height of Kate's bedroom. Which of the following statements is/are also true regarding the bedrooms of Evan, Kate, and Owen?

> I. Evan's bedroom could have the same dimensions as Kate's bedroom.
> II. Evan's bedroom must have the same dimensions as Kate's bedroom.
> III. Owen's bedroom must be directly proportional to Kate's bedroom.

A. Only I
B. Only II
C. Only I and III
D. Only II and III
E. I, II and III

4. If the six statements below are all true, what else must be true?

> Everyone who owns a pet has fleas.
> Corey does not own a pet.
> Marco has fleas.
> Julianne has fleas.
> Lacey no longer has a pet.
> Eduardo has a pet.

F. Eduardo has fleas
G. Corey does not have fleas
H. Marco owns a pet
J. Julianne does not own a pet
K. Lacey does not have fleas

5. Assume that the five statements below are true.

> There are eight bloopers and each is a different color.
> Bloopers can be tikes, kloodles, both, or neither.
> All bloopers that are tikes are kloodles.
> The red blooper is not a kloodle.
> The yellow blooper is a tike.

Which of the following must be true considering only the five statements above?
A. The red blooper is a kloodle and not a tike
B. The red blooper is a kloodle and a tike
C. The red blooper is a tike
D. The yellow blooper is not a tike
E. The yellow blooper is a kloodle

**6.** Nate said to Mark, "If you yawn in the next five minutes, then I will go to sleep by sundown." If Nate's statement is true, then based entirely on his statement and nothing else, what else is necessarily true?

    **F.** If Nate goes to sleep by sundown, then Mark did yawn in the next five minutes.

    **G.** If Mark goes to sleep by sundown, then Nate did yawn in the next five minutes.

    **H.** If Nate does not go to sleep by sundown, then Mark did not yawn in the next five minutes.

    **J.** If Mark does not go to sleep by sundown, then Nate did not yawn in the next five minutes.

    **K.** Nate and Mark have a unique relationship.

**7.** "If an apple has a worm, then it is full of protein," says a father to his daughter. If the father's statement is true, what else must also be correct?

    **A.** If an apple is full of protein, then it has a worm.

    **B.** If an apple is not full of protein, then it has a worm.

    **C.** If an apple is not full of protein, then it does not have a worm.

    **D.** If an apple does not have a worm, then it is full of protein.

    **E.** If an apple does not have a worm, then it is not full of protein.

NOTES:

# Combinations and Permutations

*In how many unique ways can you rearrange the letters in the word GRR-argh?*

**Most student cower in fear when they see permutation or combination problems.** Luckily for you, this topic looks hard but is a LOT easier when you have a plan.

## THERE ARE TWO TYPES OF PROBLEMS YOU MIGHT SEE.

**The first goes something like this:**
Bob has 6 different color shoes that fit on his left foot and 7 different color shoes that fit on his right foot. If Bob closes his eyes and randomly picks one left shoe and one right shoe, how many possible shoe combinations does he have?

Your job here is simple. It consists of three steps.

**1. Draw slots, one for each type of item that is being chosen.** Here, Bob has two choices to make: left shoe and right shoe. So we make two slots and label them.

| _____ | _____ |
| Left shoe | Right shoe |

**2. Fill in the slots with the number of options available for each choice.**

| ___6___ | ___7___ |
| Left shoe | Right shoe |

**3. Multiply.**

| ___6___ | × | ___7___ | = 42 |
| Left shoe | | Right shoe | |

**Boom. Bob can wear 42 different pairs of shoes.**
**Hopefully he picked a pair that looks good. Good luck, Bob.**

Anytime you are asked for a number of combinations on the **ACT**, the items are separated clearly into groups (such as left and right shoes). When that's the case, just follow those three steps and you will be golden.

The second type of problem will ask for the number of ways that things can be arranged. These aren't really any harder and you can use the same steps to solve.

**Here is an example of what one of these might look like:**
Bob likes to take his three cats on walks in his little red wagon. The wagon has three seats: one in the front, one in the middle, and one in the back. In how many different ways can Bob arrange his cats?

# HERE IS WHAT YOU DO:

🔎 **Draw slots, one for each space.**
**Here, Bob has three seats in his wagon.**

————————    ————————    ————————
Front          Middle          Back

**Fill in the slots with the number of each item that is available.** As you proceed, you have to ask yourself how many items are available after you place each one. In this case, you do this by subtracting one for each successive slot. Why? Because once you've placed a cute lil' kitty in a seat, you have one fewer cute lil' kitty to place in the next spot.

**Bob has three choices of cat that can fit in the first seat, but after that he only has two cats left to choose from for the middle seat, and one cat left to choose from for the last seat**

$$\frac{3}{\text{Front}} \qquad \frac{2}{\text{Middle}} \qquad \frac{1}{\text{Back}}$$

**Multiply.**

$$\frac{3}{\text{Front}} \times \frac{2}{\text{Middle}} \times \frac{1}{\text{Back}} = 6$$

**There are six cat arrangements for our weird friend Bob.**

*And now we're practicing.*

199

## EXERCISE

**INSTRUCTIONS:** Solve each problem and choose the correct answer.

1. How many ways can three letters be arranged if the first letter must be a consonant, the second must be a vowel, and the third must be a consonant?

   (Note: In the English language there are 26 letters. A, E, I, O, and U are vowels, Y can be both a consonant and a vowel, and the remaining letters are consonants.)
   A. 48
   B. 2,205
   C. 2,400
   D. 2,646
   E. 17,576

2. United States telephone area codes are formed by three digits in a row. The first digit must be 2-9 and the other two digits can have any value 0-9. How many possible area codes exist in the United States?
   F. 28
   G. 700
   H. 720
   J. 800
   K. 1,000

3. Del is on a camping trip and has packed 2 hats, 7 shirts, 3 pairs of pants, and 2 pairs of shoes. How many outfit combinations can she choose from if she will wear 1 hat, 1 shirt, 1 pair of pants, and 1 pair of shoes?
   A. 2
   B. 4
   C. 7
   D. 14
   E. 84

4. The Park Restaurant offers 3 choices of bread, 4 types of meat, 5 kinds of cheese, and 3 vegetables in its sandwiches. Cody wants a sandwich with one kind of bread, one kind of meat, one kind of cheese, and one veggie. How many possible sandwich options does he have to choose from?
   F. 12
   G. 15
   H. 60
   J. 180
   K. 636

5. Jasmine has four empty walls and four posters. She plans to hang one poster on each wall. How many unique poster arrangements are possible?
   A. 4
   B. 10
   C. 16
   D. 24
   E. 256

6. Lindsey has chosen Andy to bake the cake for her wedding. He offers her 6 cake flavors, 8 different fillings, and 7 colors of frosting. How many different possible cake combinations does Lindsey have to choose from if she picks one cake flavor, one filling, and one frosting color?
   F. 2
   G. 21
   H. 42
   J. 168
   K. 336

7. Annabelle is excited that she gets to adopt two pets from the Humane Society. Her mother tells her that she can bring one cat and one mouse home with her. When Annabelle visits, the Humane Society has 50 cats and 10 mice. How many different combinations of two pets can Annabelle pick from?
   A. 10
   B. 40
   C. 50
   D. 60
   E. 500

8. Walt has collected five signed baseballs that he would like to display on a shelf from left to right. In how many orders can Walt arrange the baseballs?
   F. 5
   G. 15
   H. 120
   J. 240
   K. 3,125

**Tutor Ted.**

NOTES:

NOTES:

# MATH: ANSWERS & SOLUTIONS

# Answers and Solutions

### Page 94 Mathcabulary

**Question 1: (D)**
The denominators are factored into primes. To find the least common denominator (LCD), we need to identify the smallest number that each denominator can divide into evenly. Let's start with 11. Since it multiplies into the second fraction twice (11^2), we will need two of them in our LCD. As for 29, we need 29^3 and for the factor 53, we need 53^2. That means our LCD equals 11^2×29^3×53^2.

**Question 2: (J)**
To find the x-intercept, let y = 0 and solve for x. 4x + 5y = 40 becomes 4x + 0 = 40 or 4x = 40 and x = 10.

**Question 3: (D)**
You can eliminate A, B and C right away— why? Because they are each two-digit integers! (It's a math test AND a reading test, people!). Both D and E are multiples of 19 and 3 and both are three digits. We are asked for the smallest value, so D is the winner.

**Question 4: (K)**
Remember that a rational number can be expressed as a ratio of two integers. In other words... a fraction. That means if you have a number that has an infinite, non-repeating decimal, then the number is irrational. If you take the square root of any number that is not a perfect square (1, 4, 9, 16,...), the result is an irrational number. √(36/9) =√4 = 2, which is the only rational choice.

**Question 5: (C)**
Domain refers to all the possible values for x. Are there any that won't work? To answer this problem, we need to check out the denominator. There are two ways that x can go wrong here. When the denominator is equal to zero, we have trouble. To avoid that issue, we need to see when x– 1 equals zero. This happens when x = 1. The other issue is that we can't have a negative value under the radical. That means that x–1 has to be greater than or equal to zero. Answer C covers both of our bases here.

### Page 105 Plugging In

**Question 1: (B)**
Here's a good opportunity to use the plug in method. Start by plugging in your own number for x. We'll say that x=5. Alright, next step: solve the problem using that concrete value for x. Okay, if x=5 then the diameter is 2(5)-5, which equals 5. Now we can divide that by 2 to get the radius of the circle: 2.5. Lastly, we use the area formula A=(π)r^2 to get A=(π)(2.5)^2 which comes out to 6.25(π). Not too hard. Now all we have to do is plug our x value of 5 into the answer choices and see which one yields that same answer or 6.25(π). It looks like B is the only one that works!

**Question 2: (H)**
Here is a perfect problem to use the trial and error method. First pick a value for y that is greater than 0 and less than ½. How about ¼? Now use your calculator to see which one of the expression produces the greatest value when y = ¼. 1/y = 1/ (¼) = 4. Surprised?

### Question 3: (D)

How do we decide this might be a good problem for plugging in? Since there are variables in the answer choices, it's a good bet that plugging in will be effective. Step 2: Plug in our own number for the variable. I want to choose a value of **"a"** that seems reasonable. Let's make "a" equal 70. Step 3: Solve the problem using your value. Okay, if **"a"** is 70, then <XYW = 2a-35 = 2(70)-35 = 105. That means that <WYZ has to equal 180-105, which is 75. Step 4: Plug our same value for **"a"** into the answer choices and see which one produces that same answer of 75. Only choice D will work.

### Question 4: (J)

Start by choosing a number for c. It will be SO much easier to solve the problem using a number. Let's pick c = 10 to make it easy on ourselves. Now solve the problem. Well, if the cow produces c+2 gallons of milk, then that would be 10+2=12 gallons of milk. How many hours would that take? Well, the cow produces 6 every 24 hours, so it produces 12 then that would take 48 hours. Finally plug in 10 for c into the answer choices and see which one produces 48 as a result. Only J will do the trick.

### Question 5: (E)

Okay, plug in method, people! Usually we start by plugging in numbers for the given variables, but in this problem is actually makes sense for us to plug in numbers for the radii first. Let's make the radius of circle A equal 10. That means the radius of circle B would have to be 2. Okay, now we can figure out what q would be. The circumference of circle B would be $2(\pi)r = 2(\pi)2 = 4(\pi)$. Now they're telling us the area of circle A is nq. Well, we can find the exact value of the area of circle A. it's $(\pi)r^2 = (\pi)(10)^2 = 100(\pi)$. So if the area of circle A is $100(\pi)$ and that's the same thing as nq, then we can set them equal $100(\pi)=nq$, or $100(\pi) = n(4(\pi))$. Great! Now just solve for n. It's 25. That's it!

### Question 6: (H)

The best way to approach this problem is to choose an original price for the app. And with percentage problems, it's easiest to use the number 100. So let's say the app started out at $100. Her discount resulted in the customer paying 60% of the original cost or, in this case, $60.00. Now she is increasing the cost by 30%. We need to multiply $60.00 by 130% or 60×1.30, which equals $78.00. That means that the new price is 78% of the original asking price. Remember to choose easy *(friendly)* numbers like 100 when you start!

### Question 7: (E)

Plug in method: choose easy numbers. If a/b has to equal 1/7, then why not just make a=1 and b=7? If b/c has to equal 7/9, then b already works as 7 and c can be 9. Now they want to know what c/a equals. Well, that's easy enough, it's 1/9. Booyahkahshah!

### Question 8: (H)

This one's a little tricky! We'll show you both the plug-in and the regular ol' math way to do it. Regular math first: Andy has completed a total of 3/7 of the required hours. That leaves him with 4/7 of the required hours to complete. He has 9 months to do this. If he wants to complete all of the necessary hours and he wants to complete the same number of hours over each of the remaining 9 months, divide 4/7 by 9. $(4/7) \div 9 = (4/7)\times(1/9)$ or 4/63

**Now the plug in method:** Start by plugging in a number for the total number of hours that Andy has to complete. We'll say he has to do 70 hours. If he did 3/7 of that in his first three months, then he's completed 30 hours and has another 40 to go. He has 9 months to do 40 hours, so each month he must do 40/9 hours, which is 4.444 hours per month. So the percentage of hours he has to complete each month is 4.444 divided by 70, which equals 0.06349. Check to see which one of the answer choices produces this decimal. It's H.

### Pages 107-109 Reality Math

### Question 1. (E)
One important thing on this problem: you've got to mind the units! The area of the floor is simple to find. 8×16 = 128 ft.2. Now we need to find out how many SQUARE INCHES each brick covers. 4× 4 = 16 in.2 We need to change the SQUARE feet to SQUARE inches. Don't even think about converting 12 inches to 1 foot! There are 144in. sq. in each square foot. Multiply 128 by 144 to get 18,432 in.2. Now each brick covers 16 in.2. To find out how many bricks we need, divide 18,432 by 16. We will need 1,152 bricks.

### Question 2: (J)
The triangular part of the sidewall is an equilateral triangle with each side equal to 8. You can find the height of this triangle by using the Pythagorean Theorem or remembering that the height of an equilateral triangle is $\frac{1}{2}s\sqrt{3}$, where s = the measure of the side of the triangle. $\frac{1}{2}(8)\sqrt{3}$ is approximately equal to 6.9 ft. The height of the barn to the base of the triangle is given as 8. Therefore, 8+6.9=14.9≈15.

### Question 3: (E)
You will need to find the total surface area of thec. Then we will subtract out the two windows and one door to determine how many square feet she wants to cover. Remember that she wants to cover both the inside and the outside! Let's wait until we get the outside area before we double.

The base structure has 4 walls, 2 at 8x8 and 2 at 8x16. Total area for these walls is 384.
The roof is made up of 2 rectangles at 8x16 or 256 total.
The remainder of the building consists of two equilateral triangles, whose area equals 2 ($\frac{1}{2}$×8×4$\sqrt{3}$). The two triangles have area of 32$\sqrt{3}$ or 55.42.
So far our total surface area is 384+256+32$\sqrt{3}$, which equals 695.43.

Now we need to remove the two windows (2×12×2) and the door (2×6). We remove 60 square feet from the total to get 635.43. Covering inside and out means we need to double this area. We want to cover a total of 1270.86 square feet.. Each can covers 140 square feet. 1270.86/140 = 9.07 cans. So 9 cans won't quite do it. Looks like we'll need 10. We'll put the leftover waterproof coating in the garage and never look at it again until we throw it away when we move!

### Question 4: (F)
24/480 = 0.05 or 5%

### Question 5: (D)
Set up a proportion that compares the current order to a larger order. 192/480=x/2000. That means that 480x=384000 or x=800.

### Question 6: (J)
The percentage of students ordering size medium is 48/480 or 10%. The percentage of those students buying small is 24/480 or 5%. That means that 15% of the pie chart represents those students who are ordering small or medium. 15% of 360° equals 54°

### Question 7: (C)
There is a fixed cost of $3000 whether or not the company sells 0 or 1000 glockenspiels. In addition, each glockenspiel will cost $150 more. To cover the costs, let's look at the following equation, where x = the number of glockenspiels sold.
3000+150x = 450x or 3000= 450x–150x. That means that x = 10. The company needs to sell 10 glockenspiels to break even.

### Question 8: (H)
Look at what the profit is if the company makes 30 glockenspiels. 450(30)-3000-150(30) = 6000, whereas making 30 euphoniums produces 150(30)-1000–(100)(30) = 500. 30 glockenspiels will make the most money.

206

### Question 9: (D)
Simply divide 5.50/50 to get $0.11.

### Question 10: (J)
To solve, find the total number of seeds. Find the sum of 10+60+40+25+50. There are 185 seeds, in total. On Kate's first choice, her probability of selecting a poppy seed is 40/185. The probability of her second seed being a poppy seed is now 39/184 and finally her third selection being a poppy has a probability of 38/183. To get the probability of selecting all three poppy seed is the product of 40/185 times 39/184 times 38/183.

### Question 11: (C)
Buying one pack of each type with the regular pricing means that the customer spent a total of $15.95. Buying the same items during the sale would total $13.45, resulting a savings of $2.50. The formula for percent change is Percent Change=(Change in amount)/(Original Amount). So Percent change = 2.50/15.95 = 0.156, which rounds up to 16%.

### Question 12: (J)
Some problems are just a pain in the butt. This is one of them. Start by writing out the relationship between the number (d, p, and s for daisy, poppy, and snapdragon) of each packet of seeds. d = 4p since the number of daisy packets is 4 times the number of poppies, and s = p + 2 since Herbert bought two more snapdragons than poppies. Next, we need to relate those quantities to each other based on the cost. 1.20d + 6.00s + .8p = 81.60 is an equation that would represent Herbert's total bill. Substitute 4p and p + 2 in there for d and s and solve for p=6. If p=6, d=24, and s=8. That's a total of 38 seed packets. Herbert has got some serious planting to do.

### Question 13: (J)
You will need to subtract each pair's data from the next pair. Between 1950 and 1970, there was an increase of 9,367. Although the difference between 1970 to 1990 is larger, it is not one of the choices. Read the questions carefully. You are supposed to consider only the ones listed!

### Question 14: (J)
The population has risen by 32,387 thousand from 1900 to 2000. Use that number and the starting value of 1,485 in 1900 plus the percent change formula (Percent Change = (Change in amount)/(original amount)*100) and you'll get a value 2181%. Rounding gives us answer J.

### Question 15: (A)
Consider the coordinates (0, 10.6), (20, 20), and (40, 30). Where did those come from? The x values represent the number of years after 1950 (so the first coordinate point IS 1950, and the second one is 1970) and the second one is the population in millions. The table gives us the population in thousands but the question asks us for it in millions, so we have to divide those numbers by 1,000. In 1970, for example, the population was 19,953 thousands...which, when rounded, is about 20 million.

The quickest way to finish the problem from here is just to test the answer choices to see which one will give the values closest to the ones listed above. When you plug in x=0, x=20 and x=40, answer A is right on the button.

---

### Pages 121-122 Using the Answer Choices

### Question 1: (C)
The best way to solve this question is to enter each value for r into the expression (27/r)-. Enter the expression exactly as it is written and stop when you get 3.25!

### Question 2: (K)
Once again, substituting each value for x will lead you to the right answer. Remember that you cannot divide by zero. If x=5 as it does in answer choice K, we will get a zero in the denominator.

### Question 3: (D)
This is an easy problem to use the answer choices. Let x = each of the values to see what makes the equation true—the right side equals the left side. Alternately, you could solve the equation: $-3(x + 7) + 4x = 8(-2)$. $-3x - 21 + 4x = -16$. $x - 21 = -16$ or $x = 5$.

### Question 4: (G)
After paying $7,000, Rohan owes $63,000 (by the way, fancy car, Rohan!). Now let's pick an answer and plug in. Start at $2,000. That means that the first year Rohan pays 2,000, the second year 4,000, the third year is 8,000, the fourth is 16,000, the fifth is 32,000, the sixth is 64,000. Well, since Rohan only needs to pay 63,000 total, this doesn't work and we should go lower. Try 1,000. You'll find that it works.

### Question 5: (E)
You can plug in the suggested values for x and see which one makes the statement true. Or if you set the equation equal to zero and see that the equation is a quadratic equation that is easily factorable into $3(x-3)(x-4)=0$. A third way would be to use a quadratic program on your calculator. No matter how you solve it, either 3 or 4 are the solutions to this equation.

### Question 6: (J)
Substitute the values in for b and check out the resulting equations. All work except $x^2 + 17x + 24 = 0$. Use a quadratic equation program to confirm this.

### Question 7: (C)
Try the answer choices. If you start with $40 you find that you run out of money too soon. But $48 works out perfectly.

### Question 8: (F)
First, list the possible answers. The integers between 1.5 and 9.5 are 2, 3, 4, 5, 6, 7, 8 9. Just start dividing the answer choices by the 8 possible integers and as soon as one doesn't work you can cross it off the list. If you want to do it the fancy way you can find the least common multiple (LCM). 2, 3, 22, 5, 2×3, 7, 23, 32 is the prime factorization of these integers. The LCM is (23)(32)(5)(7) or 2520. You should try 2520 first anyway, since it is the smallest of the choices!

### Question 9: (A)
Pick an answer choice. Let's start with 9. Okay, if y is one more than 4 times the value of 9 then y = 37. Well, 37 + 9 does not equal 22, so choice C is out. Since it was much higher than we need, let's try 2. If x = 2, then y = 9, and the relationship between x and y works! Hurray.

### Question 10: (F)
Work from the answers as usual. Start in the middle and see what happens. If he got 15 lightning round questions right, that means he got 60 regular round questions right. His point total would be $15 * 5 + 60 * 3 = 255$ = way too high. Try it again with a lower value (say, 8), and you'll see that it works and he earns 136 points. So much easier than writing and solving a system of equations, don't you agree?

### Question 11: (B)
$8^3 = 512$ and $8^4 = 4096$. Just plug in the answer choices to see which one gives you a number between 512 and 4096

### Question 12: (G)
You can certainly use a geometric sequence to see how many times John reduced his paintings or just use your calculator and start by multiplying $3000 by 0.4. Why 0.4? Because if you reduce the price by 60%, you're left with 40% (or 0.4). Continue to do this, keeping track of number of times that you do so, until you get a number less than $200.

### Question 13: (D)
Let's let x=the number of pizzas and y=the number of sodas. That means that x+y=18. Let's now look at the cost. $4.25x + 1.5y = 54.50$. Now we can start plugging in answer choices to see which one works for both equations.

## Pages 127-128 Circles

### Question 1: (C)
To find the area of a circle, we use $A=\pi r^2$. So, we need to know the radius. We are given that the circumference C is $8\pi$ and we know that $C=\pi d$. That means the diameter of the circle is 8, making the radius 4. If $A=\pi r^2$, then $A = \pi(4)^2 = 16\pi$ units$^2$.

### Question 2: (J)
Rob spent 7 out of 24 hours sleeping. That means 7/24 parts of his day. We will set up a proportion to find the part of the pie chart (central angle) that represents "sleep."
$7/24 = x/360$
$24x = 2520$, making $x = 105°$

### Question 3: (D)
The standard equation of a circle with radius, r, and center located at the origin is $x^2 + y^2 = r^2$. Knowing that the circle has y-intercepts a 6 and -6 means the radius of the circle is 6, making the equation: $x^2 + y^2 = (6)^2$.

### Question 4: (G)
If $A=\pi r^2$, then $A= 121\pi$ means that the radius of the circle is $\sqrt{121} = 11$. The diameter is 22, twice the radius.

### Question 5: (D)
The area that the transmitter covers is a circle with radius 45. Use $A=\pi r^2$ to get $2025\pi$ or approximately 6,362 square feet.

### Question 6: (H)
Remember that using the equation: $(x-h)2 + (y-k)^2 = r^2$, where (h,k) is the center and r is the radius, we can use the fact that the center is located at (-5, -5) to get: $(x+5)^2 + (y+5)^2 = r^2$. Now substitute in the values x=0 and y=-17 to solve for r or $r^2$. That will look like $(0+5)^2 + (-17+5)^2 = r^2$, which means that r = 13 and $r^2 = 169$.

### Question 7: (A)
Solve the equation so that it has the form: $(x-h)^2 + (y-k)^2 = r^2$. You'll get $(x-0)^2 + (y-7)^2 = 28$. That means that (h,k) = (0, 7), which is the center and $r^2 = 28$. The radius = $\sqrt{28}$.

### Question 8: (G)
The area of a sector/area of the circle = measure of the central angle/360. They are in proportion. Set this up as $18\pi/(9\sqrt{2})^2\pi = x/360$ and solve for x.

### Question 9: (D)
The measure of arc QS = the measure of arc RT. The measure of arc ST = the measure of arc QR. That means the circumference of the circle is $32\pi$. Since $C=(\pi)d$ we know that QT, a diameter, is 32.

### Question 10: (H)
If $A=\pi r^2$, then $r^2 = \frac{1}{4}$ and $r=\frac{1}{2}$. Remember that $C =2\pi r$, so $C = 1\pi$ or $\pi$.

### Question 11: (C)
Let's plug in for this problem. Say the diameter of this circle is 10. If the length of the arc is $7(\pi)/18$ of the diameter, that would make the arc length have a value of 10 times $7(\pi)/18$, which equals roughly 12.217. The total circumference of this circle would $(\pi)d = (\pi)(10) = 31.415$ or so. Now we can set up a proportion: $12.217/31.415 = $ central angle/360. Our central angle would equal 140.

### Question 12: (G)
If <WVZ=70 then so does <VWZ because VZ and WZ are equal (they are radii). That means that angle <VZW=40. Because <VZW and <XZY are vertical angles, we know that they are equal. So <XZY=40.

---

## Pages 131-132 Triangles

### Question 1: (B)
The sum of the three angles of a triangle is 180°. If you know the sum of two of the angles, simply subtract 94° from 180°.

### Question 2: (H)
We know that triangle RTU is similar to triangle QTS because of their congruent angles, which means that their corresponding sides are in proportion. That means QT/QS = RT/RU. Solve the proportion 6/4 =9/x for x to get the measure of segment RU.

### Question 3: (B)
Using the Pythagorean theorem, $a \wedge 2 + b \wedge 2 = c \wedge 2$, we can let a equal the missing side and r represent the side we know. That means we have: $a \wedge 2 + r \wedge 2 = 52$ or $a \wedge 2 = 25 - r \wedge 2$. To find "a", we need to take the square root of both sides of the equation, which yields $a = \sqrt{(25 - r \wedge 2)}$

### Question 4: (J)
Start by identifying all of the information that you know. Example: What does c+d equal? How about f+g+h? In this problem, it's important to know that you don't need to know the measure of each angle! So, if we want to know the sum a+b+c+d+e+f+g+h, let's substitute in what we know: a+b+(180)+e+(180). To find a+b+e, look at triangle QRS. a+b+e +36°= 180. That means that a+b+e =144. Therefore, the sum a+b+c+d+e+f+g+h=180+180+144 or 504.

### Question 5: (C)
Since we have the measures of angles QRT and SRT, we know that angle QRS = 60°. That allows us to find the measure of angle RSQ as 30°. Looking at triangle QRS, we can identify it as a 30-60-90 triangle whose shortest leg equals 20. QS is the longer leg. Therefore QS = $20\sqrt{3}$.

### Question 6: (H)
Using the Pythagorean theorem, $a \wedge 2 + b \wedge 2 = c \wedge 2$, $a \wedge 2 + 272 = 452$. Solve for "a" by isolating a. That means that $a = \sqrt{(2025 - 729)} = \sqrt{1296} = 36$.

### Question 7: (D)
What do we know here? All we know are those two side lengths. Based on that, we know that the angle opposite a side of 7.9 cannot be larger than an angle opposite a side of 8.1. The size of an angle is always relative to the size of the opposite side. Since we don't have information about side XZ, we can't draw any conclusions about angle XYZ.

### Question 8: (J)
Triangles PQR and PRS are isosceles triangles which means that the base angles are congruent. Angle PRQ = angle QRP = 70. Angle QPR in triangle PQR=40° because the other two angles in this triangle are each 70. Angles PRQ and PRS are supplementary, resulting in angle PRS=110. Using the fact that angle RSP is congruent to angle SPR, we can determine that angle SPR = 35°. Simply add 35 to 40 to get the measure of angle QPS.

### Question 9: (D)
Make a sketch! The ladder is the hypotenuse (20), one leg is the 12, now find the missing leg. Using the Pythagorean theorem, $a \wedge 2 + b \wedge 2 = c \wedge 2$, we have: $122 + b \wedge 2 = 202$. Now solve for b = 16.

---

## Pages 135-136 Percent

### Question 1: (B)
Remember to translate the words into math symbols. The word "of" means multiply (times) and the word "is" means equals (=). Change 135% into 1.35. Translation is now 1.35×(?)=270. ? = 270/1.35 = 200. Now read the problem to see what is asked for. This question is a 2-parter! Now find 0.8 of 200. That's 0.8×200=160.

### Question 2: (K)
An easy way to solve this problem is to start with the number 100 for the original profits in 2011. That means that in 2012 the profits would go up by 20% to be 120. In 2013 the new profits (120) go up by 30% to become 156. The new number is 56% higher than the original number.

### Question 3: (E)
10% off means that you are paying 90% of the original price. To find the first reduced price, multiply 0.9 by $9,000, making the first reduced price is $8,100. If you then take 15% off, multiply 0.85 by $8,100 to get $6,885. The question wants us to provide what percent is the final price ($6,885) of the original price ($9,000). Divide 6,885 by 9,000 to get 0.765. That's 76.5%.

### Question 4: (J)
Percent Change = (change in amount / original amount) x 100. James's weight change was 39 pounds. His original weight was 130. (39/130) x 100 = 30%.

### Question 5: (D)
Sometimes it is helpful to organize your thoughts. Like so:

| Mon | Tue | Wed | Thu | Fri |
|-----|-----|------|-------|--------|
| 10  | 12  | 14.4 | 17.28 | 20.736 |

Each subsequent number is found by multiplying the previous number by 1.2. By the way, do you see that this is a geometric sequence? That means that for those of you who love formulas, you could find the length on Friday by using the formula $a_n = a_1(r)^{(n-1)}$

### Question 6: (H)
Remember "of" means multiply! (1/8)(0.48)(9000).

### Question 7: (B)
There are several steps to solve this problem. Find out how much is raised by the $100 donors. (0.1×24,300×100 = $243,000). Now find out how much is raised by the $50 donors. (0.3×24300×50 = $364,500). The total is 243,000+364,500, which is $192,500 short of the goal. Divide 192,500 by 800,000 to get the % of the shortfall.

### Question 8: (G)
Find the actual dollar amount of the savings. 35-28=7. Take 7/35 (remember to use the original value in the denominator!) to find the discount percent.

### Question 9: (D)
After the 1st hour 60% of the soda was left. 0.6×200=120. After the 2nd hour, 30% of what's left was gone, meaning that 70% of 120 were left. 0.7×120= 84.

### Question 10: (H)
Translate to 1.3×680. 130% = 1.3 and the word "of" means multiply.

### Question 11: (E)
Another translation: 25 = ? percent × 5. "is" means =, "of" means multiply. Solve for the "?".

### Question 12: (J)
Let's find what the sale price of the cake is. 0.7×20=$14. If you want extra frosting, then multiply 14 by 1.1, because that's 110% of the original $14.

### Question 13: (B)
To make short order of this problem, pick a price for 12 eggs, like $2.00. That means that each egg would cost 2.00/12 or around 17 cents an egg. Using this price per egg, multiply 0.17 by 11 to get 1.8333... $2.00 minus $1.83 = 0.16, which is your savings or discount. 0.16/2.00= 0.083 or roughly 8% less than the full price.

---

### Page 138 Proportions & Ratios

### Question 1: (E)
Set up a proportion of daughter-to-father: 5/9 = x/180 or 9x = 900, x = 100

### Question 2: (J)
If the ratio of the sides is 2/7, then the ratio of the areas is 22/72 (Why?)
Set up the proportion as 4/49 = 40/x and solve for "x." You can also solve this by finding the sides of the bigger rectangle. Set up a proportion for the one side of the smaller rectangle. 2/7 = 5/x. It turns out x, one side of the bigger rectangle, is 17.5. Now do it for the other side. 2/7 = 8/x. Here x becomes 28. So the sides of the bigger rectangle are 17.5 and 28. Multiply them together to get the area of 490.

### Question 3: (C)
After making a basic recipe, you would have 8 parts. To compare the amount of salt to the total, use 4/8. Now to find how many tablespoons of salt are needed if you are making 24 tablespoons, solve this proportion: 4/8 = x/24. 8x = 96 and x = 12

### Question 4: (H)
Solve the proportion $150/10 = x/9$. Think "grams of coffee to number of cups" to get each equivalent fraction.

### Question 5: (D)
Another proportion. This one has us comparing corresponding sides. Think "longest is to longest as shortest is to shortest." That means $7/679 = 2/x$ and solve for x.

### Question 6: (F)
We have three squares of three different sizes. Let's let the length of square Z equal "z." That means that each side of square Y equals "2z" and each side of square X equals "4z." Now let's find the areas of square X and square Z. Area of square $X = (4z)^2$ or $16z^2$ and the area of square Z equals $z^2$. Comparing the areas yields $1/16$.

### Question 7: (D)
We can solve two separate proportions here: one for the length and one for the width. Solve: $1/80 = x/160$ and $1/80 = y/360$.

### Question 8: (J)
The ratio $5 : 6 : 7$ has a total of 18 parts ($5 + 6 + 7$), which means that the shelter has a minimum number of 18 pets. Now don't confuse the fact that they have 18 dogs with the least number of pets! $6/18 = 18/x$, solving for x will give us the total number of pets currently at the shelter.

### Question 9: (D)
The formula for the area of a triangle is $\frac{1}{2}bh$. That means $120 = \frac{1}{2}bh$, where b and h represent the legs of the right triangle. We know that the ratio of the legs is $3 : 5$. That means that the actual lengths can be represented as 3x and 5x. Now, further substitution into the formula yields: $120 = \frac{1}{2}(3x)(5x)$ or $120 = 7.5x^2$ or $16 = x^2$ and $x = 4$. If the longer side is represented by 5x, then the longer side is 20.

### Question 10: (J)
The fact that the ratio of the angles is $2 : 3 : 4$ means that the measures of the angles share a common factor. Let's let x represent that factor. That means that $2x+3x+4x= 180$. $9x=180$ and $x=20$. The smallest angle was represented by 2x, which means that it equals $40°$.

### Question 11: (A)
The formula for perimeter of a rectangle is $P = 2L + 2W$, where $L$ = length and $W$ = width. A 1:3 ratio means that the length and width have a common factor, which we need to find. Let's let the width equal x, which means the length can be represented by 3x. $64= 2(3x) + 2(1x)$ or $64 = 8x$ and $x = 8$, which is the width.

### Question 12: (G)
First check to see what the least number of cars can be in the lot so that this ratio works. $4+3+7 = 14$.
Now we need to check each of the statements, I, II and III.
Statement I is false since if the total is 28, then the number of blue cars would have to be 6. Statement II is true. $4x12= 48$ so there would have to be 12 times how many white cars are in the ratio: $12 \times 7 = 84$. Statement III is false, since the number of blue cars is the smallest number in any situation.

**Question 13: (B)**
Let's let the sides of the isosceles right triangle equal x. Then the hypotenuse equals x√2. We know that because an isosceles right triangle is a 45, 45, 90 right triangle. If you don't remember that short cut, you can prove this by using the Pythagorean theorem ($a^2 + b^2 = c^2$). To get the requested ratio, compare the side to the hypotenuse. That is $x/x\sqrt{2}$, which reduces to $1/\sqrt{2}$.

**Question 14: (J)**
Let's let 3x represent the price of the cheaper book and 4x the price of the more expensive book. That means that $3x + 4x = 42$, $7x = 42$ and $x = 6$, making the more expensive book cost 4×6 or $24. You could also set up the ratio $4/7=x/42$

---

**Page 142 Distance and Midpoint**

**Question 1: (B)**
The problem describes R as "exactly halfway" between Q and S. That means it's the midpoint! You can use the formula for midpoint and solve for the missing point, or you can use the logical approach, which is quicker. Look at the x-coordinates. 8 is halfway between 12 and what other number? 4, right? And -2 is halfway between 6 and -10. (4, -10), problem solved.

**Question 2: (G)**
Another "we give you the midpoint, you give us the endpoint" problem. Use the logical approach: if 0 is one x-coordinate and the midpoint is 6, then the missing x-coordinate is 12. If 5 is one y-coordinate and the midpoint is 7, then the other endpoint is 9. 12−9=3.

**Question 3: (C)**
Now we're just finding the midpoint. Use the formula, or just think: the midpoint is the average of the x-coordinates and the average of the y-coordinates.

**Question 4: (J)**
Use the distance formula, or better yet, download a distance program to your calculator. We love using that program—it's fast and it never makes a mistake!

**Question 5: (C)**
Read carefully here—we only need to find the y-coordinate of the midpoint. That's the average of the two y-coordinates, which is $(28+(-8))/2 = 20/2 = 10$.

**Question 6: (H)**
Another one where careful reading is the key! First, find the distance between those two points using the distance formula or a program on your calculator (get that program! It's legal to use on the **ACT**) to get a distance of 26. Then divide that by two to get the radius.

**Question 7: (D)**
Distance formula or distance program: your choice. One is faster. It's worth finding a cord to connect your calculator to your computer and going online to download a distance program. It would tell you that the distance between these points is 10.

**Question 8: (G)**
This is just the same as the rest of these problems, just a little more complicated. I would recommend thinking of Corey and Rachel's homes on an xy-coordinate grid. Corey is at (10, -8) and Rachel is at (-4, 16). Find the distance between them in blocks (it's about 28.635 blocks) and then multiply that by 1/8 to find the number of miles. 28.635*1/8=3.579≈3.6.

---

**Page 144 Slope Warmup**

Positive slope and positive y-intercept: B
Negative slope and negative y-intercept: D
Negative slope and positive y-intercept: C
Positive slope and negative y-intercept: A

### Page 145 Slope

### Question 1: (C)

To find the slope of a line, use $y = mx + b$, where m represents the slope and b represents the y-intercept. Let's put $2 = 5y + 3x$ into that format. Solving for y means that $2-3x = 5y$ or $5y = -3x + 2$. Now divide each term by 5 to get $y = (-3/5)x + 2/5$. The value of m (slope) is the coefficient of x. That means -3/5 is the slope.

### Question 2: (G)

You should use the slope formula here. Remember the slope formula: $m = (y2-y1)/(x2-x1)$. That means $(7-5)/(-3-1) = 2/-4$ or $-\frac{1}{2}$.

### Question 3: (A)

Slope-intercept form (the workhorse of linear equations) is: $y = mx + b$. First find the slope using $m = (y2-y1)/(x2-x1)$. $(0-2)/(-5-4) = 2/9 = m$. Now use either of the given points, let's say (4,2) along with $m = 2/9$ and solve for "b", the y-intercept. $2 = 2/9(4) + b$. $b = 10/9$—now find the correct response.

### Question 4: (G)

We need to solve the given equation for "y." In other words, isolate the "y" term. $5-y = 8x$ means that $-y = 8x - 5$ and that $y = -8x + 5$.

### Question 5: (D)

The question is asking for the slope of a line that is perpendicular to the given line. After getting our given equation in to slope intercept form, we can see that the slope of $3x = -4y$ equals $-\frac{3}{4}$. The slope of a line perpendicular to this can be found by taking its negative reciprocal, which is 4/3.

### Question 6: (K)

Substitute the known values into the given equation. $y-4x = 5q^3$ becomes $12-4(-7) = 5q^3$ or $40 = 5q^3$. Notice that you're actually done at this stage, because $5q^3$ is your b value. You might be tempted to find what q is (it's 2), but the question isn't asking for q... just the y-intercept!

### Question 7: (C)

If this system has one solution, then that means the lines cross at exactly one point. So these lines intersect and therefore are not parallel. That means that the slopes cannot be equal. In others words, $a \neq c$.

### Questions 8: (F)

If two lines are parallel, then they have the same slopes. If we find the slope of the given equation, the line in question will have the same value. $3x + 9y = 1$. Solving for "y" first produces $9y = -3x + 1$. Divide each term by 9 and the result is $y = (-1/3)x + 1/9$. The slope of each of the parallel lines is $(-1/3)$.

### Question 9: (D)

The slope of a line that is perpendicular to another line must be the opposite reciprocal of the other line. Let's solve the given equation for y to find out its slope. $4y + 3x = 5$ means that $4y = -3x + 5$ or $y = -\frac{3}{4}x + 5/4$, making $m1 = -\frac{3}{4}$. If the lines are perpendicular then $m2 = 4/3$, the negative reciprocal of $-\frac{3}{4}$. The value of the y-intercept is of no consequence and, if you look at the options, there is only one equation whose slope is 4/3. That means $y = (4/3)x - 4$ is your answer.

### Page 148 Foiling Warmup 1

$(x+4)(x-2) = x^2 + 2x - 8$
$(x-1)(x+5) = x^2 + 4x - 5$
$(3x+5)(2x+1) = 6x^2 + 13x + 5$
$(x+4)^2 = x^2 + 8x + 16$
$(a+b)^2 = a^2 + 2ab + b^2$

### Page 149 Foiling Warmup 2

$x^2 - x - 6 = (x+2)(x-3)$
$x^2 - 10x + 25 = (x-5)^2$
$2x^2 - x - 3 = (x+1)(2x-3)$

$(x+4)(x+5) = 0$
$(x-1)(x-2) = 0$
$(x-13)^2 = 0$

## Pages 150-151 FOILing

### Question 1: (E)
Use FOIL! First write the expression as (3x-2y)(3x-2y) and then multiply using FOIL. Collect like terms to get $9x^2-12xy+4y^2$.

### Question 2: (J)
FOIL again! The product is $15a^2 + 5ab - 9ab -3b^2$. Now collect the like terms to get $15a^2 - 4ab -3b^2$.

### Question 3: (D)
$(x-3)^3$ means $(x-3)(x-3)(x-3)$. Start this by finding the product of the first two factors. $(x-3)(x-3) = x^2-6x+9$. Now multiply $(x-3)$ by $x^2-6x+9$. You need to **"distribute"** each x over each term in $x^2-6x+9$ and then -3 over $x^2-6x+9$.

### Question 4: (G)
Set the equation equal to 0. That changes the equation to look like: $x^2 +x-20 = 0$. Factoring is the opposite of FOILING! Ask yourself what two numbers multiply to -20 and add to 1. $x^2 +x -20 = (x-4)(x+5)$, which means that x could equal 4 or -5. We need to find only one possible solution.

### Question 5: (A)
We have two fractions with unlike denominators. So, we need to find the least common denominator. The denominator of the first fraction can be factored into $(x+4)(x+4)$. Good news: the two fractions have a common factor. In order to make each expression have the denominator $(x+4)(x+4)$ we need to multiply $3x/(x+4)$ by $(x+4)/(x+4)$. Now that second expression becomes $[3x(x+4)] / [(x+4)(x+4)]$ Now we can add the two pieces together. The expression becomes: $[3x +3x(x+4)] / [(x+4)(x+4)]$. Simplify the numerator and the denominator to get the final answer.

### Question 6: (H)
This equation is a quadratic equation already set up to solve. Note that it is set equal to zero! Let's factor. Check out the constant. 18 has factors 1 and 18, 2 and 9, 3 and 6. Also note that 18 is positive. Now look at the middle term. Hmmm, it is 9. Since the sum of one set of factors equals 9, let's try that pair. What does $(x+6)(x+3)$ equal?

### Question 7: (C)
This can be handled easily using FOIL. The first pass through yields: $2x^2+2x-4x-4$. Simply collect like terms to get the answer.

### Question 8: (K)
Expanding the numerator (FOILING), we get $16x^2+48x+36$. You are now ready to divide each term by the denominator, which is 4. That will get you the right answer.

### Question 9: (A)
The only way that a number other than 1 raised to any power equals one is when the exponent equals zero. You will need to remember that fact! So, in this case, $x^2-1$ must equal zero. If $x^2-1= 0$, then by factoring, $(x-1)(x+1)=0$ and x can equal 1 or -1, two real solutions. NOTE: Remember that when you see things in the form $a^2 - b^2$ you are dealing with **"difference of squares."** It's always a good idea to factor such an expression into $(a+b)(a-b)$

### Question 10: (G)
The graph is that of a quadratic equation. *(A parabola only occurs with quadratic equations).* This graph intersects the x-axis in two places and the graph is in quadrants II and III, where x is a negative number. A quadratic equation can have one or two real solutions (sometimes called zeros or roots) and two imaginary solutions. From the graph, we can determine that this quadratic equation has two real negative zeros, places where the y-coordinate equals zero.

### Question 11: (D)
Check out the constant, 21. The two sets of factors for 21 are 21,1 and 3,7. We could factor this thing to be either $(x+3)(x+7)=0$ or $(x+1)(x+21)=0$. Using the first way gives the possible d value of 10.

### Question 12: (H)
If -4 is the only real solution then that means that $x^2+qx+r$ must equal $(x+4)(x+4)$. $(x+4)(x+4)= x^2+8x+16$. We can now identify both q and r from this expression. Notice all of the trap answers, like 16, which is the value of r. Be sure to go back and read the question before answering!

---

### Page 153 Inequalities

### Question 1: (A)
The graph represents an intersection. That is, it represents the part of the number line that two inequalities have in common. The word **"and"** is used to represent an intersection. The picture represents all values for x that are less than 2 AND, at the same time, greater than -4. Which of the symbolic math options represents that?

### Question 2: (K)
To solve an inequality, you can begin by treating it the same way that you do an equation. Just remember that multiplying or dividing by a negative number is an exception to the rule. When you multiply or divide by a negative number, you have to switch the direction of the inequality sign. $8(3x+2) > 6(7x-3)$ becomes $24x+16 > 42x-1$.
Now let's get the x's on one side of the equation. If you want to avoid the exception above, you can subtract 24x from each side and also add 18 to each side. That yields:
$34 > 18x$ and $17/9 > x$, which is the same as option K $(x<17/9)$.

### Question 3: (C)
We need to solve the inequality. $18-4x \le 10$ simplifies to become $-4x \le -8$. Now when we divide by-4, we must change the direction of the inequality sign. That means that $\le$ becomes $\ge$. Specifically, $-4x \le -8$ becomes $x \ge 2$. Check out your options. Which number line accurately says that x is greater than or equal to 2?

### Question 4: (J)
$5(x-6) \ge 6(x-7)$ yields $5x-30 \ge 6x-42$. At this point, you can decide if you want to avoid the exception about multiplying or dividing an inequality by a negative number or embrace it! We will avoid it. $5x-30 \ge 6x-42$ becomes $12 \ge x$, which is choice (J) in disguise.

### Question 5: (C)
$(-7/5)x + 2 \le 16$ becomes $(-7/5)x \le 14$, which means that, after dividing both sides by -7/5, the result is $x \ge -10$. NOTE: Remember that when dividing or multiplying by a negative we need to switch the direction of the inequality sign!

### Question 6: (G)
**"And"** means the intersection between these inequalities. Solve each inequality separately to get $x > 14/5$ AND $x < 6$. The only number line that fits this criteria is (G).

### Question 7: (D)
$(6+4x)/3 -4 > 0$ is the same as $(6+4x)/3 > 4$. It is legal to treat this as a proportion, which yields $6 + 4x > 12$. Solving for x, we get that $x > 3/2$.

### Question 8: (J)

When we solve an inequality with an absolute value, we need to consider all cases. That is ABS(-6x+2) > 4 means we need to look at both -6x+2 < -4 and -6x+2 > 4. Separate the two inequalities and solve each *(carefully, and reversing the inequality sign when you have to)* to get x > 1 as well as x < -1/3. Before we jump to an answer, we need to test the solutions. Choose an x less than -1/3, say -1. That works. Now let's choose an x greater than 1. Try 2. That also works. Let's focus on choices J and K. Can you think of any number that are less than -1/3 **and** greater than 1 at the same time? Nope! That means we rule out (K) and select (J).

---

### Page 154 Absolute Value Warmup

$|3| = 3$
$|-3| = 3$

$|4-7| = 3$
$|-7+4| = 3$

---

### Pages 156-157 Absolute Value

### Question 1: (B)

Think of absolute value signs as symbols of enclosure. That means you need to follow the order of operations (as you always do!). Abs(-12) = 12 and the abs(4-37)=abs(-33) or 33. The problem now looks like this: 12-33 or -21. P.S. Your calculator can do all of this for you too. On the TI-83/TI-84 family of calculators, find **"abs"** under the MATH menu.

### Question 2: (G)

The expression, 6–7(abs(-3+9–4)) = 6 – 7(abs(2)) or
6 – 14 = -8.

### Question 3: (B)

What does abs(-9+5) equal? abs(-9+5)= 4. Now multiply -4 by 4 to get the final answer.

### Question 4: (J)

You will need to clean up what is inside the absolute value sign before proceeding. What does -40 + 21 equal? Now take the absolute value of the sum.

### Question 5: (B)

What is the abs(-12)? Simple. Now solve the equation x+36=12.

### Question 6: (F)

In this problem, you need to remember that what is inside the absolute value sign can be 9 or -9. So we have to solve two easy equations: 2.5 + x = 9 and 2.5 + x = -9. A good rule of thumb is to always swing back to the original to see if both values work. But since the answer choices all include two solutions, it looks like both solutions will work.

### Question 7: (B)

The fastest way to get to this answer is by **"trial and error."** In other words, try the answer choices. The good news is that the correct answer is the second choice. Before you move on, double-check -3.5 to make sure it works. It does.

### Question 8: (F)

Remember that what is inside an absolute value symbol can be positive or negative. That means that we need to consider abs(x)≤6 as -6≤x≤6.

### Question 9: (B)

The best strategy here is to substitute the suggested values in for x. Even better is the fact that the answer is the second choice! Try it: -10 = 3abs(x)-abs(x)2 or
-10 = 3abs(±5)–abs(±5)2.
-10 = 3(15) -25.
-10 = -10

### Question 10: (J)

Solve -6 < x-7 < 6. That means pulling apart the two inequalities: -6 < x - 7 and x – 7 < 6

217

### Question 11: (A)
Try drawing a number line and place -4 where it belongs. Now count 7 units t the right. You land on 3. Counting 7 units to the left, you land on -11. Checking the answer choices, which one will yield those two solutions?

### Question 12: (H)
Take a look at that decimal. Do you recognize it? If you don't, take a second to change -1/16 into a decimal. Surprised? So basically the question is asking when, if ever, does the abs(-x/16) = -x/16. The absolute value will always be either positive (or zero), which means that the right side also needs to be positive or zero. For that to be true here, your x value has to be negative (or zero), so that the -x/16 turns out to be a positive value. Or it can be zero.

### Question 13: (A)
From the situation described, if we let d = the pet snake's total caloric intake and x = the number of calories eaten typically each day and y = the change of calorie intake from day to day, then x-y ≤ d ≤ x+y.
Does this look like a possible absolute value emerging?
Look at the choices and try some values. Let's let x = 1000 and y = ±100. That means that d can equal as few as 900 or as much as 1100. Let's plug these values into the answer choices to see what works. Looks like (A) works just fine. If it'll make you feel more confident of your answer, you can try a few of the others *(and make sure they don't work)* to convince yourself.

### Question 14: (F)
We need to remember that **"q"** is a variable that can be positive, negative or zero. The opposite of a positive number is always negative. So, q cannot be positive. That leaves two other choices. Although zero is neither positive nor negative, the best choice here is that q is either negative or zero. Example: abs(-9) = 9.

### Question 15: (C)
Plug in a few sets of values that fit the criteria. Let x = 4 and y=5. Remember to treat absolute value signs as a symbol of enclosure. That means you must clean up what is inside the absolute value sign before taking the absolute value. Try a few examples and you will find that y-x is equivalent every time.

---

## Page 159 Trigonometry Warmup

sin θ = 5/13
cos θ = 12/13
tan θ = 5/12

---

## Pages 160-162 Trigonometry

### Question 1: (E)
Tangent problem. Side PR is the side opposite angle Q. RQ is the side adjacent to angle Q. Since this is a right triangle we can use SOH-CAH-TOA. Given the information provided (side opposite and side adjacent), we determine that tangent is the trig function that we need to use. Tan 42° = PR/120°. Cross-multiply to get PR = 120tan42.

### Question 2: (J)
Cosine problem. In this right triangle, we have the side adjacent (80) and we need to find the hypotenuse (x) of the given 56° angle. That means that the cos56 = 80/x. Solving for x (carefully) yields 80/cos56°.

### Question 3: (A)
In this right triangle, with respect to angle θ, we know the hypotenuse (q), the side opposite (s) and the side adjacent (r). Using SOH-CAH-TOA, cosθ=r/q.

### Question 4: (F)
Sine problem. In this right triangle and with respect to the 42° angle, the tree's height is the side opposite (x) and the distance from the flower to the top of tree is the hypotenuse (80). SOH-CAH-TOA! Sin 42 = x/80. Since we are given sin42 ≈ .670, the proportion to solve is .670=x/80. x = 53.6 ≈ 54

### Question 5: (A)
The height of the flag pole is the side opposite the 32° angle and the wire is the hypotenuse of the right triangle formed. Looks like sine is the trig function that we need to use here. SOH-CAH-TOA! Sin 32 = ?/33.

### Question 6: (F)
If we are asked to find the sine, then we need to know the hypotenuse of the triangle. Wait, it's not provided! No problem, we can use the Pythagorean theorem: if $a^2 + b^2 = c^2$, then $32 + 82 = (RS)^2$ or RS $= \sqrt{73}$. That means that the sine of angle R = $8/\sqrt{73}$.

### Question 7: (C)
Tangent problem. We need to find the length of AC, which is the hypotenuse of right triangle ABC. Using the fact that the tangent of angle = 1.05, we can find side BC (x). That is, 1.05=x/20 or x = 21. Now we use the Pythagorean theorem to find AC. 202+212 =AC2
202+212=AC2 or 400+441=AC2 and AC = 29. Note here that ABCD is a rectangle, not a square. Don't assume anything from the **"looks"** of a diagram!

### Question 8: (H)
On this problem, you can either write out each of the trig ratios or just evaluate the answer choices. We recommend the latter option here. Just see if each answer choice is true based on your SOH-CAH-TOA expertise. Only H works.

### Question 9: (D)
Let's first identify what we know and what we don't know with respect to the 25°angle. We have the hypotenuse (9) and we are looking for the side opposite (?). Looks like we need to use the sine function! That means that sin25° = ?/9 or sin25° =x/9. Simply multiply to get x =9sin25°.

### Question 10: (K)
Using SOH-CAH-TOA, the tangent of angle C = AB/BC. So we know the length of side adjacent (8) and we need to find the side opposite, AB. Use the Pythagorean theorem to get AB = $\sqrt{57}$. That means that the tangent of angle C equals $\sqrt{57}/8$.

### Question 11: (C)
Using the fact that the sine of angle P equals 5/8, we can assign the value of 8 to the hypotenuse PQ and the value of 5 to leg RQ. Even though these might not be the actual values of the two sides, we know that this is the proportion of one side to the other. Use the Pythagorean theorem to find the leg PR, which we need to determine the cosine *(side adjacent)*. PR = $\sqrt{39}$, making cos P = $\sqrt{39}/8$.

### Page 165 Lines & Angles

#### Question 1: (E)
Make a sketch! Try to make it as accurately as possible, so that one angle looks five times as large as the other. Now let the smaller angle formed equal x. That means its adjacent angle is 5x. The angles x and 5x are supplementary, meaning that the sum of their measures is 180°. Solve the equation: x + 5x = 180 to get the smaller angle. If x equals 30°, then the larger angle equals 150°. Be sure to reread the problem. The question asks for the sum of the two larger angles.

#### Question 2: (F)
Lots to consider here! Triangle BCD is isosceles. (Whenever they tell you two sides of a triangle are equal they are really telling you that their opposite angles are equal!) If angle ABD equals 130°, then angle CBD equals 50. Angle CBD is the vertex angle of the isosceles triangle BCD. We can determine the measures of the base angles (BCD and BDC) to equal 65° each. Angle BDC is a vertical angle with angle EDF, so they are equal. Look at triangle DEF, we know the measure of two angles, 85° and 65° (angle EDF). Add 85 to 65 and subtract that sum from 180.

#### Question 3: (D)
Having two sets of intersecting parallel lines means that given the measure of any one angle in the set of sixteen formed angles, you will be able to determine all angles. If that's not initially apparent, you might try picking a real value for the first angle and solving for other angles. Basically, you have four sets of the same four angles. You can use the properties of supplementary, vertical and corresponding angles to determine the measure of all remaining angles. Be sure to carefully read the question before answering.

#### Question 4: (H)
Looking at the right triangle where we are given that one angle equals 35°. Knowing this we can determine the measure of the third angle of the triangle to be 55°. Angle GFB is a vertical angle with this angle and, consequently, the same measure.

#### Question 5: (C)
A lot of information is provided in this question. You'll have to use all of it. The fact that segments FH and IK are parallel is a very useful piece of information. Also note that triangle EFG is an isosceles triangle. (EF and FG are congruent) Triangle CDE is also isosceles. (Since CE and ED are congruent) If the measure of angle BCE measures 130°, then the measure of angle ECD measures 50°. Angle ECD is one of the base angles in isosceles triangle CDE. Therefore, angles EDC measures 50° also. We can find the measure of angle CED easily now. If angle CED measures 80°, then angle FEG (*vertical angles*) also equals 80°. Base angles of an isosceles angle are congruent, which means that angle EGF equals 80°. That means that angle FGL=100. Here's where the properties of parallel lines get us to the measure of angle IJL. Angle FGJ = 100°. Angles FGJ corresponds with angle IJL, which means that angle IJL measures 100°.

It's problems like these that show us why so many people pursue English degrees in college.

#### Question 6: (J)
If a problem talks about a shape or a line or a structure that isn't drawn, DRAW IT! Once done, it's easy to see that angles LON and NOM are vertical angles. So, if angle LON measures 82°, then angle NOM measures 82° as well.

---

### Pages 169-170 Mean Median Mode

#### Question 1: (D)
To find the mean, also called the average, add up the numbers given and divide that sum by the number of data points provided. Example 10+7+5+7+9+16=54. There are 6 data points provided So, 54÷6=9.

**Question 2: (G)**
To get the median, the first step is to arrange the data from least to greatest. 4,6,9,12,14,16,18,18,19,24. How many data points are given? Since we have 10 data points, an even number, we need to find the average between the middle two: 14 and 16.

**Question 3: (C)**
When you purchase at $1.40 each and take advantage of the deal offered, you are paying $30.80 for 22 avocados but receiving 24. What a deal! So the average cost of each avocado when you purchase 24 is around $1.28. To get this value, divide $30.80 by 24.

**Question 4: (K)**
What we need here is anticipation. We can anticipate that he will hit x homeruns this season, which will, in turn, lead to improving his average to 20. So our average formula is: $(6+18+23+x)/4 = 20$. Cleaning up the numerator of the first fraction and cross-multiplying yields $47+x=80$. Now solve this simple equation for x.

**Question 5: (C)**
There are 6 data points: 94, 94, 97, 97, 97, 97. Add them up and divide by 6. Can you see a faster way to get the sum?

**Question 6: (J)**
First, let's determine how many students are seniors. There are 180 seniors. The seniors brought in an average of 15 pounds per senior. That means the seniors brought in a total of 2700 pounds of food (180 x 15). We do the same computation for the juniors, 120×14=1680 pounds. In total, Prep High collected 4380 pounds. To get the average poundage per student, divide 4380 by 300. Note: It is tempting to average the averages but that number is not valid because there are more seniors than juniors.

**Question 7: (A)**
Start with the first average problem. 8 = sum/6. We can then figure that the sum of the scores must be 48. Let's do the same thing to find out what the sum is when the lowest score is dropped and the average is 9. Set up that equation. 9 = sum/5. So the sum must be 45. The difference between these numbers is 3, which means Denise's low score was 3!

**Question 8: (J)**
Set up the average equation. 25 = sum/6. So the sum of the data points must be 150. Removing one of the data points (20), reduces the sum to 130 and the number of integers decreases to 5. So our new average will be 130/5.

**Question 9: (C)**
How many pets do we have and how many families? There are 26 total families, which is given. To find the number of total pets will take a little arithmetic. It's 1+6+15+16+40+24+7=109. Do you understand where the data points like 40 come from? We are multiplying 8 by 5 since there are 8 families with 5 pets. Now divide 109 by 26 to get the answer.

**Question 10: (H)**
The mode is the data point that occurs most often. Looking at the table, there are 8 families who report having 5 pets. That means that 5 is the mode. Now for the median. The quickest way to find the median of a set this big is to know which term you're looking for. In a set of 26 terms, the median will be the average of the 13th and 14th terms. Let's go find them. Our two middle numbers are 4 and 5. The median is 4.5. They want the product of this and 5. 5 x 4.5 = 22.5

---

**Pages 172-173 Probability**

**Question 1: (C)**
There are a total of 15 people. Since 3 of the 15 are alternates, the probability that an alternate is the one chosen at random is 3/15 or 1/5.

### Question 2: (J)

How many black socks are in the basket? 4% of 150 is 6. That means that there are only 6 black socks, which means the remaining 144 socks are not black. 144/150 reduces to 24/25.

### Question 3: (C)

There are 52 cards in total. If there are 36 numbered cards and each of the first six players received a numbered card, the we now have 30 numbered cards left in a deck of 46 cards. So our probability is 30/46, which reduces to 15/23. Don't tell your parents that we taught you how to count cards.

### Question 4: (F)

The total number of bears is 37, so the probability of drawing a cinnamon bear is currently 7/37. That's less than 2/7. We're going to need to add some cinnamon bears. Try the first choice. That means we should look at (7+5)/(37+5). That equals 12/42, which reduces to 2/7. No need to try any other choices.

### Question 5: (E)

The sum of all of the students can be expressed as 36+45+23+n or 104+n. There are 36 freshmen. That means that the probability of the student being a freshman is 36/(104+n).

### Question 6: (J)

There are 3 sides of the die with even numbers. That means that the probability of rolling an even number the first time is 3/6 or ½. These 3 events are independent events, which means each event has the same probability of ½. ½×½×½=1/8.

### Question 7: (E)

The probability of the first shave ice being grape is 14/50. Removing that grape shave ice affects the next probability. There is one less grape shave ice and one less shave ice in total, so the chances of grabbing a grape the second time is 13/49. These two fractions get multiplied together to get the total probability. The result is choice (E).

---

### Page 176 Functions

### Question 1: (D)

When asked **"What is the value of g(-2)?"**, you are expected to plug in -2 for x in the equation: $g(x) = 3x^2-5x$. So, what does $3(-2)^2 - 5(-2)$ equal? Remember to always use the order of operations. 3(4)+10=22.

### Question 2: (F)

Let's substitute -6 for t. $h(t) = -t^2 + 4t - 4$ becomes $h(-6) = -(-6)2 + 4(-6) - 4$, which means that h(-6)= -36-24-4=-64.

### Question 3: (C)

Here we have one of those weird functions where we have to plug in two values, not just one. Using the function, we should get $3^4-3*4=81-12=69$.

### Question 4: (F)

$f(0.25) = -16(0.25)^2 + 40(0.25) + 18 =$ -16(.0625) +10 +18, which yields -1 + 10 + 18 = 27.

### Question 5: (A)

$f(-5) = -4(-5)2 = -4×25 = -100$. Don't forget the order of operations.

### Question 6: (J)

$h(1) = abs (3-1)^3 - 1 = abs(2)^3 - 1 = 8-1=7$.

### Question 7: (E)

Don't let the complexity of this fraction scare you. Just put -4 in every place that you see an x. If it makes it less scary, then work with the numerator first and then take on the denominator. So, looking at just the numerator, we get $-2(-4)^2-16(-4)-30$, which equals -32+64-30 or 2. Now let's check out the denominator. 16(-4)+48=-16.
Finally, the scary fraction ends up looking like 2/-16 or our old friend -1/8. That wasn't so bad now, was it?

222

### Question 8: (J)

To simplify f(f(2)), we need to work from the inside out. What does f(2) equal? From the chart, we see that f(2) = 4. That means we can replace f(2) with 4. f(f(2)) is actually f(4), which we can see from the chart equals 8. Start on the inside and take it one step at a time.

### Question 9: (D)

Don't be intimidated by this new rule, whatever it is. You're not supposed to be familiar with it – that's the point of the question. Think of the **"boxes"** symbol as a game where a=-5, b=1, x=3, and y=4. Now plug these values in where you see them in the equation and chug along until you arrive at an answer. When you do, you'll get a fraction that equals -11/-15 or 11/15.

### Question 10: (G)

Looks like there is a new game to play. Remember, you're not supposed to be familiar with this new symbol. Just plug the real numbers in for the given variables. The **"circle"** operation tells us to find out what 23-52 equals. Easy! 8– 25=-17.

---

### Page 177 Exponent Warmup 1

$(x^8)(x^2)=x^{10}$
$(x^8)/(x^2)=x^6$
$(x^8)^2=x^{16}$

---

### Page 178 Exponent Warmup 2

$x^{(-1/2)}=1/\sqrt{x}$
$x^{(2/5)}=$ 5th root of $x^2$
$x^{(-4/3)}=1/($cube root of $x^4)$

---

### Page 179 Exponent Warmup 3

$9.857 \times 10^{10}$
$8.3 \times 10^{-7}$
$4 \times 10^{1}$
$-8.9 \times 10^{-1}$

3,760,000
.005
-222.22
0.0000001234

---

### Pages 180-181 Exponents

### Question 1: (D)

To simplify this expression, multiply the coefficients (the big numbers!) and add the exponents of the a's. $(5a^3)(7a^3) = 35a^6$

### Question 2: (K)

When you raise a power to a power, MULTIPLY the exponents. That means that $(x^4)^{20}$ is equivalent to $x^{80}$.

### Question 3: (D)

You have a power raised to a power, so multiply the exponents to get $w^8$.

### Question 4: (F)

Change .00009856 to scientific notation. That means moving the decimal five places to the right. That means .00009856 equals $9.856 \times 10^{-8}$. If you're not sure, plug it into your calculator to check your work.

### Question 5: (A)

If you divide one base by the same base, SUBTRACT the exponents. That means $r^8/r^2=r^6$ and $q^4/q=q^3$ (Don't forget that q has an exponent equal to 1.) Now divide the coefficients, -18 by 9, to get the final answer $-2r^6q^3$.

### Question 6: (J)

Using the rules of exponents, we can simplify $(x^3x^2)^4(x)$ into $(x^5)^4(x)$ and then $(x^{20})(x)=x^{21}$. That means k =21.

### Question 7: (E)

Don't let the negative exponent knock you off your game! If the same base is multiplied, you ADD the exponents. $6+(-2)+1 =5$. That means that the answer is $a^5$.

### Question 8: (J)

Those brackets are another symbol of enclosure, just like parentheses. Also follow the order of operations. Raising a power to a power means that we MULTIPLY the exponents: $(x^4)^2 = x^8$. Inside the absolute value, we need to ADD the exponents of the base: $(x^8)$ $x^2 = x^{10}$. Now we are back to a power to a power: $(x^{10})^4 = x^{40}$.

### Question 9: (A)

One way to attack this problem is to recognize 64 and 4 can be expressed as a power of 2. Having the same base (2) will allow us to use the rules of exponents. $64(2^x) = 2^6(2^x)$ or $2^{(x+6)}$. Let's look at the right side of the equation. $((2^2)^0)^2 = 2^0$. That means that to make this equation true, the exponents must be equal, so $x+6=0$. $x=-6$. Another way to do this is to just simplify using your exponent rules until you can solve for x. Either way, you'll get $x=-6$.

### Question 10: (F)

By multiplying $-6x^2$ by each term in the parenthesis, we get $-24x^7+30x^5$.

### Question 11: (E)

Looking at $2^n = 16$, we can see that $n = 4$. Now substituting 4 in for **"n"** in the other expression, we get $(3)(3^4)$. Plug it into your calculator to get 243.

### Question 12: (J)

Fractional exponents create roots. The numerator (top of fraction) represents the power of the base and the denominator is the **"index"** of the root. That means that $6^{(1/3)} =$ the cube root of 6. Simply multiply by 8 and you have an equivalent expression.

### Question 13: (D)

We need to see what $(6.71\times10^8)/(7.61\times10^2)$ equals. Divide 6.71 by 7.61. This yields 0.8817 – don't worry that this number is less than 1 right now. $10^8/10^2=10^6$. Right now we have $.8817\times10^6$. We need to change this into scientific notation, which requires that we move the decimal one place to the right: $.8817=8.817\times10^{-1}$. The last step is to simplify $8.817\times10^{-1}\times 10^6$, which equals $8.817\times10^5$.

### Question 14: (K)

This problem is easy to solve if you look at what $6.75\times10^4$ equals. $6.75\times10^4=67500$. Now multiply $.09\times67500$ to get the final answer. The calculator is your best friend on this one.

### Question 15: (C)

Let's start by reducing each fraction. We can eliminate the x in the numerator and denominator of the first fraction. Likewise, we can eliminate the y in the numerator and denominator of the second fraction. Now turn the decimal values into their equivalent scientific notation. $0.00001=1\times10^{-5}$ and $0.001=1\times10^{-3}$. The first fraction is equivalent to $10^{-5}\div10^{-6}$, which is $10^{(-5-(-6))}$ which equals $10^1$. The second fraction simplifies down to $10^{-4}\div10^{-3}$, which equals $10^{-1}$.
The result is $10^1\times10^{-1}$, which equals $10^0$ or 1.

### Question 16: (J)

This is a question about positives and negatives as well as exponents. Look at the inequality they give you. $Z^2$ must be positive (or zero), because anything multiplied by itself (even a negative number) becomes positive. The same goes for $x^4$, because anything multiplied by itself four times becomes positive too. So if $x^4$ and $Z^2$ will both yield non-negative numbers, we need y to be less than zero if we're going to get everything on the left side to result in a negative number less than -1. Now look at the answer choices. We need one that incorporates y, since it's the key factor here, so it's either (H) or (J). In (J) we have an $x^2$, which would necessarily be positive, and since y has to be negative, we know that the product of the two must be negative.

### Page 182 Imaginary Numbers Warmup 1

real
imaginary
complex
real
real
imaginary
imaginary
complex

---

### Page 183 Imaginary Numbers Warmup 2

$4(2+i)=8+4i$
$i(3+7i)=-7+3i$
$(2+3i)(3+5i)=-9+19i$
$(1+4i)\wedge2=-15+8i$
$(5+6i)(5-6i)=61$
$(1+2i)(1-2i)=5$

$(5+i)*(5-i)=26$
$(2-2i)(2+2i)=8$
$(2-6i)(2+6i)=40$

---

### Page 184 Imaginary Numbers

#### Question 1: (D)
Take a look at the first fraction. What do you see? That's right. The numerator and denominator of the first fraction are the same. That means the first fraction is equal to 1. So, the result will be equal to the second factor. i+2 is the complex conjugate of i-2. Now let's check out the second fraction. Using the conjugate of the denominator, we multiply the numerator and denominator by 2+i. The numerator is now equal to 2i+4 and the denominator equals -5. With a slight adjustment to the negative sign, (-4-2i)/5 is equivalent to what we have as the product.

#### Question 2: (G)
Back to some old school FOILing here. Write down (3i+4)(5i−2), then find each of the four FOIL terms, then simplify to -23+14i. Even better yet, punch it into your calculator and let it do the work for you!

#### Question 3: (B)
Remember that i = i, $i\wedge2$ = -1, $i\wedge3$ = -i, $i\wedge4$ = 1, and then at $i\wedge5$ the cycle begins to repeat. So $i\wedge6$ = -1 and $i\wedge10$ = -1. Finally, -1 + -1 = -2

#### Question 4: (K)
Remember that $(6+i)\wedge2$ means (6+i)(6+i). Multiplying two binomials calls for FOIL, which produces $36+6i+6i+i2$. Collecting like terms and realizing that $i\wedge2$=-1, yields 35+12i.

#### Question 5: (E)
To make this problem more manageable, take a look at what the sum of i+ $i\wedge2$+ $i\wedge3$+ $i\wedge4$ equals. That's i +(-1) + (-i) +1... which equals 0! Not only that, but since every set of four i terms is the same, EVERY group of four in a row will add to 0. Now that we have discovered that fact, we can find the requested sum by realizing that adding the terms up to $i\wedge80$, the sum is 0. All we need now is the sum of $i\wedge81$+ $i\wedge82$+ $i\wedge83$, which is the same as i+ $i\wedge2$+ $i\wedge3$, or i+(-1)+(-i). This process is sometimes called **"projecting"**, which bases the answer for on a smaller, often repetitive, part of the problem onto the larger problem.

#### Question 6: (H)
Set up the equation n(2+i) = 5. Here is where our knowledge of complex conjugates and difference of squares come to the rescue. What happens to the imaginary part when you multiply a pair of complex conjugates? Just like a difference of squares, the **"middle term"** drops out. Let's see what that means here in this question. We need to get a real product, 5. If one of the factors is (2+i), then the other must be (2-i). Check it out.

#### Question 7: (B)
Two complex numbers with a product that is real are called complex conjugates. The complex conjugate of 4i+5 is 4i-5. To verify use FOIL (or your calculator) to multiply these two factors to convince yourself that the product is a real number.

225

### Page 187 Three Dimensions

#### Question 1: (E)
Total surface area means to find the area of each face that makes up the solid. In this case, we have a rectangular solid, which means that there are 6 rectangular faces. There are two 4x5's, two 4x6's and two 5x6's. Make a sketch to convince yourself.
40+48+60=148.

#### Question 2: (F)
Using the formula for volume, length × width × height, we have that 18×6×h=648.
Solving for h, we get 108h=648 and h=6.

#### Question 3: (C)
Make a sketch! Make a small right cylinder with radius equal to **"r"** and height of h. The larger right cylinder has radius **"3r"** and height 3h. The volume of the smaller cylinder is πr2h and the volume of the larger cylinder is π(3r)2(3h) or 27πr2h. Now divide 27πr2h by πr2h. The result is 27.

#### Question 4: (J)
We need to know Cone A's height and radius. If the volume of Cone A is 9π and its radius is the same as its height, then 9π=(1/3)πr∧3. That means that r∧3=27 and r=3. Now looking at Cone B, it has a height equal to 3 and radius equal to 4+3. Right? Now find what π(7)∧2(3) equals.

#### Question 5: (D)
Imagine uncapping both the top and the bottom and slicing a wall of this cylinder along its height. Flattening out what was once the side of this cylinder gives you a rectangle. (It's sort of like removing a label from a can). You now have one rectangle and two circles. That's where the formula comes from! Using the formula, we have 2π(15)2+2π(15)(10).

#### Question 6: (H)
The answer is computed by finding the area of 3 rectangles (5x15 each) and two equilateral triangles, 5 on each side. The area of a triangle =½bh. When you draw an altitude in an equilateral triangle, it creates two 30-60-90 triangles you can use to find the height of the equilateral triangle. That will be 2.5(√3). Thus, the area of one triangle here is ½(5)(2.5√3) or 6.25√3. The area of two triangles equals 12.5√3. Add up all the areas to get the final answer of 225+25/2√3.

#### Question 7: (D)
Tough question! We need to find the volume of the hemisphere and the cylinder then add them together. If the diameter is 6 for each, then each has a radius of 3. The volume of the cylinder equals πr∧2h or, in this case, π(3)∧2(15), which equals 135π. The trickiest thing there is that the height of the cylinder is the height of the silo minus the radius of the hemisphere. That's 18−3=15. For the hemisphere, we'll find the volume of a sphere then divide by 2. V = 4/3(π)(3)3 = 36π. Dividing 36π by 2, we get 18π. Now add this to the volume of the cylinder and we get 153π or roughly 481.

### Page 188 Adv Trig Warmup 1

540°=3π radians
45°=π/4 radians
8π radians = 1440°
π/3 radians = 60°

### Page 189 Advanced Trig Warmup 2

csc θ = 2
tan θ = 1/4
sec θ = -5

Quadrant III
Quadrant IV
Quadrants III and IV
Quadrants I and IV

**Page 190 Advanced Trig Warmup 3**

arccos 1 = 0°
arccos (1/2) = 60°
arctan 0 = 180°

---

**Pages 193-194 Advanced Trigonometry**

**Question 1: (D)**
The cotangent is the reciprocal of the tangent, which means that the cot θ=1. Can it really be that easy? Maybe you wonder why they threw in the information about the cosine? Remember that the tan and cot are positive in two of the four quadrants (Quadrant I and III). Since the cosine is negative, this angle must be in Quadrant III. Well, that's interesting but it doesn't change anything. Since the cotangent is positive in Quadrant III, cot θ=1. It really is that easy.

**Question 2: (G)**
180° < θ < 360° means that θ is located in either quadrant III or IV. Now looking at tan θ = -¾ means that θ is in quadrant IV. Make a sketch in the xy-coordinate plane using the point (4,-3) to determine the angle with the x-axis. What is the hypotenuse of the triangle formed? This is your standard right triangle with sides 3, 4, and 5. The sine of θ = (-3/5).

**Question 3: (B)**
y/x = -1 is the line y = -1x. Make a sketch. The angle formed is a 45° angle. The absolute values of the x and y coordinates must be equal. If you let x=-3 and y=3, you will quickly see that the hypotenuse of the right triangle formed is $3\sqrt{2}$. The cosine of the angle is x/r or, in this case, $3/(3\sqrt{2})$. $1/\sqrt{2}= (\sqrt{2})/2$ when rationalized.

**Question 4 (H)**
$\sin^2 θ + \cos^2 θ = 1$. If cos θ=-1, then $\sin^2 θ + (-1)^2 = 1$. That means that $\sin^2 θ=0$ and sinθ=0. Another way to do it is to ask yourself what angle has a cosine of -1. It's 180 degrees, or π radians. What's the sine of that angle? Zero.

**Question 5: (D)**
The period of a sine wave is the measure along the x-axis that the wave takes to complete one cycle. The standard form of the sine wave (y =sin x) has a period of 2π. Look at the graph provided. From the origin, a full cycle takes place in slightly more than 3 units on the x-axis. Looks like our answer is π. The fastest way of finding the answer is to take 2π (the standard period) and divide it by the coefficient of x. 2π/2=π.

**Question 6: (J)**
One revolution is 360°. 360°=2π radians. 720° equals 2×360°. Right? 2×2π=4π. Note: If you like formulas, you can change degrees into radians by multiplying the degree measure by π/180.

**Question 7: (E)**
180° < θ < 270° means that θ is in the 3rd quadrant. In the third quadrant, x<0 and y<0. Plot the point (-4,-3) and draw a segment from the origin to the point. Recognize a 3, 4, 5 triangle? cosθ=-4/5.

**Question 8: (H)**
To start with, remember that the cosecant is the reciprocal of the sine and the secant is the reciprocal of the cosine. 4/(cscθ) is equal to 4/(1/sinθ) or 4sinθ. Similarly 4/(secθ) = 4cosθ. Note that θ is located in quadrant I. If x=cosθ and y=sinθ, then $(4x)^2+(4y)^2=(hypotenuse)^2$. This yields $16x^2 + 16y^2 = (hypotenuse)^2$.

$16(x^2 + y^2)= (hypotenuse)^2$. $x^2 + y^2=1$ (because sine squared theta plus cosine squared theta = 1). That means that $(hypotenuse)^2= 16$ and the hypotenuse = 4. Pretty sweet.

**Question 9: (E)**
The standard form of a sine graph is y = a sin b(x-h) +k, where a represents the amplitude, b helps determine the period (2π/b), h represents the phase shift (movement left or right) and k represents the vertical shift. In the given equation a=4. That means that the amplitude is 4.

### Question 10: (H)
Where do we have a negative value for sine? $\theta$ could be located in quadrants III and IV. Therefore there are two values for $\theta$ such that $\sin\theta = -\sqrt{3}/3$.

### Question 11: (C)
Let's let the distance between Rebecca and Pepe equal x. Using the law of sines, we get $x/\sin75 = 30/\sin36$. After cross-multiplying and solving for x, we get
$x = (30\sin75)/\sin36$.

---

### Pages 196-197 Logic

### Question 1: (E)
Think contrapositive here. The only choice that is equivalent to the original statement (**"If A, then B"**) is its contrapositive: *"If not B, then not A"*.

### Question 2: (H)
It will be very helpful to make an Euler diagram here. (Euler diagrams are sometimes called Venn diagrams, which are similar but slightly different.) Think of one large circle that is labeled **"Pirates."** Now inside that circle draw two non-overlapping circles: one for vampires and one for zombies. Inside the vampire, place a smaller circle labeled demons. Got the picture? From the list, we need to find a statement that, based on the given information, is always true. Looks like we can say, with confidence, **"Every demon is a pirate."**

### Question 3: (C)
If Evan's bedroom in proportional to Kate's, and Owen's and Evan's bedrooms have the exact same dimensions, then Owen's bedroom has to also be proportional to Kate's. So III is logically sound. If Evan's bedroom is proportional to Kate's then it's possible that the two rooms have identical dimensions, but it is not necessarily the case, so II is wrong but I is right.

### Question 4: (F)
The only safe answer here that must be true is that **"Eduardo has fleas."** That is based on the fact that he has a pet, and **"everyone who owns a pet has fleas."** Have you heard the phrase **"All men are mortal. Socrates is a man. Therefore, Socrates is mortal."** Our situation is a bit less grand but it's the same idea. P.S. For the record, Eduardo is also mortal.

### Question 5: (E)
You can crack the code here one of two ways: first, you can draw a diagram. It's a little tricky here but it can be done. The other way (that is probably easier) is to evaluate the answer choices themselves to decide if they are true or not. Answer (E) is right: we know that the yellow blooper is a tike from the given statements. We also know that all bloopers that are tikes are kloodles. Thus, the yellow blooper has to be a kloodle.

### Question 6: (H)
The statement that will be true here is the contrapositive. The narrative says that, **"If Mark yawns, then Nate goes to sleep."** Its contrapositive is, **" If Nate does not go to sleep, then Mark did not yawn."** The only viable choice is (H).

### Question 7: (C)
Think of the problem as telling you that, **" If apple has worm, then apple has protein."** The contrapositive of this conditional is, **"If the apple has no protein, then the apple has no worm."** Which one of the options sounds like that?

## Page 200 Combinations and Permutations

### Question 1: (D)
There are 26 letters in the alphabet, with 6 possible vowels, leaving 21 consonants. (Remember that the letter **"y"** can be considered both a vowel and a consonant.) That means we have 21 possibilities for the first letter, 6 possibilities for the second letter and (since there is nothing preventing us from using the same consonant twice) we have 21 possibilities for the third letter. To get all possible arrangements, simply multiply 21 times 6 times 21.

### Question 2: (J)
There are 8 possible digits for the first number (2-9) and 10 possibilities for each of the next two digits (0-9). 8×10×10=800. Tricky

### Question 3: (E)
2 hats × 7 shirts × 3 pants × pairs of shoes. That means she can be out in the wilderness for 84 days and never once repeat herself. Del is a fashionista.

### Question 4: (J)
Cody can choose from 180 different possibilities. Simply multiply 3×4×5×3.

### Question 5: (D)
For the first wall, Jasmine has 4 posters to choose from. For the 2nd wall, she has 3 posters to choose from. For the 3rd wall, she has 2 posters to choose from and for the last wall she has the last remaining poster to place on the wall. That means 4×3×2×1 (or 4!), which equals 24.

### Question 6: (K)
Lindsey has 6×8×7 possible choices for her cake. 336 cakes.

### Question 7: (E)
Annabelle can choose 1 cat from 50 and one mouse from 10. That means she has (50×10) = 500 different possible pairings of pets.

### Question 8: (H)
Walt needs to choose one of his five signed baseballs to be first in line. Once he has done so, he has four remaining and so on until he has one left. We can use a factorial here: 5!=120. If you take a look at Walt's choices, we will get the same result: 5×4×3×2×1=120. Walt has 120 different ways to arrange his five signed baseballs.

229

1_Prose Fiction

**?**

# HOW MANY?
**35** minutes
**40** questions
over **4** passages

**35**

**40**

2_Social Science

That's **8 minutes**
and **45 seconds**
per passage

8 min.
45 sec

NOW
INCLUDING
**DOUBLE
PASSAGES!**

That's **2** related passages
**for the price of 1 !!!**

# READING

## The Breakdown

3_Humanities

# 4

## 4 PASSAGE TYPES
### ALWAYS PRESENTED IN ORDER:

> **Prose Fiction**
*(or Literary Narrative)*

> **Social Science**

> **Humanities**

> **Natural Science**

4_Natural Science

The questions ask you what is either **directly stated or implied** in the passage.

**Do...** work fast, and **ALWAYS** practice with a timer.

**Don't...** think too hard. If an answer **feels right**, **pick it & move on.**

**Tutor Ted.**

NOTES:

# Introduction

You know that **"Fast & Furious"** movie series?
That could be the name of the **ACT** Reading test.

"Fast & Furious 11: Social Science's Revenge," or something like that. The point is *(and there is a point here... somewhere...)* that the **ACT** Reading section **is FAST.** Maybe a little bit furious too, **but mostly just fast.** Hand this section to a student to complete for the first time and 95% of them won't have enough time to finish it.

**Here is the good news: although it is fast, it is designed to be finished in time.** Let that soak in for a second. The test makers created the test in order to give you enough time to finish it.

**Why, then, do so many students not finish in time?** The answer is that they are not solving the test the way it is designed to be solved.

## Here is the best piece of advice on the **ACT** Reading section.

*Ready for it?*

**Don't think too hard. Does that go against everything you've ever been taught in school?** Sure does! Is the **ACT** part of a strange, perverse system meant to frustrate students until they can be sorted and categorized by score? You bet! Does it make sense, then, that the **ACT** Reading test asks you to work in a way that goes against your training AND your common sense? *Sadly: yes.*

**The good news is that once you adopt techniques that allow you to move at a quicker pace, you'll be able to get through the whole ACT Reading test.** And once that happens, you'll score higher. You'll be playing the **ACT**'s game the way it was meant to be played. Is it a fun game? Not really. You'd probably rather watch a **"Fast & Furious"** film than take an **ACT** Reading test. Unfortunately, watching the movie won't get you into college.

**Here are our key strategies** to get you working at the right pace:

- ✒ Practice @ 8:45
- ✒ Play Offense
- ✒ Make Caveman Notes
- ✒ Create a Mental Map
- ✒ Easy Money
- ✒ Be a Search Engine
- ✒ Answer It Yourself

# Key strategies

## 1 PRACTICE @ 8:45

Here's your job in the Reading Test: read 4-5 passages and answer 40 questions in 35 minutes.

**The good news?** Most of the questions on the reading section are very straightforward. **The bad news? You gotta do 'em fast.**

**You have 8 minutes, 45 seconds per passage.** You won't necessarily spend that exact amount of time on each passage, but you don't want to look up after the first passage and see that you've already used 12 minutes. For that reason, timed practice is key. You will learn to pace yourself by becoming mindful of what 8 minutes and 45 seconds feels like.

**Whenever you practice, practice at 8 minutes and 45 seconds per passage.** That's the speed you need to maintain in order to finish the section in less time. If you finish one passage 30 seconds ahead of time, you can budget those extra seconds to another passage. If you finish a passage at 9 minutes and 30 seconds, then you have 45 seconds to allot to the rest of the passages. Play the game at their speed and work to find the pace that gets you through a set of four passages in time to finish.

**Two things to remember:** the test IS designed to be finished in time, and it doesn't matter if you finish with 2 minutes or 2 seconds to spare —you just need to finish.

Let's dig in!

## PLAY OFFENSE

**2**

**Many students treat the Reading section as a passive experience.** They sit on their hands and stare at the passages while trying to absorb enough information to answer the questions. **They are doing it wrong.**

**When we tell you to Play Offense, we are reminding you to read actively while you attack this section.** Here are some techniques we strongly recommend you adopt. When you Play Offense, you'll arrive at the questions better informed and more equipped to find the right answers.

> How to Play Offense: Use your pencil. Underline key ideas, or transitions within the passage. Draw a box around important or unfamiliar terms. Circle the names of characters as they appear. Draw a star next to anything you find especially important or interesting.

**Ask yourself questions.** What is the author trying to say? What is the style of this passage? Do you agree or disagree with the author's point of view? What are the most interesting and/or important aspects of the characters in the story? On a double passage, how do the two passages connect to one another?

**The most important thing you can do while you're reading is to pay attention to what is happening in each paragraph.** What is its purpose? What jumps out at you? Is there any notable action, character development, or discovery? After you finish reading each paragraph, make a very brief note based on your interpretation. **We call these "caveman notes."** More on those in a second.

When you Play Offense while you read, you will be more engaged and **less prone to getting sidetracked** by the occasional momentary daydream.

## MAKE CAVEMAN NOTES

**3**

**How would a caveman summarize the purpose of a paragraph in 4 words or fewer?**

🔍 Ex: PETA angry! Make law.

*Caveman notes good!*

Writing "caveman notes" after each paragraph will increase your comprehension AND save you significant time on most of the questions.

**After you finish reading the passage, quickly review your caveman notes and think of them as a whole.** What was that passage about? How does the author feel? Who had conflicting opinions? What was the point?

**Play offense / caveman notes activity. Try Playing Offense on the passage on the following page.** You don't have to answer any questions yet—we just want to see what you can do when attack a passage instead of sitting on your hands.

# EXERCISE

**INSTRUCTIONS:** While you read this passage, **underline key ideas or terms. Put a box around unfamiliar terms. Draw a star if you find an idea you think is really important.** Make caveman notes—**2-4 words that summarize the big ideas** within a section. We did this with the same passage, so after you're done you can look over to see how our version compares to yours.

Legend has it that coffee was first discovered in Ethiopia when a goat herder ate some berries that seemed to make his goats surprisingly energetic. Sometime around 1000 AD, people in Arabia began to use the coffee bean to brew a drink. One thousand years later, coffee is not just a beverage—it is a worldwide cultural and economic institution. Picture the more than 21,000 Starbucks locations worldwide as evidence. Or consider the fact that coffee is the lead export of 12 different countries. Or simply consider this staggering fact: humans consume four hundred billion cups of coffee annually, making it the second most popular beverage in the world behind water.

The popularity of coffee has much to do with an alkaloid crystalline compound commonly known as caffeine. During the millennia that humans have consumed coffee and tea, the caffeine found in these plant-based beverages has been utilized to increase alertness in the morning or enhance productivity throughout the day. The eye-opening power of coffee is so well known that it's a cliché—mugs with cute sayings like "I don't start working until my coffee does," and television characters who seem to spend at least half their lives inside of coffee shops attest to that. It's almost enough to make you think that coffee's appeal is limited to its caffeine content. The question arises: are coffee and caffeine inseparable?

The question can be answered on two levels: the hypothetical (do people really want coffee that does not deliver caffeine?) and the practical (is it possible to effectively remove caffeine from coffee?). It makes sense to answer the questions in order: if people don't want coffee without caffeine, why should we bother to try?

Is caffeine the sole reason for coffee's appeal? Some say that they crave coffee for the smell or the taste. Others would say that those aspects are simply reminders of the caffeine content, a signal to the human brain to "get excited" about the energy boost to come. One factor to consider is that caffeine consumption has negative side effects such as anxiety and sleeplessness; these symptoms are so acute in some people that they cannot consume any caffeine at all. Other people simply do not desire the physical effects of caffeine. Anecdotally, some members of both of these groups still enjoy the ritual and taste of coffee. Though it's not a scientific result, we know that there are people who enjoy coffee but actively avoid caffeine.

The existence of this group who say "yes" to coffee but "no" to caffeine has led coffee producers to believe in the significant commercial potential of coffee without caffeine, which in turn has led to the science of decaffeination. Practically, decaffeinating a coffee bean is about as easy as unscrambling an egg. Caffeine molecules permeate the bean and are dispersed over the entirety of its contents. Not only that, but the flavor of coffee comes from more than 400 separate chemical compounds in the coffee bean. Taking the caffeine out of the bean without disturbing that delicate balance is nearly impossible. Yet, despite these logistical difficulties, modern science has managed to create a product: the "decaffeinated" coffee bean.

The most popular method of removing caffeine from the coffee bean relies on the use of a chemical solvent. Unroasted green coffee beans are steamed to force the caffeine in the beans to surface; then the caffeine is removed by washing the bean in the solvent. Methylene chloride is the chemical solvent most used in decaffeination and, even though it has been found to be toxic in high doses, the amount found in an average cup of coffee is well within the limits that the US Food and Drug Administration deems acceptable.

Recently, however, science has come up with a less toxic method. Known as the Swiss Water Process (despite the fact that the only factory that uses this process is located in Canada), it involves soaking coffee beans in water saturated with the flavor compounds in coffee. When a batch of new beans is soaked in this compound, the caffeine is free to leave the beans, but the saturation of flavor in the water prevents the beans from also giving off their delectable, non-caffeinated compounds.

Hope for an easier way to brew "decaf" arose in 2004 when scientists discovered a strain of coffee plant in Ethiopia that produces caffeine-free beans. The strain is not hardy enough to stand up to the rigors of commercial production, so it will have to be crossbred with a commercial variety before it is ready for market. The energy dedicated to taking the caffeine out of coffee attests to the popularity of the ritual born so many years ago, when some goats enjoyed the first ever "coffee buzz."

# EXERCISE

**INSTRUCTIONS:** While you read this passage, **underline key ideas or terms. Put a box around unfamiliar terms. Draw a star if you find an idea you think is really important.** Make caveman notes—**2-4 words that summarize the big ideas** within a section. We did this with the same passage, so after you're done you can look over to see how our version compares to yours.

Legend has it that coffee was first discovered in Ethiopia when a goat herder ate some berries that seemed to make his goats surprisingly energetic. Sometime around 1000 AD, people in Arabia began to use the coffee bean to brew a drink. One thousand years later, coffee is not just a beverage—it is a worldwide cultural and economic institution. Picture the more than 21,000 Starbucks locations worldwide as evidence. Or consider the fact that coffee is the lead export of 12 different countries. Or simply consider this staggering fact: humans consume four hundred billion cups of coffee annually, making it the second most popular beverage in the world behind water.

*coffee is big*

The popularity of coffee has much to do with an alkaloid crystalline compound commonly known as caffeine. During the millennia that humans have consumed coffee and tea, the caffeine found in these plant-based beverages has been utilized to increase alertness in the morning or enhance productivity throughout the day. The eye-opening power of coffee is so well known that it's a cliché—mugs with cute sayings like "I don't start working until my coffee does," and television characters who seem to spend at least half their lives inside of coffee shops attest to that. It's almost enough to make you think that coffee's appeal is limited to its caffeine content. The question arises: are coffee and caffeine inseparable?

*coffee = caffeine*

The question can be answered on two levels: the hypothetical (do people really want coffee that does not deliver caffeine?) and the practical (is it possible to effectively remove caffeine from coffee?). It makes sense to answer the questions in order: if people don't want coffee without caffeine, why should we bother to try?

Is caffeine the sole reason for coffee's appeal? Some say that they crave coffee for the smell or the taste. Others would say that those aspects are simply reminders of the caffeine content, a signal to the human brain to "get excited" about the energy boost to come. One factor to consider is that caffeine consumption has negative side effects such as anxiety and sleeplessness; these symptoms are so acute in some people that they cannot consume any caffeine at all. Other people simply do not desire the physical effects of caffeine. Anecdotally, some members of both of these groups still enjoy the ritual and taste of coffee. Though it's not a scientific result, we know that there are people who enjoy coffee but actively avoid caffeine.

*why people like it*

The existence of this group who say "yes" to coffee but "no" to caffeine has led coffee producers to believe in the significant commercial potential of coffee without caffeine, which in turn has led to the science of decaffeination. Practically, decaffeinating a coffee bean is about as easy as unscrambling an egg. Caffeine molecules permeate the bean and are dispersed over the entirety of its contents. Not only that, but the flavor of coffee comes from more than 400 separate chemical compounds in the coffee bean. Taking the caffeine out of the bean without disturbing that delicate balance is nearly impossible. Yet, despite these logistical difficulties, modern science has managed to create a product: the "decaffeinated" coffee bean.

*decaf hard to make*

The most popular method of removing caffeine from the coffee bean relies on the use of a chemical solvent. Unroasted green coffee beans are steamed to force the caffeine in the beans to surface; then the caffeine is removed by washing the bean in the solvent. Methylene chloride is the chemical

*chemical decaf*

solvent most used in decaffeination and, even though it has been found to be toxic in high doses, the amount found in an average cup of coffee is well within the limits that the US Food and Drug Administration deems acceptable.

Recently, however, science has come up with a less toxic method. Known as the Swiss Water Process (despite the fact that the only factory that uses this process is located in Canada), it involves soaking coffee beans in water saturated with the flavor compounds in coffee. When a batch of new beans is soaked in this compound, the caffeine is free to leave the beans, but the saturation of flavor in the water prevents the beans from also giving off their delectable, non-caffeinated compounds.

water
decaf

Hope for an easier way to brew "decaf" arose in 2004 when scientists discovered a strain of coffee plant in Ethiopia that produces caffeine-free beans. The strain is not hardy enough to stand up to the rigors of commercial production, so it will have to be crossbred with a commercial variety before it is ready for market. The energy dedicated to taking the caffeine out of coffee attests to the popularity of the ritual born so many years ago, when some goats enjoyed the first ever "coffee buzz."

NEW
way?

## 4 CREATE A MENTAL MAP

**One more strategy to apply before attacking the questions: use your caveman notes and your understanding of the passage to create a mental map.** A mental map is a sense of the organization of the passage. The test makers do not give you enough time to read the passage to the extent that you can absorb all of the details within it. That's how we read in the normal world, but this is not the normal world! Instead, you want to read and remember what happens where. Your brain should say to itself, **"this is the part where they talked about how bees make honey. Over here is where they talked about the stages of bee maturation."** Don't memorize the details; just know where the details will be when you need them.

**Your caveman notes will be essential in helping you create your mental map.** This step should not be a time-consuming process; rather, it's a technique you want to use while you are reading. Don't drown in the details—ride the wave of the bigger ideas. When you need to find the details, those ideas will help you know where to look.

## HOW TO ANSWER THE QUESTIONS QUICKLY?

Since speed is the number one challenge on the **ACT** Reading section, we need to know how to find answers quickly. **Try these techniques to pick up speed on the test.**

## 5 EASY MONEY

**ACT Reading questions are NOT organized in sequence with the passage, so feel free to bounce around.** Identify the simplest questions and answer those first. We call these the **"easy money"** questions. As you read about the different question types, think about which questions look like they might be easier to answer. Find your favorite type of question. Jumping around within the questions can make the test less monotonous, and it can also help you figure out what the **ACT** thinks about the passage.

## 6 BE A SEARCH ENGINE

**Wouldn't it be great if you had a "find" command on the ACT?** That would make the Reading test so easy it wouldn't even be funny. Since we don't have that luxury, we have to be our own search engine.

**What does that mean?** There are key words on every reading question, words that point towards the right answer. If you could type the key words into a search command, where would you look? Since we already have our mental map, we can use that to remember the section of the passage where the author mentioned the key words. Now you have a vital head start on answering the questions —you know where to look.

## ANSWER IT YOURSELF

**Now that you've jotted your caveman notes, made a mental map, and found the key words in the passage, let's do what we came here for: answer some questions.**

**Which is faster, finding one correct answer or finding three incorrect ones?** Hopefully you said, **"the correct one."** Once you know where to look, challenge yourself to answer the question on your own. When you do that, you can pounce on the right answer.

Sometimes you'll be able to answer a question without even looking back, but you don't have to rely solely on your memory bank to solve the question—look back at your caveman notes and underlines/circles/boxes. When you find it in the passage, you'll know you've got the right answer.

**Here's a metaphor to explain why it's valuable to Answer It Yourself: you shouldn't go to the grocery store hungry.** Why? When you do, you end up buying a LOT more than you actually need, because your hungry stomach takes priority over your brain. On the **ACT**, don't rely on the answers to solve the question for you. If you try to figure out whether each of the answer choices is right or wrong, you'll be overwhelmed by too much information. Not only that, but you'll spend more time trying to find three wrong answers than you will finding one correct one. Know what you're looking for, and go get it. Did you really need those Oreo cookies, bag of Doritos, and donuts, anyway?

**Last thing:** Answer It Yourself does not apply to **NOT** or **EXCEPT** **questions**—on those fun guys you need to **use the answers to solve** the question.

## PLAN B: PROCESS OF ELIMINATION

Whenever you're not able to Answer It Yourself, **don't sweat it.**

Find the CLEARLY wrong answer choices. Justify why you are eliminating them. Make an educated guess and, when in doubt, double-check your answer!

Students often make mistakes by not reading the answer choice carefully before moving on.

> **🔥 HOT TIP**
> **If you see an answer choice that you know is right, choose it and move on.** This is the value of Answering It Yourself; it can save you serious time because you don't even have to read the wrong answers. This tip is a little bold—less intrepid test prep people would tell you to read every answer choice NO MATTER WHAT. It won't happen on every question, and it might even happen on less than half of the questions, BUT... **if you know what you are looking for and you see it right away, choose it and move on!**

# Passage Types

**There are four types of passages on the reading section** prose fiction/literary narrative, social science, humanities, and natural science and each one has its own particular style, content, and presentation.

For that reason, it's important for you have a unique strategy to attack each of the four passages.

> Word to the wise: read the brief introduction to each passage *(This passage is adapted from...some sort of book or article)* to get a brief overview of what the passage is about.

## PROSE FICTION/LITERARY NARRATIVE

**The first passage of any ACT reading section is always a fiction/narrative passage.** Everyone has his/her own preference, but we think that the fiction/narrative passages, adapted from novels or short stories, are usually slightly more interesting to read than the others.

Some passages will focus on a single character, while other passages will have multiple characters and differing viewpoints. Prose Fiction/Literary Narrative passages are more likely than the other types of passages to rely on symbols and metaphors to convey something.

### Key strategies
**Circle character names and underline key details.** Seemingly small things can be surprisingly important. Note when a character or narrator presents a new perspective. Don't memorize the details. Write caveman notes not for each paragraph but for larger blocks. Be aware of emotions and plot developments. Get into the story. Lastly, get through it fast. This is the first passage and we've still got a ways to go. **Practice with a timer! 8:45 *(or under)* is your target.**

## SOCIAL SCIENCE

**The second passage on the reading section covers social science.** What is social science? It's the study of human society and social relationships. That means this section can discuss anything from politics to economics to anthropology.

### Key strategies
**Focus on ideas and points of view as you read this passage. CAVEMAN NOTES GOOD!** Really good on this passage, in fact. Don't memorize the details. Underline or draw stars by any key points. Social science passages can be denser than other passages. Make mental maps. **Practice with a timer!**

# HUMANITIES

**The humanities passage, third on the reading section, will discuss various forms of art including music, personal essays and memoirs.** Think of these passages as cousins of the fiction passage—they're more metaphorical and less concrete than the other two passage types.

**Key strategies**

Humanities passages often express one key, abstract idea. For that reason, you want to go **"big game hunting."** Look for ideas that are global to the passage. Mark up the passage with stars *(or arrows, since we're hunting)* when you spot a big idea. Pay attention to the author's tone and feelings throughout the piece—they could be essential to understanding those big ideas. **Practice with a timer.**

# NATURAL SCIENCE

**The fourth *(and final)* passage covers natural science. You may read a passage about biology, meteorology, physiology, or other similar sciences.** Some say it is cruel to read a science passage immediately before having to do the Science test. Others are either the creators of the **ACT** or their mothers.

**Key strategies**

**Don't box names here.** Sorry scientists—we don't care who you are. Find and summarize discoveries, predictions, and conflicting opinions. Underline quotations. Note big stuff, like scientific theories or laws, but don't get bogged down in technical details. Cavemen don't get science, and you don't need to either on these passages. Extract information but don't worry if you don't fully comprehend it. Take your cues from the questions. Make mental maps—these passages may contain a high level of detail, so organizing your thoughts is a must. **Practice with a timer.**

# DOUBLE PASSAGES

**The ACT now features double reading passages — two related, shorter passages instead of one longer passage.** You'll recognize a double passage when you see one. The first passage is called Passage A, and the second one Passage B. The reason they are paired together is that they are related in some interesting way that the **ACT** is going to ask you about.

**Key strategies**

**The strategy for attacking double passage differs slightly from how we attack the other passages.** The questions are grouped so that all of the Passage A questions come first, then all of the Passage B question, then the questions that are about the relationship between the passages come last.

We can take advantage of that set-up: read Passage A first, then immediately answer all of the Passage A questions. Now read Passage B and answer all the Passage B and comparison questions. When you do Passage A's questions first, you'll be more focused on what happened in that passage, which will make answering the questions easier. Same goes for Passage B. Then, once you've answered all of the (A) and (B) questions, you'll have a good idea what is going on in both passages, and drawing any comparisons will be easy. With that strategy might at hand, double passages might be EASIER than single passages!

243

# The 9 Essential Question Types

It pays to know what kinds of questions you will encounter. You will know how to approach each question, avoid common answer traps, and further economize your time.

## 1 BIG PICTURE

**Guess what? This is exactly what it sounds like!** On nearly every **ACT** passage you will encounter one or more questions referring to the main idea of the passage. Good thing you've already underlined it!

Understanding the main idea of most **ACT** passages is pretty simple, but if for some reason you don't know it or find yourself strapped for time *(a likelier scenario)*, the main idea can usually be found at the beginning or end of a passage.

**What are those called when you're writing an essay? Oh yeah! The introduction and the conclusion! And what do introductions and conclusions do? Introduce and then summarize the main idea!**

Main ideas almost always come in two parts: "**What?**" and "**What about it?**"

> 🔍 **For example:**
> **What:** This passage is about President James Garfield.
> **What about it:** It's about how he would have been an amazing President if he hadn't been assassinated by that crazy guy who thought he was going to be named ambassador to France.

Sometimes, there is a third part to the main idea: "**What,**" "**what about it,**" and "**that's good/bad.**"

> **What:** This passage is about antibiotics.
> **What about them:** It's about how our overuse of them is leading to the creation of drug-resistant "superbugs."

**And that's...**
> **Part 3:** Oh, and that's bad.

**Or...**
> **What:** This passage is about dance therapy
> **What about it:** It's about how dance therapy is helping veterans with PTSD.
> **Part 3:** Oh, and that's good.

# JUST THE FACTS

**The most frequently asked questions on the ACT Reading are those that test your ability to find specific details in the passage.** These questions are very straightforward because they want **"just the facts."** And, since you've marked up the passage as you read, you've set yourself up to quickly find or recall where in the passage a particular detail is discussed.

### TRY THIS:

Similar to butterflies, moths have four stages in their life cycle. In the first stage, moths exist as microscopic eggs, often laid on the underside of a host plant. Within the course of a week the eggs hatch and a caterpillar emerges. In this second stage of a moth's life, the newly hatched caterpillar's first meal is the shell from which it hatched. Caterpillars continue to grow and feed on their host plant. In the third stage, after the moth spins a cocoon, the process of histolysis changes the physical form of the caterpillar, and the process of histogenesis transforms it into a moth. Trigger signals, such as changes in light or temperature, help the moth emerge from its pupal stage into an adult, the final stage of its life cycle.

1. According to the passage, a newly hatched caterpillar's first meal is:
   A. its own shell.
   B. its mother's shell.
   C. its host plant.
   D. ribs.

**The answer is (A), its own shell.** Simple, right? Most people miss **"just the facts"** questions just because they get a little bit careless, or because they don't bother to look back at the passage to confirm their answer. The answer to the question is pretty clear, but a student who isn't quite paying attention could see that the passage mentions something about a host plant around the place it mentions a caterpillar's first meal, and erroneously choose (**C**).
**You won't do that, obviously.**

## 3 INFERENCE

**This question type is also pretty common** (*especially on the fiction/narrative passage*) and, unfortunately, it requires a little more thinking than the previous question types. Inference questions, by nature, ask for implied rather than explicitly stated information. That means you need to "read between the lines." Even though you will be interpreting a bit on these questions, any inference you make must still be based on actual evidence in the passage. So, the question here is: how much can I infer from a given line or statement?

### 🔍 LET'S TRY A QUESTION.

Molly felt sorry for Mr. Taschen each time she watched him taking his daily walk through the park. Mr. Taschen walked along the same route that he and Mrs. Taschen used to take together. Once, from a distance, she even saw him hold out his hand as if to take hers. Then, realizing his folly, he awkwardly stuffed his hand back into his trouser pocket.

2. It can be reasonably be from the passage that Mr. Taschen likely:
   F. fell in love with Molly.
   G. suffers from dementia.
   H. left his wife.
   J. is a widower.

**None of these details are explicitly stated in the lines, and yet you can confidently infer the answer: (J).** Answer choice (**F**) is not justified by the passage at all. (**G**) is hoping you will infer too much from the line about Mr. Taschen trying to hold Mrs. Taschen's hand. It is more than possible to forget things from time to time without suffering from a severe neurological disease. (**H**) is technically possible, though it seems to be reversed—why is he so sad if he is the one who left his wife? Mr. Taschen most likely reaches out for his wife's hand out of nostalgia; therefore, it is most likely that Mr. Taschen's wife has died.

## 4 COMPARISON

**Comparison questions ask you to...you guessed it...compare!** You will see 3-4 comparison questions whenever you have a double passage, but comparison questions appear on single passages too. You could be asked to compare two characters within a story, or the opinions of two experts within a passage, or the opinion of one expert to the author's opinion.

Whenever you are given a double passage, think about the similarities and differences between the passages as you read. A key to comparison questions is to keep track of who's who. **"Okay,"** you remind yourself, *"this question is asking about this guy, Mark, who was the one that thought Pablo Picasso was kind of a hack, whereas the author thinks he's the best flippin' artist ever."* That's how you want think through these questions. As you read a passage, if you see that there are multiple opinions presented, you can be pretty sure that you will be asked at least one comparison question.

## PASSAGE A

The novel, as a work of imagination, is neither good nor bad, but is one or the other according to its own individual character. And yet novel-reading has become one of the great vices of our age. Multitudes care for nothing but light reading. The records of our public libraries show that there are more readers in this department than any other—perhaps more than in all the rest. As all kinds of readers become addicted to fiction, so all sorts of writers press into this wide and productive field, and produce books of every degree of badness, with now and then something of better quality. It is not easy for the young to find their way through this labyrinth of good and evil, the good little and the evil infinite. The safest rule, in whose application the fewest mistakes will be made, is that of total abstinence.

## PASSAGE B

When we imagine an intellectual person who is well read, we don't picture a person scrolling through tweets and Facebook posts on a laptop. Between questionable content and the numerous ads and links vying for our attention, online reading is assumed to be frivolous and unreliable. Reading novels, on the other hand, is deemed a respectable pastime. And yet, a couple hundred of years ago, novel reading wasn't regarded as quite so wholesome an activity.

Novels were believed to have a negative effect on impressionable young women who were unable to differentiate fact from fiction. Reading novels was thought to ignite sensuality and spark radical notions. Not everyone agreed with this sentiment, though. In Northanger Abbey (1817), Jane Austen satirized the supposed impact of novels with her depiction of Catherine Moorland, an avid reader who starts to believe that a man with whom she is living is a murderer.

*Let's give it a go!*

3. Both Passage A and Passage B describe how reading novels has been characterized as:
   A. a respectable pastime.
   B. frivolous and unreliable.
   C. influential and harmful.
   D. neither good nor bad.

**All four answers are words mentioned in the passages, so at first glace the question may seem difficult.** The comparison question is asking what Passage A and Passage B have in common in regards to how novels have been characterized. Both passages include the idea that young minds can be swayed by content that is not suitable for them to read in the first place; therefore the answer to number 3 is (C), influential and harmful.

4. Unlike Passage A, Passage B presents:
   F. multiple perspectives.
   G. a single subjective perspective.
   H. a single objective perspective.
   J. the writer's opinion.

**The answer to number 4 is (F).** Passage A is written from the perspective of one individual who is really, surprisingly sour on novels. Haters gonna hate! Clearly this person has never read the Harry Potter series. On the other hand, Passage B presents multiple perspectives: one about the positive implications of reading, one about the harmful effect of reading on young women, and another satirizing the impact of reading.

# 5 CHRONOLOGY

**Chronology questions are a subset of "just the facts" questions.** These ask you about a specific kind of detail: the order of events. You may find these questions in any passage, but it is most prevalent on the natural and social science passages. Many science passages will describe a process that occurs in a particular sequence. When you see a sequence like that, it is likely less important that you understand each step of the process in depth than it is for you to keep the order straight. You may also see chronology questions about the initial or final event in a series —it is important to look for key words in these questions to answer them correctly.

*Go get it!*

As Dr. Rebane walked onto the stage her heart was pounding so loud it nearly drowned out the sound of the audience clapping. Even before the presentation was announced, there were rumors spreading among her colleagues about her controversial theory. Clicking the remote to move to the first page of her presentation, Dr. Rebane started to explain her interest in Capgras Syndrome: her brother suffered a traumatic brain injury that caused him to think that she, his sister, was an impostor. The audience was silent. Later she explained her theory: combining anti-psychotics with mild electroshock therapy and visual stimulation with personal photographs will help patients to become conscious of their delusion, thereby reversing it. She noticed inquisitive looks and a few frowns, but she also observed several of her colleagues listening intently. One colleague actually approached her at the end of the presentation to express interest in learning more about her theory.

5. According to the passage, how did Dr. Rebane's colleagues initially react to her theory?
   A. They applauded her efforts.
   B. They expressed interest in learning more.
   C. They spread rumors.
   D. They seemed interested and appeared to be more engaged.

**The correct answer is (C).** You got that right, didn't you? Don't tell me... you found the key word **"initially,"** and then quickly recalled that her colleagues had started spreading rumors. **Right on!** It can be very tempting to select answer (D) or even (B) *(though only one of her colleagues reacted this way)* if you are not careful and don't pay attention to the word **"initially."**

248

## CAUSE & EFFECT

**6**

**Like chronology questions, cause and effect questions concern the sequence of occurrences, but cause and effect questions take it a step further.** For these questions you have to keep track of the order in which things happened and their relationship to one another as well.

On June 7, 1892, Homer Plessy was arrested for violating a Louisiana law passed in 1890, which required blacks and whites to use separate railway cars. The Supreme Court contemplated the constitutionality of this law in 1896, in *Plessy v. Ferguson*, as it pertained to the equal protection clause of the Fourteenth Amendment. The Court ruled against Plessy, claiming that the protection clause only extended to political and civil rights, not social ones. *Plessy v. Ferguson* essentially paved the way for pervasive segregation throughout the South. It was not until the 1954 *Brown v. Board of Education* ruling that the equal protection clause extended to social equality.

6. According to the passage, institutional segregation prevalent in the South was bolstered by:
   **F.** Homer Plessy's arrest.
   **G.** the court ruling in *Plessy v. Ferguson* in 1896.
   **H.** the Louisiana law passed in 1890.
   **J.** the court ruling in *Brown v. Board of Education* in 1954.

*OK, you try!*

**This passage has one law, two court cases and four dates referenced in this passage... so it can seem overwhelming at first.** However, the correct answer **(G)** *the court ruling in Plessy v. Ferguson* is said to have **"paved the way"** for segregation. Answer **(H)** might be a tempting choice since the Louisiana law required segregation on the railway prior to Plessy's case. And yet it was Plessy's case at the Supreme Court that established that social equality was not covered in the constitution, thereby making segregation acceptable and the norm.

## VOCABULARY IN CONTEXT

**7**

**Peppered throughout the reading section are questions about how a word or phrase is used in the passage.** These questions rely more on context than on knowing an extensive list of definitions—you can often answer these questions right without knowing the exact dictionary definition of a word.

The bazaar teemed with life. Amara was in a state of euphoria as she experienced a welcome onslaught of new sights, smells, and sounds. Vendors shouted the prices of their wares as a crush of humanity weaved its way through the lanes of colorful stalls, selling everything from fresh figs to hookahs and hides. The jewel-colored garments flapped in the wind beckoning her onward.

7. As it is used in the passage, the word crush most nearly means:
   **A.** passion.
   **B.** horde.
   **C.** trample.
   **D.** devotion.

*Your turn!*

**The correct answer here is (B).** The easiest way to test the answers is by replacing the word **"crush"** with each of the answer choices and reading the sentence. Even if you don't know that horde means **"a large crowd,"** none of the other words make sense in the sentence.

## 8  POINT OF VIEW

**Here's another question type on which we try to get into an author's (or a character's) head.** Point of view questions can be straightforward: they can ask how the author *(or a character)* feels about something. They can also be comparative: they might ask what the author thinks about the opinion of the expert who is cited. Does he/she agree or disagree? A question can also ask you about a character's point of view. On these, you really do want to get into the character's perception of the situation: how the character feels or thinks might differ from our perception of their reality.

*Let's get crackin'*

*Dive in!*

More than half of all American households own one or more pets. Pet ownership is thought to provide many benefits, not the least of which is health improvement. Stroking a pet has been shown to reduce stress and decrease blood pressure. One study, by the National Institutes of Health, looked at 2,500 adults aged 71 and above, and concluded that pet owners had increased mobility as a result of daily walks with their pets. However, many other indicators may affect the mobility of this study group and the benefits of pet ownership on the whole, including lifestyle, health history, and genetics.

8.  The author would most likely agree with which of the following statements?
    F.  Americans would be much healthier if everyone owned a pet.
    G.  Pet ownership does little to improve a person's health.
    H.  It is difficult to attribute health improvement to pet ownership alone.
    J.  Not owning a pet can be very stressful.

**What is the author's perspective?** First, she lays out some of the health benefits of having a pet. That might make answer choice (**A**) tempting to you. Eventually, the author lands on the idea that there may be factors beyond pet ownership that explain positive health outcomes. The right answer is (**H**); the author brings up evidence of the benefits of pet ownership and then says that it is not yet fully convincing.

# EXCEPT/NOT

**THE SCAVENGER HUNT IS ON!** Some of the most annoying questions on the **ACT** are **EXCEPT or NOT** questions.

**They are not necessarily more difficult than others—indeed most are simple "just the facts" questions—but they can be more tedious than other questions because you have to find three "right" answers in the passage in order to select the one that is the odd man out.** This is when knowing what type of question you are looking at can help you make effective decisions about time management! Could I complete two or even three other questions in the time it will take me to do one EXCEPT question? The answer is likely yes. Based on how much time you have left on a given passage, it may be smarter to skip that question for now and move on to questions that require less time and energy to answer.

Divers who fail to equalize throughout their descent may experience middle ear barotrauma. The air spaces between the sinuses and middle ear must be equalized to the pressure of the surrounding water, which increases with depth. The most common technique used to equalize is the Valsalva maneuver, whereby a diver pinches and blows through his nose. Similarly, a diver may pinch his nostrils and swallow, a method know as the Toynbee maneuver. Edmonds technique— tensing the soft palate and throat muscles then pushing the jaw forward and down—is slightly more challenging with a regulator in the mouth. Regardless of which technique is used, divers must equalize early and often to protect the inner workings of their ears.

**9.** According to the passage, all of the following techniques may be used to equalize the ears EXCEPT:
   **A.** Vinyasa.
   **B.** Edmonds.
   **C.** Valsalva.
   **D.** Toynbee.

**Lots of funny words here. Imagine this was a full-length passage, and all of these techniques were spread throughout; you would have a much harder time finding the right answer, (A).** Perhaps trying some sort of Vinyasa yoga pose might help a diver equalize, but it is certainly not mentioned in the passage.

# Wrong Answer Traps

**Here's another useful skill we can develop:** how to spot incorrect answers by knowing common wrong answer traps. Sometimes identifying wrong answers is all you need to do to get a question right. Here are some ways in which those no-good, wrong answers are well...wrong.

*Hoh Trap.*

## BAIT-AND-SWITCH

**Have you ever had an almost-winning raffle ticket only to get to the last number and lose?** It's the same emotional ride with bait-and-switch answers. The trap here is that these answers are 90% right. They lure you in with the seductive charm of their oh-so-rightness, only to throw in a teensy bit of wrong information at the end. If you don't read carefully to the end of the answer choices you may miss that final detail and fall right into their evil trap.

### Remember: 90% right = 100% wrong.

 **Here's a bait-and-switch statement for your reading pleasure:**
"Abraham Lincoln, America's 16th President, was assassinated in 1865 by John Wilkes Booth, a vampire hunter."

**See how right that was... up until the very end?** You're getting pretty excited by the beginning and middle there, and then, boom! That snake might look like a leaf from far away, but be careful: if you come any closer it will bite you!

## RIGHT ANSWER, WRONG QUESTION

**Here's another heartbreaker. An answer is 100% right...just not in response to the question that being asked.** It's not only crucial to look at the specific wording of each answer choice but also the question itself. Sure, Sally sells seashells by the seashore, but is that what the question is asking about? Oh wait, the question asks what Sally sells on the sidewalk—knockoff Rolex watches in case you are wondering. **Make sure you read the question carefully, or you may end up the target of those seagulls flying over Sally's shop.**

## MISUSED DETAIL

**Misused detail answers simply incorporate information from a different part of the passage than the one being discussed.** You don't just want to pick an answer choice because you **"remember reading about it somewhere."** We know that reading the answers carefully is not difficult in a relaxed, un-timed setting, but this is the **ACT**, and you are racing against the clock.

*I knew it! It's a trap.*

**Careful and fast is trickier—difficult, but not impossible if you work at it. Whoa!** What's that noise? Is that a boulder rolling down that mountain headed right towards you?

## SCOPE

**"Scope" trap answers are either over or under exaggerated. Be wary of answers that are too broad, too narrow, or too specific. Look out for words like CERTAINLY, ALWAYS, NEVER, EVERY, and ONLY.** Those words sounds pretty sure of themselves, don't they? The reading section is all about **"provability,"** and the more extreme a statement is, the harder it is to prove. It's almost impossible to prove that all eccentric old ladies love cats, even if the passage claims that eccentric older women are prone to owning cats. **Don't fall for these—they are a one-way ticket to trap city.**

*Let's see these tempting-but-deadly traps in action!*

## EXERCISE

**INSTRUCTIONS:** Read the passage and then try to spot the trap in each of the three wrong answers.

As Roland marched down the corridor, resignation in hand, he felt a kind of relief in the finality of it all. For months, he had been under such a dark cloud of uncertainty that he had barely been able to breathe, he now realized. He spent most of his day at the office and hated his job. He had let the fear of the unknown get the better of him. His father had told him never to quit a job if you do not have a new one lined up. What would he do with his newfound free time? What if he couldn't find another job? Only a fool would quit with the economy in its current state!

Roland could only imagine how angry his boss, Grant, would be—what he would say! "Roland, you ungrateful, worthless scoundrel," he could hear Grant say. He didn't care. With each step, he could feel the sweet air of freedom fill his lungs.

Walking out of Grant's office a few minutes later, he was shocked by how calm Grant actually appeared. Grant even congratulated him for his moxie. Roland walked away without a care in the world.

10. According to the passage, Ronald believes that his boss would respond to his decision to leave by:
    A. feeling relieved.
    B. congratulating him for his moxie.
    C. *correct answer omitted*
    D. getting angry and feeling like a fool.

11. It can reasonably be inferred from the passage that Ronald's next step will be to:
    F. *correct answer omitted*
    G. take a vacation and never work another day in his life.
    H. find a job that he enjoys more as a salsa instructor.
    J. spend the rest of his days at a job that he hates.

**Question 1:** The question is asking how Ronald thought his boss would respond, not how he actually responded. The specific wording of the question makes all the difference here.

**Answer (A) is a classic example of misused detail.** Ronald felt relieved after deciding to quit—not his boss. How would you fall for this trap? You might recall something about someone feeling relieved
and confuse the two characters.

**Answer (B) is the correct answer to the wrong question.** **(B)** is answering the question how does Ronald's boss respond to his decision to leave, not how Ronald thought his boss would respond.

**Answer (D) draws you in with correct information only to throw in wrong information at the end**
*(feeling like a fool).* It is important to read the entire answer. If you read getting angry *(which is
correct)* and bubbled in **(D)** right away, you succumbed to this Bait and Switch trap.

**Question 2:** is an inference question, which might make it seem like a tough question for wrong answer traps. Remember that even on these questions you want to draw evidence from the passage to justify your answer.

**Answer (G) is a great example of the Scope answer trap.** You might be able to get away with an answer that indicated he would take some time off from working to further enjoy the sweet air of freedom fill[ing] his lungs. To say he would NEVER work another day in his life is too extreme—it's too much of
a leap.

**Answer (H) is another Bait and Switch trap.** You think you have the right answer, you have your pencil poised to bubble in **(H)**, then you hear screeching tires as you slam on the breaks! A salsa instructor? While it is always nice to have some moves on the dance floor, that information came out of nowhere.
If the passage mentioned that Ronald had an interest in dance, **(H)** would be a reasonable inference, but it doesn't.

**Answer (J) would be the right choice if the question had asked:** It can reasonably be inferred from the passage that had Roland stayed at his current job, he would: **(J)** spend the rest of his days at a job that he hates. Right answer. Wrong question.

# EXERCISE

**INSTRUCTIONS:** You've learned the strategies to approach the reading section, the types of questions you'll see, and the wrong answer traps that the test makers set for you. Now it's time to see all of that stuff in action! Here are four passages for you to use as a warm-up. **Important:** remember to use a timer to see if you can finish each one under the 8 minute, 45 second time limit!

## Passage I

**LITERARY NARRATIVE:** This passage is adapted from the essay "Capri" by Cody Webber (©2013 by World Traveler).

I had begun my vacation with such intense fervor to see, do, eat, and drink everything. Italy, after all, was supposed to be the place that nourished the senses! Nothing can bring one quite as low as
5   unmet expectations, however, and after two weeks spent fighting for sidewalk space with scooters zig-zagging through the streets of Florence and arguing with cabbies over clearly inflated fares in Rome, I was not surprised when a delayed train
10  to Sorrento caused me to miss my boat to Capri. I played out my tragic opera to the front desk girl at my hostel; she, in turn, dutifully kept one eye on me while the other wandered with the move-ments of a dark-haired young man just outside
15  the window. After my curtain call, she shrugged. "Tomorrow another boat, but the cost will need to be made again." Of course, I thought. I muttered "ciao" and headed to my room for a nap.

"You want to go to Capri?"

20  The question jolted me from sleep, and I smacked my head into the top bunk. A sun-ripened face greeted meme with a grin. "Excuse me?" I asked groggily. "Capri! Giana tells me the American want to go to Capri." I stammered something about
25  a boat tomorrow, but the man waved my concerns off like he was brushing away a cloud of gnats. I sat on my bunk, trying to comprehend. Who was this ebullient Italian? And what was the catch?

Marco was waiting for me outside next to his
30  skiff, a modest 12-foot fishing vessel that looked like something out of The Old Man and the Sea, save for the addition of a little outboard motor. As we approached Capri, we sailed to the south where sheer 100-foot cliffs dropped right into the
35  sea. Marco dropped anchor. "Now, we swim," he declared. I declined, mostly because I was still unsure whether Marco wasn't a little unhinged.

Marco stripped his shirt, jumped in the water, and
40  began stroking energetically away from the boat. Was he abandoning me? Was this the con revealed? Was a shipload of pirates waiting to strip me of all my valuables? Finding no answers in the blue-pink early evening sky, I jumped in, following Marco's
45  wake towards the island.

When I reached the cliffs, Marco surfaced just beside me. "Swim under!" Before I could protest, he had disappeared beneath the rocks. After a long
50  moment of consideration, I did the same, feeling my way through the underwater tunnel. Seconds later, a hand pulled me above the surface. "Grotta di Champagne!" he said excitedly. The interior cave ceiling was three feet above the water and
55  the space was maybe ten feet wide. Every time the ocean swelled and then receded, a burst of sea spray would force its way through a tiny opening in the rock. The rapid shifts created millions of tiny bubbles inside the grotto—the Champagne Cave.

60  As I soaked in the scene, I felt something I hadn't since Sarah left. When Marco cried, "Meduse!" I was too enraptured with my surroundings to respond. When he repeated himself in English, "Jellyfish!" I looked down and saw two dozen
65  of them as large as softballs. Marco grabbed my shoulder, "Wait one minute, then follow." Suddenly, he was gone. I watched in a mix of horror and relief as the jellyfish swarmed him, then followed him out. Once I had escaped the cave, I swam as fast as
70  I could, swallowing seawater and flailing my arms and legs.

Back in the boat, I saw Marco's battle scars. He shrugged, pulled a soda from the cooler, and pressed it against his swollen skin. I couldn't quite
75  get the "thank you" right. Every time I tried to go at it directly, Marco waved my words of apprecia-tion away like he had my protestations. But I would not be able to convey to him the profundity of my gratitude. How I felt during those brief moments in
80  the cave before the jellyfish arrived. How deeply I feared I would never feel that again.

1. The statement "Nothing…expectations" (lines 4-5) functions in the passage to support the narrator's position that:
   A. his high expectations directly caused his initial troubles.
   B. his disappointments were exacerbated by the extent to which they differed from his expectations.
   C. one can improve one's circumstances through the power of positive thinking.
   D. it is unrealistic to expect any one place to nourishes all one's senses.

2. In the first paragraph, the narrator portrays the front desk girl's demeanor as:
   F. frustrated.
   G. distracted.
   H. condescending.
   J. attentive.

3. The narrator's comparison of Marco's skiff to "something out of The Old Man and the Sea" (line 31) is meant to suggest that:
   A. it is somewhat archaic
   B. it is new and well-maintained.
   C. its owner, Marco, is elderly.
   D. it is large and powerful.

4. Which of the following statements most accurately expresses the narrator's emotional state when he decides to ride with Marco to Capri?
   F. He is both intrigued by and fearful of Marco.
   G. He is exhausted and not looking forward to any more adventures.
   H. He is relieved that something is finally going right.
   J. His past disappointments have made him wary.

5. According to the passage, the narrator experiences all of the following difficulties while traveling in Italy EXCEPT:
   A. delays on public transportation.
   B. being charged too much by cabdrivers.
   C. being conned and robbed by pirates.
   D. chaotic, urban streets.

6. Which of the following best describes the way the last paragraph functions within the passage as a whole?
   F. It provides clear evidence of how an experience has changed the narrator.
   G. It bookends a humorous tale of foreign travel misadventure.
   H. It serves to highlight the pros and cons of Italy as a travel destination.
   J. It contrasts the narrator's fantasy of what Italy would be like with reality.

7. As it is revealed through his decision to join Marco to go swimming, the narrator can best be characterized as:
   A. hesitant, then reluctantly accepting.
   B. overly fearful, then confidently excited.
   C. somewhat defensive, then increasingly angry.
   D. quite confused, then somewhat annoyed.

8. The narrator's attitude after discovering the "Champagne Cave" is best described as:
   F. unimpressed.
   G. scared.
   H. euphoric.
   J. perplexed.

9. It can reasonably be inferred from the passage that, prior to his trip to Italy, the narrator:
   A. experienced the painful end of a romantic relationship.
   B. suffered from a lack of self-esteem.
   C. left a promising career opportunity to travel the world.
   D. studied the Italian language but did not become fluent.

10. Which of the following is the most likely reason why Marco dismisses the narrator's thanks?
    F. Marco regrets taking the narrator into the cave.
    G. Marco is not bothered by the jellyfish stings.
    H. Marco has an easygoing personality and does not need thanks.
    J. Marco doesn't understand the narrator's English.

## Passage II

SOCIAL SCIENCE: This passage is adapted from "Markets" by Charlotte Sienknecht ( ©2010 by Charlotte Sienknecht).

As late as the year 1986, nobody in the finance world had heard of collateralized debt obligations (CDOs) because they did not exist. 22 years later, CDOs would play a pivotal role in the greatest
5 housing crisis in American history, one that sent the ripples of recession and depression throughout the world.

Before understanding CDOs and their role in the U.S. economic crisis of 2008, it is first necessary to
10 understand mortgages. A mortgage is a loan given to a homebuyer, typically through a bank or mortgage broker. In return for the money required to purchase the home, the buyer becomes indebted to the bank, owing them regular payments with inter-
15 est until the mortgage loan is paid off, a process that typically takes 15 to 30 years. If the loan is unable to be repaid at any time, the bank reserves the right to take possession of the home. Since the home is a physical commodity, it is considered an
20 "asset," something with actual value that can be bought, sold, or traded on the market.

U.S. mortgages of the early 20th century were simpler than the mortgages today. Only two parties entered the transaction—the borrower and the
25 lender—and the latter was almost always a bank. In handing out the mortgage the bank did not take much of a risk since the required initial down payment was high and the loan itself typically covered only 40% of the property. It took a mere six years
30 on average for the borrower to pay off the mortgage, and the profit made by the lender was tidy but by no means extravagant.

By the 1980's, down payments had shrunk to 20% or less of the purchase price of the home. The
35 mortgage business was booming, but banks and mortgage brokers saw an opportunity to make even more money. In 1987, the collateralized debt obligation (CDO) was born. A CDO is an amalgam of multiple loans (as many as tens of thousands) and
40 their promised payments. This mixture of loans is broken up into many pieces and sold to investors who hope to collect profits as the loans are repaid with interest. Once this financial Frankenstein was pieced together, the CDO would then be divided
45 into tranches, slices of debt that were given specific letter ratings based on risk. The highest rating, triple-A (AAA), meant a guaranteed return on investment with a lower overall yield, while the lowest B rating held greater risk but also a slim chance of a high return.
50

The dot-com crisis of 2000 made investors wary of CDOs not backed by real assets, and at that point mortgage-backed CDOs surged in popularity. Mortgages were seen as safe since they were
55 asset-backed securities attached to tangible properties, not investments in dicey commodities like websites. The value of CDOs in the United States grew from $20 billion in 2004 to a staggering $520 billion in 2006. A great deal of this tremendous cash flow was predicated on a simple assumption:
60 the price of housing would always increase.

That assumption proved to be incorrect. Overinflated housing prices plummeted, at which point it became clear that most CDOs carried rat-
65 ings that didn't accurately reflect their risk and were therefore overvalued. In addition, the practice of subprime lending was rampant, wherein high-interest mortgages were sold to customers with little chance of repaying them. The majority of CDOs
70 were tainted with subprime mortgages. As a result, many CDO investors were only able to recoup a small fraction of their investments. The damage wasn't contained to the U.S. The U.S.-based bank Lehman Brothers had sold slices of these weak CDOs across the globe; the resulting market crash
75 sent the bank into bankruptcy and caused financial distress around the world.

CDOs still exist today, yet the global market is warier. The world now realizes that simply because
80 something is touted as a sound investment doesn't necessarily make it so. From its height of $520 billion in 2006, the value of worldwide CDOs bottomed out in 2009 at a paltry $4.3 billion, and the burden of this evaporation in capital was felt all
85 over the globe.

1. As it is used in line 32, the word *tidy* means:
   A. clean.
   B. considerable.
   C. orderly.
   D. insignificant.

2. The passage suggests that in the 2000s, mortgages were seen as safe investments because they:
   F. had a long history of high returns.
   G. were regulated by the federal government.
   H. had low interest rates.
   J. were attached to tangible assets.

3. Which of the following best describes the way the fourth paragraph functions in the passage as a whole?
   A. It explains how CDOs are both riskier and more lucrative than traditional lending.
   B. It highlights the fact that mortgages began as a simple and low-risk form of lending.
   C. It portrays banks as historically willing to take great risks to lend money to homebuyers.
   D. It points out that homebuyers were once more conservative than they are now.

4. The passage indicates that the first collateralized debt obligation (CDO) was created in the year:
   F. 1987.
   G. 1981.
   H. 1986.
   J. 1929.

5. It is most accurate to say that the information about CDOs in the passage is presented in a way that is:
   A. comprehensive and mathematical.
   B. entertaining but historically inaccurate.
   C. primarily factual but occasionally subjective.
   D. strongly opinionated and condemnatory.

6. The reference to the dot-com crisis is included to indicate why American investors:
   F. stopped investing in new web technologies.
   G. slowed their investment in mortgages.
   H. began to have less faith in certain types of CDOs.
   J. invested more heavily in websites.

7. Which of the following is NOT given as a reason why CDOs were unreliable investments?
   A. CDOs were given inflated ratings.
   B. The excessive complexity of CDOs confused investors.
   C. Investors assumed that the price of housing would always increase.
   D. Mortgages were given to people who might have trouble paying back their loans.

8. According to the passage, if a homebuyer defaults on their mortgage, the lender may:
   F. increase their interest rate.
   G. issue a warning.
   H. sue for damages.
   J. take possession of the home.

9. The statement "simply because something is touted as a sound investment doesn't necessarily make it so" (lines 80-82) functions in the passage to express the view that:
   A. assertions about financial products are not wholly reliable.
   B. investment firms often engage in fraudulent practices.
   C. bankers prioritize profitability over ethics.
   D. the American financial system needs more oversight from the government.

10. The last paragraph leaves the reader with the clear impression that:
    F. CDOs are complex financial structures with little effect on the global marketplace.
    G. Although CDOs still exist, their popularity with investors has declined.
    H. The reputation of CDOs suffered during the 2008 housing crisis, but they are likely to increase in popularity as the market recovers.
    J. Because of the high risk such financial instruments entail, CDOs should be regulated by the federal government.

## Passage III

**HUMANITIES:** This passage is adapted from "The American Museum" by Denise Werkle (©2011 by Denise Werkle).

Art has the power to entertain, but it can also serve a greater purpose: to inform and ultimately change the viewer. Nowhere is this more evident than in the New England Holocaust Memorial
5 (NEHM) in Boston, Massachusetts.

Designed by architect Stanley Saitowitz and constructed in 1995, the NEHM consists of six glass towers that symbolize the six major death camps in Germany and Poland. Two black gran-
10 ite memorial stones bearing statistics and inspirational quotes flank the glass towers. When viewed from afar, the entire construction resembles a menorah, the sacred lamp that was the centerpiece of the ancient Jewish temple. On the glass of each
15 three-story tower are inscribed six-digit numbers, each one representing a Jewish person who lost his life in the Holocaust. The memorial is interactive as visitors can walk through the open bottoms of the glass towers and read quotes, poems, and
20 accounts of survivors along the way.

Perhaps most remarkable of all, the NEHM is a work of art that engages three out of five senses in order to create an emotional impact on viewers. Our vision is most heavily involved when experi-
25 encing the memorial, and its sheer size allows it to be seen from nearby historical landmarks Faneuil Hall and Quincy Market. In addition to engaging our sight, the memorial connects on an auditory level. When walking through each of the glass
30 pillars, the visitor will hear a faint hissing noise coming from below. At the bottom of each tower is a metal grate with faux embers and steam that billows into the air. The sound of a steady fire is meant to remind the viewer of the fate of many
35 Jews who lost their lives in the Holocaust. As for our tactile sense, the gravestone-like black granite stones encourage visitors to place a small rock or two on top of them, simulating a tradition of Jewish gravesites. The ritualized act affords a meditative
40 moment before and after the intense experience of the memorial itself.

When considering the NEHM in the context of the larger city of Boston, it becomes evident that it is a work of art that engages with history as well.
45 Soon after its construction, the memorial became an official part of Boston's Freedom Trail, a 2.5-mile walk through the city that stops at 16 historical landmarks. Why is the memorial included in a historical tour of Boston, when it does not specifi-
50 cally refer to a piece of Boston's history? Created in 1958, the Freedom Trail sought to encourage tourism and protect the city's history "when the wrecking ball threatened." On the first monument stone of the NEHM is written, "Here we create a
55 marker—a place to grieve for the victims and for the destruction of their culture—a place to give them an everlasting name." Thus, the Freedom Trail and the NEHM share a goal: the preservation of history. Both offer a testament to the high
60 cost of freedom—evident throughout the Freedom Trail tour, which catalogues Bostonians' struggle against England during the Revolutionary War. Additionally, the NEHM was strategically placed in the middle of Boston's modern city space, in
65 between bustling "Pub Row" and the seat of the city's power, Government Center. Thus, when passing through and experiencing the NEHM, the viewer can't help but put it into the context of both the history of the Freedom Trail and modern
70 society.

In the canon of modern art, the most significant works are united by one common quality: the power to change us. From the moment we begin to engage with a work to the moment we conclude, we
75 should be an altered person, even if the change is minor. When visiting the New England Holocaust Memorial, a unique transformation occurs between the entrance and exit, a product of a construction that engages the intellect and emotions on the pro-
80 foundest of levels.

1.  The author would most likely agree with which of the following statements about the New England Holocaust Memorial?
    A.  It is a memorial that makes an unnecessary contribution to Boston's cultural landscape.
    B.  It is a major architectural achievement that lacks emotional impact.
    C.  It is a work of art with the power to change its viewers.
    D.  It is an architectural icon directly connected to the history of Boston

2.  The author indicates that the value of engaging visitors through sensory stimuli is that it will:
    F.  aid those for whom some senses that are stronger than others.
    G.  help them remember historical events effectively.
    H.  leave a deeper emotional impression on viewers.
    I.  provide a welcome distraction from painful topics.

3.  According to the passage, the museum's architectural design, when viewed from afar, most closely resembles:
    A.  a menorah.
    B.  a smokestack.
    C.  a collection of headstones.
    D.  a large hand reaching skyward.

4.  Which of the following questions is NOT answered by the passage?
    F.  What is the name of the architect who designed the New England Holocaust Museum?
    G.  What are the names of the six major death camps in Germany and Poland?
    H.  Where is the New England Holocaust Museum situated in relation to downtown Boston?
    J.  What are the primary materials used in the construction of the New England Holocaust Museum?

5.  The author characterizes the NEHM as:
    A.  impactful and evocative.
    B.  historical and simplistic.
    C.  melancholic and innovative.
    D.  striking and controversial.

6.  According to the passage, the act of placing rocks on the black granite stones is partially meant to:
    F.  symbolize the museum's connection to the Freedom Trail.
    G.  provide a meditative moment for visitors to reflect on their experience.
    H.  give visitors a multi-sensory way to interact with the subject matter.
    J.  replicate an ancient Jewish prayer of hope.

7.  The author indicates that one priority when creating the NEHM was to:
    A.  situate it in a well-traveled downtown location.
    B.  create an unprecedented work of architecture.
    C.  appeal to both a Jewish and non-Jewish audience.
    D.  incorporate the direct participation of Holocaust survivors.

8.  The author asserts that the NEHM and the other memorials on the Freedom Trail are connected because both provide:
    F.  a stark reminder of the horrors of war.
    G.  a portrayal of Bostonians' struggle during the Revolutionary War.
    H.  architecture that symbolizes cherished icons.
    J.  a means of preserving the past.

9.  Which of the following characteristics would the author most likely say indicates that a work of art is significant?
    A.  aesthetic completeness
    B.  impact on the viewer
    C.  harmony with its environment
    D.  ability to engage both intellect and emotion

10. The fourth paragraph is primarily concerned with:
    F.  the materials used in the construction of the museum.
    G.  the museum's ability to engage the senses.
    H.  the visual design of the museum.
    J.  the museum's interaction with the city.

## Passage IV

**NATURAL SCIENCE:** Passage A is adapted from "The Science Behind Drought" (©2014 by Nancy McNish). Passage B is adapted from "Thirsty Planet" (© 2015 by Savannah Marquez).

## Passage A by Nancy McNish

The weather phenomenon known as drought occurs, put most simply, when a certain area does not get enough water to support the habitats of the plants and animals that live there. Droughts
5 can occur worldwide, can at times last decades or longer, and most certainly can have devastating effects on ecosystems—and the people who live within them.

But how does a drought come to be? Droughts
10 are created over time by weather patterns caused by changing atmospheric conditions. At the beginning of the water cycle, water from lakes, rivers, and oceans evaporates and moves into the atmosphere, forming clouds. Wind moves these clouds
15 around the globe, but these patterns of movement can change depending on changes in air pressure. When winds are blocked by high-pressure zones called "ridges"—the atmospheric equivalent of mountain ranges made purely of air—the winds
20 are forced to redirect clouds along with the potential precipitation they carry. Areas that have been blocked from receiving rainfall by a particular ridge over time become susceptible to drought. The case of the California drought, which began in the
25 early 2010s, is thought to have been caused by one such ridge. Nicknamed the "Ridiculously Resilient Ridge" for its refusal to break down, this ridge is a vast zone of high pressure in the atmosphere nearly four miles high and over 2,000 miles long.

30 Scientists do not yet know exactly what is causing atmospheric ridges from the U.S. to Australia to become so powerful and long lasting, but evidence suggests that the phenomenon is due, in part, to climate change. In Australia, for example,
35 researchers have established a strong relationship between increasing global surface temperatures and the growing intensity of the sub-tropical ridge.

## Passage B by Savannah Marquez

"Water, water everywhere but not a drop to drink." That is, at least, what millions of people
40 throughout human civilization have thought while gazing out over a wide expanse of sea, for, although most of the surface of the Earth is covered by water, 97.5% of Earth's water is salt water and therefore not able to be consumed.

45 Since so much of Earth's water is non-potable, efforts to find a reliable way to desalinate water are as old as civilization itself. As early as 350 B.C., Aristotle talked about removing salt from water using a series of filters. The U.S. Navy has used
50 solar stills, devices that desalinate water using solar energy, since the 1700s. However, only recently have scientists figured out how to make desalination possible on a scale large enough to serve as a possible water source for communities who deal
55 with scarcity for a number of reasons: some do not live close to fresh water, others live in places where the existing fresh water has largely been polluted or contaminated, and still others face ecological crises like long-term drought. With scientists pre-
60 dicting that climate change will worsen drought in the decades to come, and the global population continuing to increase, research into sustainable, cost-effective desalinization methods has never been more needed.

65 Currently, there are two methods by which most large-scale desalination operations remove salt from seawater: reverse osmosis and multistage flash. To set up a reverse osmosis desalinator, one must first set up an intake pump at the source of
70 the seawater. Next, you need to create flow through the membrane, just as the process of osmosis works through cells in the body, only in reverse. You then add pressure by pumping in feed water, forcing water molecules through the membrane but trap-
75 ping the salt behind. The multi-stage flash method, on the other hand, uses heat to separate water molecules from salt by turning fresh water into water vapor, which is then collected while leaving behind salt molecules in a concentrate called brine.

80 These are the most effective methods of desalination science has come up with to date, but they are not perfect. Desalination on a large scale is currently expensive and requires a tremendous amount of energy, and if the use of energy from
85 fossil fuels is partly causing the problem, detractors say, it is not a net benefit to use additional energy to solve a problem created by too much energy use. Another issue is what to do with the

enormous amounts of brine that are left over after
90 salt has been removed from the water. Returning it
to the ocean raises environmental concerns: brine,
which is denser than the normal ocean water into
which it is released, depletes surrounding waters
of oxygen, thereby threatening marine plants and
95 animals living in ecosystems where the brine is
returned.

Still, there is great hope, especially in areas
facing the likelihood of more frequent drought,
that scientists and researchers will find more
100 cost-effective ways to desalinate large amounts of
water without the use of fossil fuels and without
harming marine life.

Questions 1-3 ask about Passage A.

1. According to Passage A, which of the following is
the first stage of the water cycle?
A. Precipitation
B. Cloud formation
C. Movement of clouds via wind
D. Evaporation from lakes, rivers, and oceans

2. Based on the information presented in Passage A,
atmospheric "ridges" are:
F. zones of strong winds that can block or redirect clouds.
G. zones of strong winds above mountain ranges.
H. high pressure zones that can block or redirect clouds.
J. high pressure zones above mountain ranges.

3. Passage A indicates that the link between the
intensity of atmospheric ridges and climate
change is largely based on evidence that ridge
intensity increases with:
A. increasing temperatures.
B. increasing rainfall.
C. decreasing temperatures.
D. decreasing rainfall.

Questions 4-7 ask about Passage B.

4. The purpose of the first paragraph of Passage B is
most likely to:
F. remind readers that they are not so different
from their ancient ancestors.
G. engage readers through imagery and the presentation of an interesting fact.
H. warn readers that salt water is not safe for
drinking.
J. introduce surprising facts about the Earth's
water.

5. Passage B answers all of the following questions
EXCEPT:
A. How long have humans been attempting to
desalinate water?
B. Why can't humans safely consume salt water?
C. Which populations have the most to gain
from desalination technology?
D. How does reverse osmosis differ from multistage flash?

6. Which of the following is NOT mentioned as a
drawback of modern, large-scale desalination
techniques?
F. Financial cost
G. Excess oxygen in ocean water
H. Effects on marine life
J. Energy consumption

7. The method of desalination that separates water
from salt using heat is called:
A. multistage flash.
B. solar stills.
C. osmosis.
D. reverse osmosis.

|||||||||||||||||||||||||||||||||||||||||||||||||||||||||||||||||||||||||||

> **Questions 8-10 ask about both passages.**

**NOTES:**

8. The authors of both passages would probably agree that:
   F. modern water challenges are likely caused by climate change.
   G. most areas of the world are in danger of running out of water.
   H. the need to address water scarcity is crucial for the continued success of human populations.
   J. humans are both the cause of the problem and the source of the solution when it comes to handling challenges relating to water.

9. Which of the following statements best describes the relationship between the two passages?
   A. Passage B describes historical efforts to address a challenge presented in Passage A.
   B. Passage B underestimates the urgency of a crisis depicted in Passage A.
   C. Passage B discusses a possible solution for a problem presented in Passage A.
   D. Passage B presents a way in which scientists are trying to reverse a trend discussed in Passage A.

10. Unlike the author of Passage B, the author of Passage A:
   F. proposes a solution to an existing problem.
   G. describes an ecological phenomenon.
   H. traces the history of a technology.
   J. discusses the possible cause of a problem.

# READING:
# ANSWERS &
# SOLUTIONS

# Answers and Solutions

## PASSAGE 1

**Page 257**

**Question 1: (B)**
First off we can throw the real stinkers off the boat. In this case, that's **(C)** and **(D)** because they have nothing to do with anything. **(A)** is a little tricker, but the word **"directly"** is a problem. Did his high expectations literally cause the narrator's cab driver to gauge him or make his train late? Unlikely.

**Question 2: (G)**
This question does not say **"infer,"** but you do have to do a little inferring here. Here, we must look at the context clues. The passage describes the front desk girl as keeping one eye on the narrator while the other is watching some guy out the window. Do we know who this guy is? Nope. But do we know she's focused more on him than on the narrator? Yup.

**Question 3: (A)**
The evidence for this answer comes just after this reference, when the narrator says **"save for the addition of a little outboard motor."** Why would a person add anything to anything? To make it better! So if the motor is an upgrade, we can infer that the rest of the boat is less modern, i.e. **"somewhat archaic."**

**Question 4: (J)**
If you don't know the answer right away you can eliminate incorrect answers. The word **"fearful"** in **(F)** makes it a scope wrong answer trap. The narrator seems wary, but we can't prove that he is outright afraid. **(G)** is a bait and switch. The narrator does seem exhausted, but the second part of the answer choice is not provable. **(H)** is the right answer to the wrong question. Perhaps if we are asking about the narrator's state of mind at the end of the passage, this answer choice would work *(but even then not perfectly)*, but there is certainly no evidence to prove this as the answer to question 4.

**Question 5: (C)**
Ooh! Our first EXCEPT question. Lucky us. Take a look back at your caveman notes and annotations. If you can't find the answer we'll need to do a little scavenger hunt to find evidence for the three wrong answers. Thankfully, evidence for **(A)**, **(B)**, and **(D)** can all be found in the first paragraph. **(C)** is a little tricky, since later in the passage the narrator does reference pirates: **"Was a shipload of pirates waiting to strip me of all my valuables?"** However, this is clearly a hypothetical possibility, not something that actually happens.

**Question 6: (F)**
**(F)** is clearly the best answer here, but there are ways to work this one backwards if you are uncertain. **(G)** and **(H)** are out because they are both way too broad in scope. **(J)** is the second best answer, but if you look closely, there's no contrast. The narrator's fantasy was that Italy would be amazing, and in the last paragraph, the narrator is reflecting on an experience that actually was amazing.

**Question 7: (A)**
Do you see how each of these answer choices is broken up into two parts? That means that you can eliminate answer choices easily based on half of the information! If it's half wrong, it's all wrong. That helps us get rid of **(B)** because the narrator is not **"confidently excited,"** **(C)** because...well...both parts don't work, and **(D)** because while the narrator certainly is confused, there is no evidence that he is **"somewhat annoyed."** The narrator is definitely hesitant to join Marco at first, but then he follows suit and jumps in, so the answer is **(A)**.

### Question 8: (H)

First of all, we can break this down by tone. Does the narrator feel generally positive or negative about discovering the cave? Positive! (**And if you're not sure, look at context phrases like "I was too enraptured by my surroundings..."**). Even if you don't know the word "euphoric," all three other choices are negative, so it has to be (**H**).

### Question 9: (A)

This is a good news bad news situation. The bad news is that you've got to dig a little deep into the context to answer this one correctly. The good news, however, is that the wrong answers are really really wrong. As in **"no evidence at all" wrong. The evidence for (A), on the other hand, can be found in the phrase "I felt something I hadn't since Sarah left,"** in the sixth paragraph.

### Question 10: (H)

You can eliminate (**F**) and (**J**) pretty quickly since neither of those answers are mentioned in the passage. The fact that Marco puts a cold soda can on his stings is evidence that he is bothered by them, so (**G**) is also out. Based on the development of Marco's character throughout the passage, we can confidently say that (**H**) is the best choice.

PASSAGE II

### Page 259

### Question 1: (B)

You can answer vocab-in-context questions correctly every time by utilizing one of two strategies: 1) try each word in place of the current word and see what sounds best, and 2: use context clues to discern the meaning. As you learned in the English section, this question is an exercise in diction, or word choice. If we take out the **"Clean"** and **"orderly,"** while synonyms for tidy, simply do not work in this sentence. The same thing goes for **"insignificant,"** since it doesn't make sense based on the context. What we're looking for here should mean **"a lot but not so much as to be extravagant,"** which is basically (**B**): considerable.

### Question 2: (J)

Just the facts. Woohoo! What's even better is that having a name or number in a question can be a gift when it comes to knowing where to look in the passage, as these can stand out. If you scan you eye across the passage for the number **"2000,"** you'll quickly find the answer to this question in the fifth paragraph.

### Question 3: (A)

Make sure you're looking at the right paragraph! This paragraph explains in detail how CDOs are organized and how they operate. That's basically what (**A**) is saying as well. (**B**) is the right answer to a different question, as it talks about the beginning of mortgages, and we're past that now. (**C**) is out because of the word **"historically,"** and (**D**) can be eliminated because the paragraph does not address homebuyers.

### Question 4: (F)

Numbers! Look for 'em but be careful not to mix them up! The fourth paragraph: 1987. Easy money!

**Question 5: (C)**
Be careful here! This is less about what information the author is presenting, and more about how the author is presenting that information. That means we're talking about tone. The tone of this passage is mostly neutral, though at times the author indicates that maybe—just maybe *(ya know, because they helped cause a global economic recession)*—CDOs are not the greatest thing. That is evidence for (**C**).

**Question 6: (H)**
If we work this one backwards, we see that (**F**) is the right answer to the wrong question because it tells us what the dot-com crisis was but not why anything. (**G**) and (**J**) are wrong because the passage indicates that the opposite was true in both cases. (**H**) is supported by the rest of the paragraph, and is our winner.

**Question 7: (B)**
Evidence can be found for (**A**), (**C**), and (**D**) in the passage. That leaves (**B**)!

**Question 8: (J)**
Just the facts! This is all about knowing where to look, and in this case, evidence for (**J**) can be found in the second paragraph.

**Question 9: (A)**
Answer choice (**A**) seems pretty straightforward, and it is. The rest of the answers are too broad in scope and generalizations not supported by the passage.

**Question 10: (G)**
Where should we look for the main idea of a particular paragraph! Why, the topic sentence, of course! There's all the evidence you need for the right answer to this question. Watch out for (**F**)—it's a classic bait-and-switch. Yes, CDOs are complex financial structures, but **"little"** effect? I think not.

PASSAGE III

**Page 261**

**Question 1: (C)**
We're lookin' at the Big Picture, baby. No trees, all forest. What is the main idea of this passage? (**C**).

**Question 2: (H)**
This paragraph is all about how the sensory aspects of the museum's exhibits are intended to enhance visitors' experiences by making them feel more involved. Therefore, it's fundamentally not a **"distraction,"** as in (**J**). (**F**) is too literal and therefore out of scope, and (**G**) is close, but it's not as much about literally remembering the events as it is leaving with a more powerful emotional connection to them.

**Question 3: (A)**
Evidence for this just the facts question can be found in the second paragraph: **"When viewed from afar, the entire construction resembles a menorah, the sacred lamp that was the centerpiece of the ancient Jewish temple."**

**Question 4: (G)**
Oh goody! We get to trek through the passage all over again looking for tiny, insignificant details that seem to have nothing to do with the overall point of the passage! Evidence for (**F**) and (**J**) can be found in the second paragraph, and evidence for (**H**) can be found in the fourth paragraph. The passage mentions that the museum consists of six tours in remembrance of the six death camps, but it does not name the six individually.

**Question 5: (A)**
Big picture! Pick the thing that's closest to the main idea! Also, since each answer choice contains 2 words, you can eliminate any answer choices if even one of those words doesn't work! **"Simplistic?"** Be gone (**B**)! **"Melancholic?"** I melan-call that wrong! **"Controversial?"** Unless there's a holocaust-denier paragraph somewhere in the passage that I missed, you can eliminate this one too.

269

### Question 6: (G)
Evidence for the correct answer can be found in the third paragraph: **"As for our tactile sense, the gravestone-like black granite stones encourage visitors to place a small rock or two on top of them, simulating a tradition of Jewish gravesites."**

### Question 7: (A)
The right answer, (**A**), almost seems too obvious to be the right answer, but it's the only one we can back up with any kind of evidence from the passage. In this case, the evidence can be found toward the end of the fourth paragraph.

### Question 8: (J)
Fourth paragraph: **"Thus, the Freedom Trail and the NEHM share a goal: preservation of history."** This would have been a great sentence to underline as you were reading through the passage.

### Question 9: (B)
Big picture, people! What's the main idea? If you're still not sure, travel to the lands where main ideas roam free: the introduction and conclusion! There you will see all the evidence you need for answer choice (**B**).

### Question 10: (J)
To be honest, the only way you can get this question wrong is to miscount your paragraphs. Don't do that.

## PASSAGE IV

### Page 263-264

### Question 1: (D)
Evidence for this question can be found toward the beginning of the second paragraph. Just the facts, folks! Welcome to the natural science passage.

### Question 2: (H)
Be very careful here, as these answer choices are all very similar but with crucial differences. The only one that is fully correct is answer choice (**H**), and the evidence for it can be found in the second paragraph: **"When winds are blocked by high-pressure zones called "ridges"—the atmospheric equivalent of mountain ranges made purely of air—the winds are forced to redirect clouds along with the potential precipitation they carry."**

### Question 3: (A)
Treat this question as you would a question in the actual science section: get rid of answer choices as you fight the battle of **"temperatures v. rainfall"** and **"increasing v. decreasing."** You can also use a little common sense. What is happening with climate change? Oh yeah, temperatures are increasing!

### Question 4: (G)
What do we sometimes call the very beginning of an essay or other piece of non-fiction writing. The hook! What is the purpose of a **"hook"**? To engage the reader and make him or her want to read more. That's what's happening here. (**F**) is stupid, (**H**) is off in scope and tone, and (**J**) is out because of the plurality of **"facts,"** as well as the fact that learning that you can't drink salt water is not—or at least it shouldn't be if you've lived on this planet long enough to be taking this test—very surprising.

### Question 5: (B)
This one's a bit nit-picky, so let's work it backwards. You can definitely find proof for (**A**) *(efforts are "as old as civilization itself")*, (**C**) *(people in drought-prone areas, those with few fresh water sources, and those whose water is polluted)*, and (**D**) *(all of paragraph 3)*. The passage does state that salt water is undrinkable, but not why.

270

**Question 6: (G)**
Keep your scavenger hats on, people, because we've got another EXCEPT question on our hands. There is evidence in the passage that **(F)**, **(H)**, and **(J)**, are all drawbacks, and **(G)** is the correct answer because it's a misused detail. The drawback is actually a deficit of oxygen in the water, not an excess. Those tricky tricksters!

**Question 7: (A)**
Just the facts. Find this one in the third paragraph.

**Question 8: (H)**
This is a tough one. Working it backwards, **(G)** is probably the worst answer because of the word "most." Then **(J)** is out because the author of Passage B never mentions that people are the definitive cause of the water problem. That leaves us with **(F)** and **(H)**, and while **(F)** is tempting because it seems so reasonable, there is more evidence supporting **(H)** than **(F)**.

**Question 9: (C)**
This is another two-parter answer, and if we know a half-wrong answer is a completely wrong answer, we can save ourselves a lot of time and frustration. **(A)**: is Passage B primarily "historical"? No it is not. **(B)**: does Passage B underestimate anything? Nope. **(D)** is out because the trend in Passage A is drought, and Passage B does not discuss attempts to reverse drought. It does, however, discuss a possible solution to drought—desalination!

**Question 10: (G)**
The answer is right in the first sentence of Passage A: "The weather phenomenon known as drought occurs…" While **(J)** might be tempting it is wrong. In the final paragraph the author states: Scientists do not yet know exactly what is causing atmospheric ridges from the U.S. to Australia to become so powerful and long lasting, but evidence suggests that the phenomenon is due, in part, to climate change." The author mentions a possible cause but does not all of the possible causes. **(F)** and **(H)** would be right it was asking about Passage B.

NOTES:

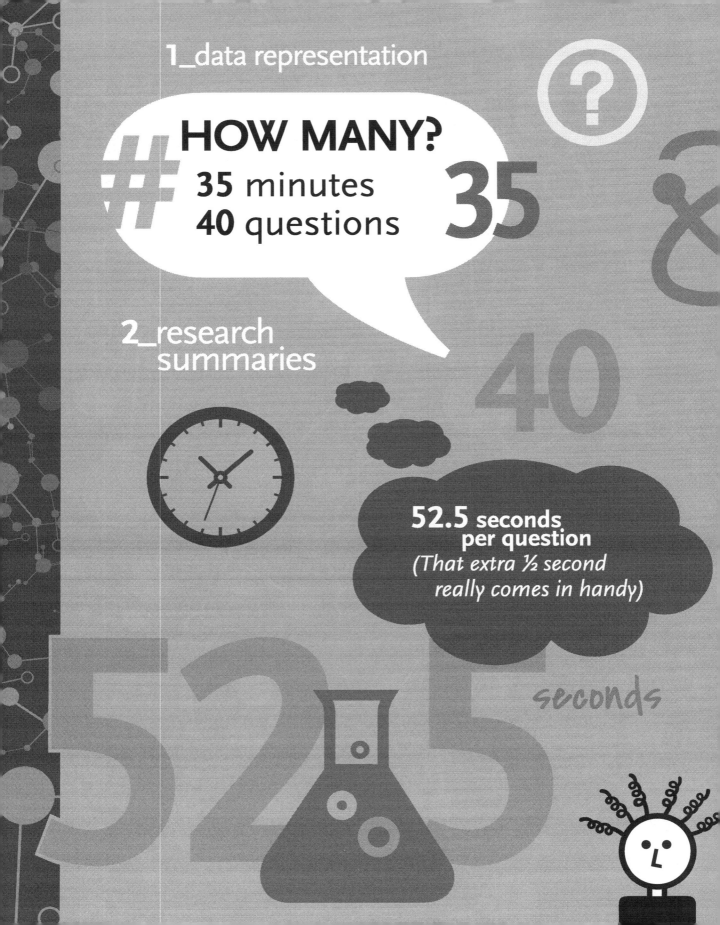

# SCIENCE

## The Breakdown

# 3 TYPES
# OF PASSAGES

> **Data representation 30-40%**
*tables and graphs*

> **Research summaries 45-55%**
*studies and experiments*

> **Conflicting viewpoints 15-20%**
*differing opinions*

**Do...** keep it simple.
It's easier than it looks.

**Don't...**
get **bogged down
in the details.**
Read what you need to read
and **ignore the rest.**

3_conflicting
viewpoints

# Introduction

## Why the **ACT** Science Test is Easier Than You Think.!?

*Ah, the Science Test—the most dreaded section of any standardized test in the modern era.*

At first glance, this section looks complicated beyond reason—you are staring down six or seven passages, each loaded with more data than you could interpret in a week, much less in 35 minutes. **And yet... This section is utterly simple, and the secret to doing well is to keep your thinking simple too.**

What are they testing on this section? **If you said, "science," you are wrong.** A science test asks you how much stuff you know—the structure of a molecule, Avogadro's Number, rotational acceleration—science class stuff.

Now, the **ACT** Science test DOES require some basic science knowledge—**on up to four questions on a given test...but that means 36-40 questions do NOT test science knowledge.**

**So what are they testing?** We call it **basic science** reasoning. **What happens at a particular data point on a graph?** As one quantity goes up, does the other one go up or does it go down? Maybe it goes up and then down? What would happen if the experiment had tested a value just above the values given in a table or chart?

**On these questions, you are thinking—reasoning—and you're doing it with scientific data.** A more useful way to think of it, though, is this: this section is the equivalent of the Reading test, but with charts, tables, and graphs instead of reading passages.

Pacing: the number of questions **(40)** and the amount of time you have on this section **(35 minutes)** is identical to what you have on the Reading test.

## That should make you realize that you need to work fast.

**Really fast.** The best way to do that is not to rush, but to make quick, confident decisions and move along.

**Difficulty:** the questions within each passage go from easy to difficult, but the tests as a whole also vary in difficulty. Take a look at portions of two Science test curves, excerpted from real **ACT** exams.

On Test A, if I miss two questions I still get a 36. On Test B, if I miss two my score falls all the way to 31. The reason for that is simple: Test A was way, way, way harder than Test B.

*Wait, whaaaaat?*

| # of questions correct | Score on Science Test A | Score on Science Test B |
|---|---|---|
| 40 | 36 | 36 |
| 39 | 36 | 33 |
| 38 | 36 | 31 |
| 37 | 35 | 30 |
| 36 | 34 | 29 |
| 35 | 33 | 28 |

**You never know what kind of test you're going to get until you take it.** It could be hard, it could be easy, and it could be somewhere in the middle. Just keep in mind that the score curve will make up for any major differences in the difficulty of the test.

## Here is a list of the strategies presented in this section:
- Learn as Little as Possible
- Think Like the Test
- Just Keep Swimming
- Pick Your Battles
- Follow the Clues
- Keep It Simple

On ACT Science, you'll answer 40 questions in 35 minutes on 6-7 passages. The passages fall under three different categories:

*That's the warm-up; time to start working out.*

**Data Representation** *(30-40%)*: on these you're given tables, graphs, and figures and asked to find information, make inferences, and draw conclusions.

**Research Summaries** *(45-55%)*: these passages give you several related experiments. Questions will ask you to perform simple data retrieval, compare two or more data points, and interpret or analyze experimental procedure.

**Conflicting Viewpoints** *(15-20%)*: you'll typically only see one of these passages per test. These passages, which often consist of text only, present two or more scientific viewpoints. Questions typically ask you to identify similarities and differences between those views.

275

# strategies

SCIENCE

## LEARN AS LITTLE AS POSSIBLE

**This one makes us laugh every time. Why?** Because it sounds like the worst advice ever but turns out to be the best way to approach the Science section. **Here's what we mean:** you will be swamped with information on the Science.

**Flooded with figures. Overwhelmed by unfamiliar terms. To get through this test, you want to process the bare minimum amount of information.** We estimate that you only need about 40% of the information given to you to solve the problems. If you tried to process or understand 100% of it, you wouldn't get halfway through it. Here's HOW you do it: as soon as you turn to a passage, go straight to the questions.

The ONLY passage on which you don't want to do that is the "**Conflicting Viewpoints**" passage. We'll discuss that one a little later.

**When you start trying to solve, you'll notice that you DO have to go back to the information in the passage.** You might need data from a table or a chart. You might even have to read the introductory information. Who knows? By the time you answer all of the questions on a particular passage, you may have read most or even all of the passage. That's cool! You still only read the minimum amount that was required, and that's important. On another passage, you'll find that you only read 10-20% of what was given to you. When you finish that one, won't you be glad that you didn't read the entire passage?

**Keep in mind that this strategy is not called Don't Learn Anything.** You will have to go back and find stuff in the passage, and yes, that's going to take some reading and some learning. Here is another way of thinking about this strategy: you want to find what they want you to find—and nothing more.

## THINK LIKE THE TEST

**So far we've told you what NOT to do on the test—DON'T treat this like a regular science test, and DON'T start by reading the whole passage. Now, to tell you what you DO want to do.**

**Look for relationships.** By relationships, we do not mean the rumors that your friends Madeline and Colin are dating (though that one caught us by surprise too...those two together? Really?!). We're talking about relationships between data points. The table below shows the average tail length of tadpoles at a certain age. **Take a look.**

| Age (days) | 2 | 3 | 5 | 6 | 7 | 8 | 11 |
|---|---|---|---|---|---|---|---|
| Tail Length (mm) | 15 | 14 | 12 | 9 | 8 | 5 | 1 |

**What is the relationship there?** As the age of the tadpoles goes up, the tail length goes down. That's an example of the type of question you will see on the **ACT** Science.

You can also assess relationships from a graph. What's the connection between these two quantities?

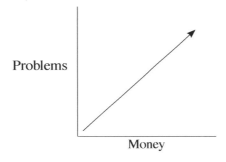

**Hopefully you can see from the graph that as money increases, problems steadily increase.** In other words: Mo' money, mo' problems. If that '90s hip-hop reference is lost on you, may we recommend a Google search and a quick study break.

🔎 **Interpolate and extrapolate. Aren't those fancy words! Here's what they mean:**
Interpolation: 1, 2, ___, 4
Extrapolation: 3, 5, 7, 9, ___

**What would go in each of those blanks?** 3 and 11, right? Congrats! you just interpolated and extrapolated. To interpolate is to estimate a value within a given set of data, and to extrapolate is to estimate a value outside the data set. The names of these procedures are not important, but using them to find an answer to a question is something you'll do on every single ACT.

Let's give that a shot.

Here is some super-serious data followed by some super-serious **ACT** questions.

🔎 The table below shows the Vapor-Liquid Equilibrium of Ethanol-Acetone at various levels of pressure (kPa) at a temperature of 305.15 Kelvin.

| Pressure (kPa) | Vapor-Liquid Equilibrium (mol/mol) |
|---|---|
| 11.679 | 0.00000 |
| 14.999 | 0.04220 |
| 16.585 | 0.06730 |
| 19.358 | 0.11300 |
| 22.571 | 0.17870 |
| 24.811 | 0.23610 |

1. At a pressure of 21 kPa, the Vapor-Liquid Equilibrium of Ethanol Acetone would most likely be:
   A. less than 0.06730.
   B. between 0.06730 and 0.11300.
   C. between 0.11300 and 0.17870.
   D. greater than 0.17870.

2. Suppose that the procedure were repeated at higher pressure values. At a value of 30 kPa, the Vapor-Liquid Equilibrium of Ethanol-Acetone would most likely be:
   F. less than 0.06730.
   G. between 0.06730 and 0.11300.
   H. between 0.17870 and 0.23610.
   J. greater than 0.23610.

**First off, did you get (C) and (J) as your answers?** Here's why you should have: on question 1, the given pressure value of 21 is between the table's values of 19.358 and 22.571. Thus, we can draw the really simple conclusion that the Equilibrium value would be between the two corresponding values on that table.

**On question 2, the pressure value is above any of our listed values.** Since the Equilibrium values increase as the pressure increases, we assume that they will continue to do so, and our answer should be higher than the values listed on the table.

That's interpolation and extrapolation, in that order.

**Now, one other important point to make based on those questions.** Did you need to know what Vapor-Liquid Equilibrium meant to answer those questions? Nope. Did you need to think about what the pressure unit kPa is? Sure didn't! All you needed to do is find a value between two other ones, and another value that's higher than what was in the table. **Learn as little as possible...it really is the way to do this test.**

## The scientific method

**You don't need to know a lot of science content *(and the content you do need to know we present you later in this book)*, but you do need to know how science gets done. That's the scientific method.**

### Here are the key principles in layman's terms:

Before you conduct an experiment, you start with a hunch: a feeling that something will happen in a certain way. That's a hypothesis. Background research is the next step. You learn as much as you can about the topic you're studying. OK, now you're ready to conduct an experiment. How do you do it?

**Experimental design is a topic that we could dedicate 500 highly unnecessary pages to covering, but let's just keep it simple.** You set up a process that will methodically change one or more variables and measure the effect of the change(s) on other variables. What are those variables called? Good question.

Variables that you control—like how much water you give to a plant, or the weight of a sphere that you drop to the floor—are called independent variables. You get to do whatever you want with those ones. They're independent.

Variables that are affected as a direct result of changes to the independent variable—how much the plants grew after you watered them, how much time it took for your sphere to hit the floor—are dependent variables. What happens to them depends on what you did with the other variables.

**When we graph them, we almost always put the independent variable on the x-axis and the dependent variable on the y-axis.**

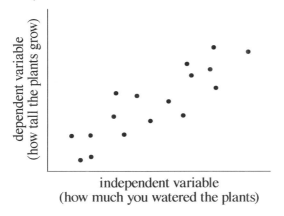

independent variable
(how much you watered the plants)

**A control group is a set of subjects within the experiment that receive no treatment.** If you were to test the effectiveness of a new medication, you'd give it to one group *(the experimental group)* and you'd give a fake pill *(called a placebo)* to the control group. The point of having a control group is to establish what happens when you do nothing. That makes it easier to draw conclusions from an experiment.

**Once you run your experiments, you look at the data to see if they prove your hypothesis.** If they do, congrats! You just drew a conclusion. If they don't, whoops! You should adjust your hypothesis and try again.

## JUST KEEP SWIMMING

**The questions on the Science test are, for the most part, really quite simple.** Still, this test intimidates and overwhelms students. Why is that? Part of the reason is that there is just so much information to process. Your brain, which has been working on this test for over two hours at this point, will begin to mutiny. **"I don't want to look at this crap anymore! I just want to watch funny web videos, or better yet, curl up in a ball and take a nap,"** your brain will say.

One solution to your brain's problem is to know that you don't have to process all of that crazy data; as we discussed earlier, you want to Learn as Little as Possible, processing as little of that information as you can. The other solution is that you just have to keep swimming. Keep going! Keep turning the page, keep answering all of the easy questions. Keep finding what they ask you to find. Grind your way through those 35 minutes. Tell your brain, **"you'll be free soon, sweet, courageous brain, but for now I need you to look at just a couple more tables and graphs."**

## PICK YOUR BATTLES

**Skipping questions *(and guessing on them at the end if you don't have time to look back)* is a terrific tool.** Here are the facts: Just like on the entire **ACT**, there is no penalty for guessing. In addition, the correct answer to the easiest problem is worth exactly the same as the correct answer to the hardest problem. For those two reasons, it is a good deal for you to skip one difficult question in order to get four easy ones right.

**How do you know which ones are the hard ones?** Within each passage, the questions ascend in difficulty and complexity. Did you know that? Aren't you glad you do now?
The first question will ask you the simplest type of stuff. It might ask you to report one data point. These questions are softballs.

**Later questions will do stuff like introduce a whole new idea and ask you to apply it.** Or they'll ask you to compare up to four different elements within the experiment. They might even ask you what would happen if you changed one element of the experiment. They're a pain in the ass—believe me. Do you want to solve these questions? You sure do, especially if you're trying to score 33+ on the test. Do you want to spend 3-4 minutes on this one crazy question? No. No, you don't.

**So pick your battles.** On any given passage, answer all of the questions you can handle *(which should be the first few questions on each)* and skip any that give you a headache *(typically the last 1-2 questions on each passage)*. Clearly mark the ones that you skip. Then move onto the next passage and repeat the process. Once you get through all of the passages, come back to the ones you've skipped. When you look at them with fresh eyes, you may have a better chance of solving them.

> **HOT TIP:** it's a good idea to mark on your answer sheet which questions you skip. We recommend drawing a small circle around the number of the question to remind yourself that you haven't answered that one yet. Two advantages to doing that: you won't accidentally try to grid an answer to another question in that spot, and you'll quickly know which questions you need to guess on at the end of the section. The test instructions say that you should not make any **"extraneous marks"** on your answer sheet, so you might want to erase them at the end if you have time to be on the safe side. We've submitted answer sheets with extraneous marks and it hasn't caused us any trouble, so draw your own conclusion.

## FOLLOW THE CLUES

**One of the nicest things that the test does for you is tell you where to look.** If the question mentions Figure 1, guess where the answer comes from? If the question says, **"according to Table 1 and Figure 2,"** you're going to need both Table 1 and Figure 2 to get that question right.

> You'd probably file this strategy under **"common sense."** Common sense is pretty much what the whole Science test is about.

**We want to encourage you to push this strategy to the extreme.** Follow all of the geographical clues they give you, like **"in Experiment 1,"** of course, but you should also hunt down the exact words a question mentions. For example, if a question asks you to compare the resonant angular frequency of two different circuits, do not start attacking that question by asking yourself, **"what does resonant angular frequency mean?"** We don't have time to care what it means. What we should do is Follow the Clues, and scan quickly for those exact words. Guess what? They'll be there! Once you find them, you'll be in the right spot to solve the question.

**Be a bloodhound for those clues. Match words from the questions to the tables, the charts, and the introductory information. Pretend you're a detective. It might actually be kind of fun.**

## KEEP IT SIMPLE

To a student who is brand new to the **ACT**, this strategy might seem like the most ridiculous, nonsensical advice of all time. How can you keep it simple when you're staring down at 500 pieces of data?

The funny thing is that keeping it simple is the whole point of the test. The test makers want to see if you can find a path through all of that information. You want to be a magnet for everything that's important and ignore everything else.

A really important thing to keep in mind is that every question is correct in a black-and-white way. That's true for the entire **ACT**, but it's especially helpful here. You want to turn yourself into a professional finder-of-information on the Science test. When you do that, you'll be finding answers that you are confident are correct. That's where you want to be.

**HOT COLLEGE TIP:** the fact that this college entrance exam tests you on your ability to extract information efficiently is no coincidence...it's a skill you'll use all the time in college. You'll learn how to read 30% of a research paper in order to understand 95% of it. You'll even use this skill in English and History classes. It's a funny transition to go through from reading every last word when you're in high school to learning how NOT to read every word in college. It's a good one, though.

**Here's a guarantee: on every ACT Science test, you'll see something that you've never seen before.** There is just too much damn science for you to know it all. That doesn't mean you can't get the questions right—it's actually a reminder that you need to **Keep It Simple** and solve the questions using your good reasoning skill rather than your encyclopedic science knowledge.

All of the strategies we've mentioned so far culminate in this one. We could have called this strategy **"Don't Overthink It,"** but we think it makes more sense as a positive strategy, a way of approaching the test. To demonstrate, we're going to **"think through"** a passage with you. On the next page you'll see a typical **ACT** Science passage. On the page after that, you'll see how we would approach this passage, with our thoughts written out on the page. Start by trying the passage for yourself. Then turn the page to see how your answers—and your thought processes—match up with ours.

Don't Overthink It!

NOTES:

# EXERCISE

**INSTRUCTIONS:** Work through this sample passage. Then, compare your thinking to ours on the following page.

The ideal gas law, which represents the state of a hypothetical ideal gas, approximates the behavior of many gases under various conditions. The ideal gas law is written as $PV = nRT$ in which $P$ is pressure, $V$ is the volume of the gas, $n$ is the number of moles of the gas, $R$ is the ideal gas constant, and $T$ is the temperature.

A group of students devised and carried out the following experiments to test whether or not air, a mixture of 78% nitrogen, 21% oxygen, and trace amounts of other gases, obeys the ideal gas law.

### Experiment 1

An experiment was conducted in which the quantity of gas molecules $n$ was held constant and the temperature $T$ was held constant at 25° C. The teacher filled a syringe with 20 milliliters of air and connected it to an absolute pressure gauge (see Figure 1). The students hypothesized that if air obeys the ideal gas law, the initial pressure multiplied by the initial volume will be equal to the final pressure multiplied by the final volume ($P_i V_i = P_f V_f$).

Figure 1

The teacher asked the students to predict the pressure in the syringe at different volumes based on the ideal gas law. She then took pressure readings as she decreased the volume of the air by closing the syringe. The results are shown in Table 1.

| Table 1 | | | |
|---|---|---|---|
| Volume (mL) | Predicted pressure (kPa) | Measured pressure (kPa) | Error (%) |
| 20 | – | 101.2 | – |
| 14 | 144.6 | 141.2 | 2.35 |
| 10 | 202.4 | 186.4 | 7.91 |
| 6 | 337.3 | 297.1 | 11.9 |
| 4 | 506.0 | 423.1 | 16.4 |

### Experiment 2

An experiment was conducted in which the volume of gas $V$ and the quantity of gas molecules $n$ were held constant and the temperature was varied. The teacher attached an absolute pressure gauge to a canister and submerged it into a hot water bath with a thermometer (see Figure 2). The students hypothesized that initial pressure divided by initial temperature will be equal to final pressure divided by final temperature ($\frac{P_i}{T_i} = \frac{P_f}{T_f}$) if the ideal gas law accurately describes air under these conditions.

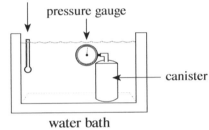

Figure 2

She then gradually added ice to decrease the temperature of the bath, and recorded the pressure of the canister and temperature of the water bath at regular intervals. The results are shown in Table 2.

| Table 2 | | | |
|---|---|---|---|
| Temperature (°C) | Predicted pressure (kPa) | Measured pressure (kPa) | Error (%) |
| 56.12 | – | 116.88 | – |
| 42.37 | 88.24 | 82.13 | 6.92 |
| 31.22 | 65.02 | 70.49 | 8.41 |
| 20.60 | 42.90 | 47.70 | 11.2 |
| 13.49 | 28.10 | 32.48 | 15.6 |

1. Which of the following best describes the difference between the procedures used in Experiments 1 and 2? In Experiment 1, the:
   A. temperature was varied while in Experiment 2, pressure was varied.
   B. temperature was constant while in Experiment 2, volume was constant.
   C. pressure was varied while in Experiment 2, volume was varied.
   D. volume was constant while in Experiment 2, temperature was constant.

2. Based on the results of Experiment 1, which of the following graphs best shows the relationship between volume and pressure of a gas?

   F.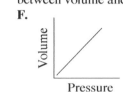

   G.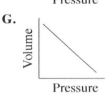

   H.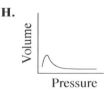

   J.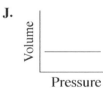

3. Based on Table 2, if the pressure meter had showed a reading of 92.00 kPa, temperature would most likely have been closest to:
   A. 121.34 °C
   B. 82.78 °C.
   C. 46.17 °C
   D. 31.21 °C

4. One student hypothesized that air under low pressure adheres to the ideal gas law more closely than air under high pressure. Do the results of the experiments support this hypothesis?
   F. Yes; in both experiments, the error was higher when the pressure was higher.
   G. Yes; in both experiments, the error was higher when the pressure was lower.
   H. No; in Experiment 1, the error was lower when the pressure was lower, but in Experiment 2, the error was higher when the pressure was lower.
   J. No; in Experiment 1 the error was lower when the pressure was higher, but in Experiment 2 the error was lower when the pressure was lower.

5. Which of the following procedures would best help the students to determine an approximate value for the constant $R$? The students could:
   A. maintain constant pressure but vary the amount of air in the syringe to measure the effect on the volume.
   B. maintain a constant quantity of gas molecules but vary the pressure by conducting the experiment at various altitudes then measure the change of temperature.
   C. measure the quantity of gas, the pressure, and the volume at several temperatures.
   D. measure the quantity of gas, the pressure, the volume, and the temperature and use the ideal gas law to calculate an $R$ value.

6. A student claimed that the error in Experiment 2 may have been caused by the gas in the canister failing to change temperature as quickly as the bath water. Do the results from Experiment 2 support this hypothesis?
   F. Yes; as the temperature of the water bath decreased, the error increased.
   G. Yes; as the temperature of the water bath decreased, the error decreased.
   H. No; as the temperature of the water bath decreased, the error increased.
   J. No; as the temperature of the water bath decreased, the error decreased.

# EXERCISE

**INSTRUCTIONS:** Use this completed passage to check your work and your thinking from the previous page.

*Blah blah blah...let's skip to the questions.*

The ideal gas law, which represents the state of a hypothetical ideal gas, approximates the behavior of many gases under various conditions. The ideal gas law is written as $PV = nRT$ in which $P$ is pressure, $V$ is the volume of the gas, $n$ is the number of moles of the gas, $R$ is the ideal gas constant, and $T$ is the temperature.

A group of students devised and carried out the following experiments to test whether or not air, a mixture of 78% nitrogen, 21% oxygen, and trace amounts of other gases, obeys the ideal gas law.

*Experiment 1*

An experiment was conducted in which the quantity of gas molecules $n$ was held constant and the temperature $T$ was held constant at 25° C. The teacher filled a syringe with 20 milliliters of air and connected it to an absolute pressure gauge (see Figure 1). The students hypothesized that if air obeys the ideal gas law, the initial pressure multiplied by the initial volume will be equal to the final pressure multiplied by the final volume ($P_i V_i = P_f V_f$).

Figure 1

The teacher asked the students to predict the pressure in the syringe at different volumes based on the ideal gas law. She then took pressure readings as she decreased the volume of the air by closing the syringe. The results are shown in Table 1.

| Table 1 | | | |
|---|---|---|---|
| Volume (mL) | Predicted pressure (kPa) | Measured pressure (kPa) | Error (%) |
| 20 | – | 101.2 | – |
| 14 | 144.6 | 141.2 | 2.35 |
| 10 | 202.4 | 186.4 | 7.91 |
| 6 | 337.3 | 297.1 | 11.9 |
| 4 | 506.0 | 423.1 | 16.4 |

*Experiment 2*

An experiment was conducted in which the volume of gas $V$ and the quantity of gas molecules $n$ were held constant and the temperature was varied. The teacher attached an absolute pressure gauge to a canister and submerged it into a hot water bath with a thermometer (see Figure 2). The students hypothesized that initial pressure divided by initial temperature will be equal to final pressure divided by final temperature ($\frac{P_i}{T_i} = \frac{P_f}{T_f}$) if the ideal gas law accurately describes air under these conditions.

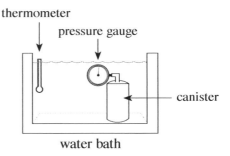

Figure 2

She then gradually added ice to decrease the temperature of the bath, and recorded the pressure of the canister and temperature of the water bath at regular intervals. The results are shown in Table 2.

| Table 2 | | | |
|---|---|---|---|
| Temperature (°C) | Predicted pressure (kPa) | Measured pressure (kPa) | Error (%) |
| 56.12 | – | 116.88 | – |
| 42.57 | 88.24 | 82.13 | 6.92 |
| 31.22 | 65.02 | 70.49 | 8.41 |
| 20.60 | 42.90 | 47.70 | 11.2 |
| 13.49 | 28.10 | 32.48 | 15.6 |

*92 kPa would go here*

*Sweet! I found the proof for B. in the first sentence of each passage*

1. Which of the following best describes the difference between the procedures used in Experiments 1 and 2? In Experiment 1, the:
   A. temperature was varied while in Experiment 2, pressure was varied.
   **B.** temperature was constant while in Experiment 2, volume was constant.
   C. pressure was varied while in Experiment 2, volume was varied.
   D. volume was constant while in Experiment 2, temperature was constant.

2. Based on the results of Experiment 1, which of the following graphs best shows the relationship between volume and pressure of a gas?

   F.
   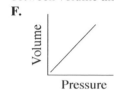

   **G.**

   *As volume goes down, pressure goes up. That's this one.*

   H.
   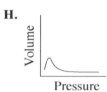

   *Kind of a math question...keep all the variables constant and solve!*

   J.
   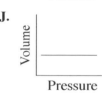

3. Based on Table 2, if the pressure meter had showed a reading of 92.00 kPa, temperature would most likely have been closest to:
   A. 121.34°C
   B. 82.78°C.
   **C.** 46.17°C *←---- only value that's*
   D. 31.21°C *between 42.37 and 56.12 so that's gotta be it.*

*Looks like I answered all the questions but only had to read about 20% of the passages. Sweet.*

*Answer choices extremely helpful on this one!*

4. One student hypothesized that air under low pressure adheres to the ideal gas law more closely than air under high pressure. Do the results of the experiments support this hypothesis?
   F. Yes; in both experiments, the error was higher when the pressure was higher.
   G. Yes; in both experiments, the error was higher when the pressure was lower.
   **H.** No; in Experiment 1, the error was lower when the pressure was lower, but in Experiment 2, the error was higher when the pressure was lower.
   J. No; in Experiment 1 the error was lower when the pressure was higher, but in Experiment 2 the error was lower when the pressure was lower.

5. Which of the following procedures would best help the students to determine an approximate value for the constant $R$? The students could:
   A. maintain constant pressure but vary the amount of air in the syringe to measure the effect on the volume.
   B. maintain a constant quantity of gas molecules but vary the pressure by conducting the experiment at various altitudes then measure the change of temperature.
   C. measure the quantity of gas, the pressure, and the volume at several temperatures.
   **D.** measure the quantity of gas, the pressure, the volume, and the temperature and use the ideal gas law to calculate an $R$ value.

6. A student claimed that the error in Experiment 2 may have been caused by the gas in the canister failing to change temperature as quickly as the bath water. Do the results from Experiment 2 support this hypothesis?
   **F.** Yes; as the temperature of the water bath decreased, the error increased.
   G. Yes; as the temperature of the water bath decreased, the error decreased.
   H. No; as the temperature of the water bath decreased, the error increased.
   J. No; as the temperature of the water bath decreased, the error decreased.

*Lots of moving parts here, but it's true that as the temp. went down, error got worse. The canister adjusting slowly could have caused that problem.*

# Passage Types

That's what we mean when we say Keep It Simple.
Find what you need to find and ignore the rest—it's the secret to success on the Science. **Now we're going to move onto some more specific content.** Let's get into the nitty gritty of how you'll get these questions right.

To remind you, there are three passage types:
- Data Representation
- Research Summaries
- Conflicting Viewpoints

## DATA REPRESENTATION

You'll be given a brief introduction plus a pile of information—graphs, diagrams, charts, you name it. Questions focus on extracting information from the data, identifying relationships, and interpolation/extrapolation.

**Key strategies: Since these passages are data driven, you really want to learn as little as possible.** These passages require less thinking and more finding. Jump straight to the questions. Be familiar with the different types of graphs and charts. Keep it simple. Look out for the unusual (and sneaky) ways of formatting graphs later in this chapter. Work quickly and don't overthink.

## RESEARCH SUMMARIES

The fraternal twin of the Data Representation passages, these passages describe specific, related experiments/studies, and also include a pile of data. Questions will ask you to find one basic data point, compare data points from multiple studies, find the relationship between the studies and the data, and think about experimental procedure.

**Key strategies: Jump straight to the questions, but don't be shy about looking back at the passage and reading part (or all) of it.** Learn as you go—it's more likely that you will need to understand what's actually going on these passages than it is on Data Representation. Note the differences between the different studies. Look out for what changes and what stays the same. Think like a scientist—you're likely to see questions about experimental procedure or the scientific method. Keep it simple—a fair number of the questions on these passages are as basic as data questions. Work quickly—do we sound like a broken record with that one?

## CONFLICTING VIEWPOINTS:

The redheaded stepchild of the Science test, this passage will present you with 2-4 (get ready for it) conflicting viewpoints on a scientific topic. Sometimes the characters are students, and sometimes they're scientists, but they always disagree. A passage could include several possible theories about what specifically caused dinosaurs to go extinct, or alternate theories about plate tectonics and how earth's landmasses came to be located where they are. On a typical test you'll only see one Conflicting Viewpoints passage. That's a good thing because they take the most time and energy—conflicting viewpoints passages are often composed of just text and no data.

**Key strategies: Know which passage is the Conflicting Viewpoints passage.** If you see a section that is all text *(or almost all text)* with headings like Scientist 1, Scientist 2, and Scientist 3, that's the one. Look for multiple viewpoints, explanations, or hypotheses—that will confirm that it is. Since these passages can be all text, we recommend reading the passages in their entirety. When you read, look for similarities and differences because nearly every question is going to ask you about those. Make **"caveman notes"** *(like we did in the Reading section)* identifying the key aspects of each theory. Underline important ideas. Because this passage takes the most time, you may want to consider skipping and coming back to it after you finish everything else. Work quickly.

**Speaking of Conflicting Viewpoints, let's take a look at a sample one of those right now!** Here is another **"think through"** passage. You take a shot at it first, then flip the page to see how we thought our way through it. Most important thing to remember about Conflicting Viewpoints: this is the one that you actually have to read.

Be an active reader—note similarities and differences
and make notes as you read.

# EXERCISE

**INSTRUCTIONS:** Read the conflicting viewpoints passages and answer the questions.

A geological phenomenon is a natural occurrence related to the structure or composition of the earth. Racetrack Playa, a flat, dry lake in Death Valley National Park, California, is home to a geological phenomenon in which rocks, some up to 18 inches in diameter and weighing 700 pounds, leave trails stretching hundreds of meters, making it appear as though the rocks have glided across the sand. Four scientists attempt to explain what causes these "sailing stones" to move.

## Scientist 1

During periods of heavy rain, water from the nearby mountain drains into the playa and forms a shallow, temporary lake. When the hot desert sun returns, the water quickly evaporates and leaves behind a surface layer of soft, slick mud for a certain period before it dries completely. During this period, high winds would be able to push the rocks across the playa due to the reduced friction between the rocks and the surface.

## Scientist 2

On rare occasions when rainfall is heavy enough to flood the lakebed, the water flowing down from the mountains that border the playa would apply a substantial amount of force on the rocks in the direction of the current. The force of the flowing water applied to the stones and the reduction in friction between the stones and the lakebed allows the rocks to move across the playa.

## Scientist 3

During periods of heavy rain, water runoff from nearby mountains drains into the lakebed, saturating a clay compound 0.75" beneath the surface of the playa sand. The rain causes this clay layer to become a smooth, fluid surface. When high winds arise concurrently, they are able to propel the rocks across this slick layer.

## Scientist 4

Rapid changes in temperature are required for the Racetrack Playa stones to move. When periods of heavy rainfall are followed by extreme temperature drops in the evening, thin sheets of ice form. When the morning temperature warms quickly, these sheets of ice crack into large, rigid pieces. These pieces function as sails, carrying the rocks along the lakebed with the help of a light wind

1. Scientist 2 would most likely agree with the statement that the cause of the movement of the rocks is:
   A. ice.
   B. high winds.
   C. clay.
   D. the force created by moving water.

2. In the year 1995 the playa did not experience any heavy rain, but evidence showed that the stones moved. This information would most likely weaken the viewpoint(s) of:
   F. Scientist 1 only.
   G. Scientist 2 only.
   H. both Scientists 2 and 3.
   J. Scientists 1, 2, 3, and 4.

3. Scientist 4's views differ from Scientist 3's views in that only Scientist 4 believes that the movement of the rocks requires:
   A. ice.
   B. high winds.
   C. clay.
   D. the force created by moving water.

4. Is the claim "Freezing temperatures are a necessary factor for the rocks to move" consistent with both Scientist 1 and Scientist 4's explanations?
   F. Yes, because both Scientists 1 and 4 explain that slick ice is an important secondary factor causing the rocks to move.
   G. Yes, because the reduction in friction causes an increase in the speed of an object moving across an icy surface.
   H. No, because Scientist 1 explains that the evaporation of water, not the formation of ice, is a necessary factor for the rocks to move, while only Scientist 4 discusses the necessary function of rigid pieces of ice as sails.
   J. No, because Scientist 4 explains that liquid water mixed with a clay substance is necessary for the rocks to move, while only Scientist 1 discusses the necessity for rapid changes in temperature and the formation of ice.

**5.** Which of the following diagrams showing the relationship between temperature and time of day is consistent with Scientist 4's assertion about temperature fluctuations required for the rocks to move?

**A.**

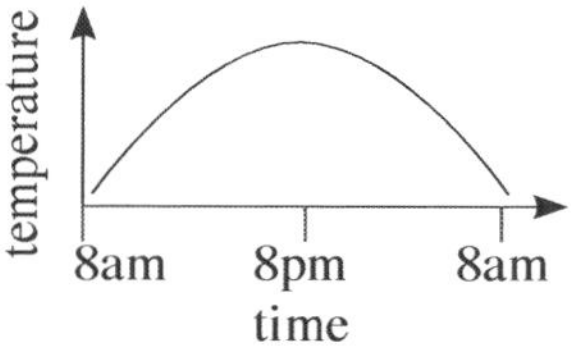

**B.**

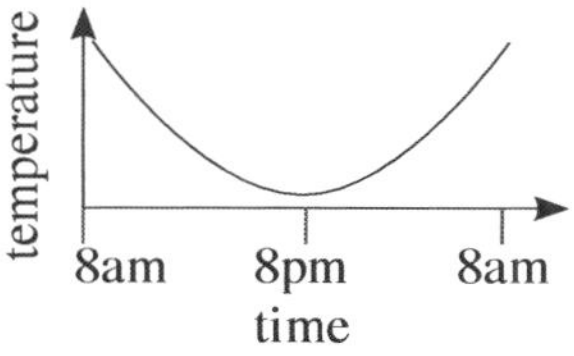

**C.**

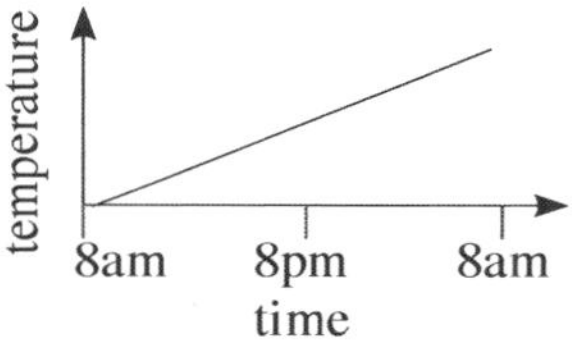

**D.**

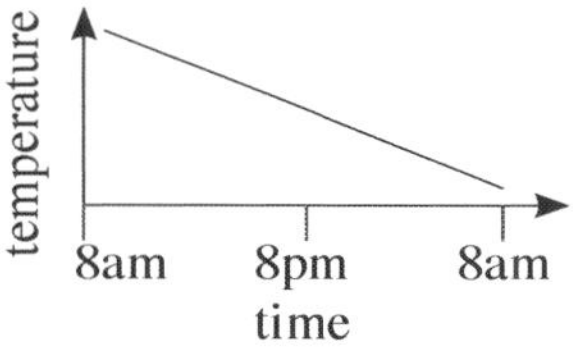

**6.** Which of the following pairs of statements best explains the cause for the sailing stones according to the viewpoints of Scientists 1 and 3?

| | Scientist 1 | Scientist 3 |
|---|---|---|
| **F.** | Periods of heavy rain | Light wind pushing rocks |
| **G.** | High winds pushing rocks | The force created by moving water |
| **H.** | Slick muddy surface and high winds | Clay-based fluid surface & high winds |
| **J.** | Sheets of ice and low winds | Periods of heavy rain |

**7.** All of the scientists would most likely agree that which of the following natural characteristics of Racetrack Playa is essential to the movement of the rocks?

**A.** Rapid changes in temperature
**B.** High winds
**C.** The flat surface of the lakebed
**D.** Distance above sea level

Did that feel like a crossover between the science and the Reading section?

If so, good—that means you handled it the right way!

# How to be a Science Ninja

When a ninja prepares for battle *(and just so you know, we are making this up right now)*, he or she studies the opponent. What weaknesses do they have? What tendencies can I predict and take advantage of?

**ACT** ninjas do the same thing: they learn the tendencies of the test in order to reach maximum, Bruce Lee-style performance level. Here are some tendencies of the **ACT** Science test that can help you *(yes, YOU)* become an **ACT** ninja.

The kids' show **"Sesame Street"** used to include a song called, **"Which of these kids is doing his own thing?"** The screen was divided into four quadrants and in three of the quadrants the kids would be doing one thing, like swinging a baseball bat. In the fourth quadrant, the kid would be wearing a football helmet. Then the really sweet, very 1970's song would ask you to play the game, **"which of these kids is doing his own thing?"** It was not a very difficult game.

Amazingly, this very same game can be played on the **ACT** Science, and it isn't any more difficult to play than when you were a four-year-old watching **"Sesame Street."**

**Here's an example:**
Each of the four lotions was tested using a sample of synthetic skin. One of the four samples showed signs of increased cell damage. The damaged skin sample most likely had been treated with:

| Lotion | SPF | UVB Filtration (%) |
|--------|-----|--------------------|
| A      | 5   | 51%                |
| B      | 15  | 97%                |
| C      | 30  | 98%                |
| D      | 40  | 99%                |

**A.** Lotion A.
**B.** Lotion B.
**C.** Lotion C.
**D.** Lotion D.

**Now, you can solve this using the information in the passage as well as your science common sense. For now, let's play another game: which of the four lotions is doing its own thing?** Since three of them (B, C, and D) are within 2% of each other on UVB filtration, and the other one (A) is lower by almost 50%, guess what? A is the answer.

It's surprising how often that strategy works on this test. The rule of thumb here is that if three of the answer choices are very similar and the other one is way different than those, it's probably the right answer.

## WHEN IN DOUBT, READ THE INTRO

**When the ACT wants to mess with you... it will include the critical information you need to answer a question in the most obvious of places: the introduction.** If you find yourself struggling to find an answer to a question—you've searched every table and figure to no avail—glance back at the introduction. You might just find it there.

## DON'T DO *(Too Much)* MATH

Although the **ACT** Science is loaded with numbers... remember that you're not allowed to use a calculator. The implication of that policy is that you don't need one. Avoid the temptation to do a bunch of calculations. Most **ACT** Science tests don't require a single calculation *(unless you consider "finding the highest or lowest value in a group" a calculation)*, and when you do have to do math, it is the simplest kind. Here are some examples of mathematical calculation we've ever seen on the **ACT** Science.

- Adding two numbers together
- Subtracting a percentage from 100
- Finding the average of a set of 5 numbers

**If you find yourself doing math more difficult than that, take a step back and look at the question fresh—it's probably simpler to solve than you think.**

## LEARN SOME UNUSUAL WAYS DATA CAN BE PRESENTED

What follows is a quick lesson in some funky styles of graphs and charts that you might see on the **ACT**. It's worth getting to know these guys—as G.I. Joe says, **"knowing is half the battle."**

### GRAPHS WITH MULTIPLE Y-AXES

Here's a fun one: they can give you a graph with more than one quantity represented on the y-axis. Take a minute to look at this graph. See if you can figure out what it means.

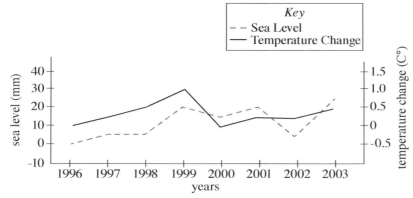

The scientist who created this graph wanted to show the relationship between changes in temperature and sea level. The two separate y-axes are labeled, and then a key is included to help you figure out which plot is which—the little squares tell you what happened to sea level and the closed dots show the temperature change values. In the year 1999, for example, the sea level had risen 20mm while the temperature increased by 1 degree Celsius.

293

## TABLES WITH THE SAME VARIABLE ON BOTH AXES.

We just showed you how you can put three values on two axes. Here's how to include just one value!

| °C | 0 | 1 | 2 | 3 | 4 | 5 | 6 | 7 | 8 | 9 | 10 | °C |
|----|------|------|------|------|------|------|------|------|------|------|------|----|
| | Thermoelectric voltage (mV) | | | | | | | | | | | |
| 0 | .000 | .039 | .079 | .119 | .158 | 1.98 | .238 | .277 | .317 | .357 | .397 | 0 |
| 10 | .397 | .437 | .477 | .517 | .557 | .597 | .637 | .677 | .718 | .758 | .798 | 10 |
| 20 | .798 | .838 | .879 | .919 | .960 | 1.000 | 1.041 | 1.081 | 1.122 | 1.163 | 1.203 | 20 |
| 30 | 1.203 | 1.244 | 1.285 | 1.326 | 1.366 | 1.407 | 1.448 | 1.489 | 1.530 | 1.571 | 1.612 | 30 |
| 40 | 1.612 | 1.653 | 1.694 | 1.735 | 1.776 | 1.817 | 1.858 | 1.899 | 1.941 | 1.882 | 2.023 | 40 |
| 50 | 2.023 | 2.064 | 2.106 | 2.147 | 2.188 | 2.230 | 2.271 | 2.312 | 2.354 | 2.385 | 2.436 | 50 |
| 60 | 2.436 | 2.478 | 2.519 | 2.561 | 2.602 | 2.644 | 2.685 | 2.727 | 2.768 | 2.810 | 2.851 | 60 |
| 70 | 2.851 | 2.893 | 2.934 | 2.976 | 3.017 | 3.059 | 3.100 | 3.142 | 3.184 | 3.225 | 3.267 | 70 |
| 80 | 3.267 | 3.308 | 2350 | 3.391 | 3.433 | 3.474 | 3.516 | 3.557 | 3.599 | 3.640 | 3.682 | 80 |
| 90 | 3.682 | 3.723 | 3.765 | 3.806 | 3.848 | 3.889 | 3.931 | 3.972 | 4.013 | 4.055 | 4.096 | 90 |

**Notice how this table has just one unit in each corner, °C?** That's because this table is given in terms of degrees Celsius both vertically and horizontally. The vertical axis contains all of the multiples of 10 from 0 to 90, and the horizontal axis contains all of the units from 0 to 10. What that allows you to do is find any value from 0 up to 100°C. Say you want to find the value for 84°C. Start in the 80°C row, then slide over to the 4°C column. That value is 3.848.

These are two of the many wacky ways that the ACT can present science data.

**Here's a really good rule of thumb:** check the axes on every graph and the labels on every table that you use!

# ACT Science Knowledge

**As you know by now, ACT Science is barely a science test.** A little scientific common sense is handy, but the vast majority of the questions simply ask you to find data and interpret experimental outcomes. It's reading comp—not hard science.

**That said, the ACT does ask some questions** *(no more than four on any test we've seen)* **that require fundamental science knowledge to solve.** We scoured real ACTs to find all of the science concepts that have appeared on those exams. You're welcome!

## A couple of points to make about this list:

- You'll notice right away that a lot of this science content is the most fundamental, essential kind. That is not by mistake. The ACT is not going to ask you to know Planck's Constant or the atomic number of iridium. Much of this stuff you probably already know—and that's good news.

- What's on this list is literally all of the outside science information from over a decade's worth of real ACT tests. This is the stuff that you had to know in order to get a question right. This list might seem long or intimidating at first, but remember that only 3 or 4 of these concepts showed up on any given test.

- **We put in bold the concepts that showed up over and over again. Make sure you know those ones in particular.**

## EXPERIMENTAL PROCEDURE
- **Independent variables are directly controlled by the experimenter.** They are usually plotted on the x-axis of a graph.
- **Dependent variables are the measured outcomes of an experiment.** They are not directly controlled by the experimenter. They are usually plotted on the y-axis of a graph.
- Control groups receive no experimental treatment.
- Experimental design: to test the effect of one variable, an experiment should vary only that one variable and leave all of the others constant.
- A hypothesis is a yet-unproven proposal based on preliminary data.
- Unsterilized equipment may have microorganisms that could contaminant experiments.

## TERMINOLOGY
- When two things are described as **directly proportional**, it means that when one of them goes up, the other one goes up. Likewise, if one goes down, the other goes down.
- When two variables are **inversely proportional**, as one goes up, the other goes down.

## PHYSICAL PROPERTIES

- Mass is the amount of matter in an object. A pool ball has more mass than a tennis ball. Mass is typically measured in grams and kilograms.
- Volume is the amount of space occupied by a substance. That pool ball and tennis ball have approximately the same volume. Volume is typically measured in liters and cubic meters.
- **Density equals mass divided by volume.** Density measures how much matter an object has per unit of space.
- The freezing point of a substance is the same as its melting point.
- The boiling point of a substance is the same as its condensation point.
- The melting/freezing point of water ($H_2O$) is 0° C.
- The boiling/condensation point of water is 100° C.
- Stirring a substance helps to maintain the uniformity of its temperature.
- Evaporation is when liquid turns into a gas form due to heat.
- Insulation slows heat loss or gain.
- When water is heated it becomes less dense.
- A heterogeneous mixture contains different substances that remain physically separate. Chicken noodle soup is heterogeneous.
- A homogeneous mixture is a mixture with a uniform composition. Salt water is homogeneous.
- **Substances with lower density float above substances of higher density.**
- Objects with greater mass produce a greater gravitational force.
- The more surface area of an object is exposed to a solvent, the more quickly it will dissolve.
- Permeability describes the ability of a material to allow liquids or gases to pass through it. Something that is impermeable does not allow any other substance to pass through it.
- **Viscosity is a measurement of the speed at which something flows.** Higher viscosity is correlated with slower flow.
- The volume of a cube equals the length of a side raised to the third power.

METHODS OF HEAT TRANSFER:
- Conduction: the transfer of heat between substances that are touching. Example: if a heated block of aluminum sits next to a cool block, the heated block's temperature will fall and the cool block's temperature will rise.
- Convection: the transfer of thermal energy when a warmer area rises and circulates past a cooler area. Example: when water boils, the hotter water rises past the cooler water, pushing the cooler water to the bottom where it will be heated.
- Radiation: the transfer of heat through thermal, infrared radiation. Does not require contact. Example: warmth from the sun.

## BIOLOGY

- Mitosis is a part of the cell cycle through which one mother cell separates into two identical daughter cells. It is associated with asexual reproduction.
- Meiosis is a type of cell division associated with sexual reproduction.
- Gametes are sexual reproduction cells.
- Water is required for living creatures to survive (hint: this is a useful one to keep in mind in your everyday life too).
- A cell membrane is a thin barrier that separates the interior of a cell from the outside environment.

- The ribosome is a structure within every cell that serves as the site of protein synthesis. The protein synthesis process is called "translation."
- Chloroplasts are the site of photosynthesis in plants.
- Photosynthesis is the process by which plants turn light (typically sunlight) into chemical energy (in the form of sugar).
- Plants absorb $CO_2$ (carbon dioxide) and produce $O_2$ (oxygen).
- Endothermic animals are "warm-blooded." Examples include mammals and birds.
- Ectothermic (or "cold-blooded") animals include fish, reptiles, and amphibians.
- ATP is a basic unit of energy in plants and animals.

## GENETICS

- Genes are dominant or recessive. Dominant genes are expressed using a capital letter, and recessive genes using a lower-case letter.
- An organism is "homozygous" for a trait if its two genes are either both dominant or both recessive, i.e. GG or gg.
- An organism is "heterozygous" for a trait if it has one dominant and one recessive gene, i.e. Gg.
- Genotype refers to the specific set of genes in an organism, i.e. BbCc.
- Phenotype refers to the expression of genes in an organism, i.e. offspring with the genes BbCc have curly tails.
- Genus and species are the last two parts of an organism's taxonomy, and these parts are typically used to identify an organism. For example, house cats are categorized as Felis catus. They belong to the genus Felis and the species catus.

## CHEMISTRY

- The kinetic theory of gases states that gas is made of many small particles that are always moving and bouncing off each other randomly.
- **Liquids with pH values lower than 7 are acidic, and liquids with pH values higher than 7 are basic. Water has a pH of 7 and is neutral.**
- Oxides (like peroxide) are molecules that must contain at least one oxygen atom.
- A mole is a unit of measurement that expresses the amount of a chemical substance present.
- Balanced equations: on both sides you must have the same number of atoms of each kind. For example, the equation: $4 NH_3 + 5O_2 \longrightarrow 4 NO + 6 H_2O$
- is balanced, because you have 4 Ns on each side, 12 Hs, and 10 Os.
- Reactants are the starting material in a chemical reaction.
- Products are the substances that are formed in a chemical reaction.
- **A solute is a substance dissolved into another substance, called a solvent.**
- A solution is a mixture of a solute into a solvent. Salt water is a solution in which salt is the solute and water is the solvent.
- Distilled water is water that has many of its impurities removed.
- Protons are positively charged.
- Electrons are negatively charged.
- Neutrons are neutral.
- An ion is an atom or molecule with a net electric charge due to the gain or loss of electrons.

## STATIC ELECTRICITY

- "Like" charges (such as + and +) repel each other, and opposite charges (+ and −) attract each other.
- As current flows through a resistor, heat is produced. The more current, the more heat is produced.
- Ohm's Law (don't worry about the name): Current (I) = Voltage (E) / Resistance (R)
- Electromagnets have north and south poles.

## PHYSICS

- **Potential energy is the energy an object has due to its position.** You can think of it as "stored" energy ready to be used. A bowling ball on top of a table has potential energy because it would fall to the ground (and release energy) if it were pushed off the table.
- Elastic potential energy is stored in an elastic object (i.e. a spring or a slingshot).
- **Kinetic energy is the energy of a moving object.** Remember that bowling ball? Once it falls off the table, it has kinetic energy because it is moving. When it lands on your toe, it will transfer its kinetic energy into your body (and you will scream a word your mother taught you not to say).
- Kinetic energy is directly proportional to mass and velocity. A larger object moving slowly and a smaller object moving quickly can have the same kinetic energy.
- Heat is the same thing as average kinetic energy. The hotter something is, the higher its average kinetic energy.
- In a frictionless world, potential energy (PE) is equal to kinetic energy (KE). The real world has friction and air resistance, which cause KE to be less than PE for moving objects.
- Newton's First Law of Motion: an object at rest tends to stay at rest, while an object in motion tends to stay in motion. Also referred to as the Law of Inertia.
- A vacuum is a space without air (and therefore without air resistance).
- Fire requires oxygen in order to burn.
- Velocity (speed) = distance traveled / time
- Acceleration = change in velocity / time
- Amplitude is the distance between the maximum height of a wave and its resting position. It is equal to half the peak-to-trough height of the wave.
- Wavelength is the distance between one peak and the next in a wave.
- Period is the length in time it takes for one wave to pass.
- Frequency is a rate, measured as the number of waves that pass a certain point in one second.
- Period and frequency are reciprocals.
- Pressure and temperature are directly proportional.

## ENVIRONMENTAL SCIENCE

- The ozone layer absorbs ultraviolet radiation from the sun. The more ozone present, the more UV is absorbed.
- A drought is a prolonged period of decreased rainfall resulting in a drier than normal habitat.
- An invasive species is a non-native plant or animal that threatens to harm an ecosystem.
- Pressure is greater deeper inside earth and deeper in the ocean.

## ASTRONOMY

- The planets in our solar system, from nearest to the sun to furthest from the sun: Mercury, Venus, Earth, Mars, Jupiter, Saturn, Uranus, Neptune (Sorry, Pluto.)
- The planets in our solar system, from smallest to biggest: Mercury, Mars, Venus, Earth, Neptune, Uranus, Saturn, Jupiter
- The bigger the planet, the stronger its gravitational impact.
- The earth rotates about 365 times per year.

That's it—all of the science content we have found on the **ACT**! If you find anything that we missed, email us and we'll add it to the list! Write to us at **actscience@tutorted.com**.

**Tutor Ted.**

NOTES:

# SCIENCE: ANSWERS & SOLUTIONS

### Page 284 - Think Through

**Question 1: (B)**
Look at the first sentence of both Experiment 1 and 2. In Experiment 1, gas and temperature are held constant, and in Experiment 2, gas and volume are held constant.

**Question 2: (G)**
Since this is Experiment 1 you want to look at Table 1. Notice how as volume decreases, pressure increases. Therefore the two variables have an inverse correlation, and the only graph that shows that is (G).

**Question 3: (C)**
Let's head to Table 2. 92.00 kPa lies between 82.13 kPA and 116.88 kPA, so it's interpolation time! That means the temperature value should be between those given at the two pressures, so 56.12°C at 116.88 kPa and 42.37°C at 82.13 kPa.

**Question 4: (H)**
This question is tough just because it is asking us to keep a bunch of different moving parts in our head all at the same time. We need to look at the relationship between pressure and error. Look for the highest error in both Tables 1 and 2. We can see that the highest error appears in the same row as the highest pressure in Table 1, and the highest error occurs with the lowest pressure in Table 2. That means that the student's claim is not proven for the reason stated in (H).

**Question 5: (D)**
For this question we need to refer to the equation provided in the passage and put our math thinking caps on—don't worry it is simple algebra. To solve for R we just need to have the value of every other variable.

**Question 6: (F)**
For Experiment 2 we refer to Table 2. If the temperature inside the canister failed to change as quickly as the bath water, then we would expect that as the temperature decreased (by gradually adding ice) the percentage of error would increase. This is indeed the case.

### Page 290-291 - Conflicting Viewpoints

**Question 1: (D)**
If you marked up the passage you might be able to glance over and find your answer. Otherwise skip through Scientist 2's explanation. The answer is in the last sentence.

**Question 2: (J)**
The explanations of all four scientists involve heavy rain and water flowing in from the mountains into the lakebed. If this doesn't happen then all of the scientists' positions are weakened.

**Question 3: (A)**
Both Scientists mention wind, but it is Scientist 3 who mentions highs wind are needed. What other mechanism does Scientist 4 claim is necessary for the rocks to move, that Scientist 3 does not? Ice!

**Question 4: (H)**
We recall from the previous question that Scientist 4 asserted that extreme temperature drops cause ice to form, which allows the rocks to move. On the other hand, Scientist 1 mentions that the "hot desert sun" and evaporation are necessary factors. So eliminate the two "Yes" answer choices and you'll find that (H) is the correct answer.

**Question 5: (B)**
Scientist 4 again! Scientist 4 mentions "extreme temperature drops in the evening" and later he say "the morning temperature warms quickly." Therefore, we would expect a drop from 8 am to 8 pm (morning to evening) and a corresponding rise from 8 pm to 8 am.

**Question 6: (H)**
Remember just because the first column is correct, doesn't mean it's the right answer—you need explanations that cover both Scientists' views. If you didn't mark up the passage, one way to tackle this question is to cross off which explanations don't work for Scientist 1, and the go back over the answers left, and see which don't work for Scientist 2.

**Question 7: (C)**
Time for process of elimination. Rapid changes of temperature are mentioned by Scientist 4, but by no one else. High winds are mentioned by Scientist 1 and 3, but not by Scientist 2 or 4. The flat surface is not explicitly mentioned, but would logically be needed, otherwise the stones would all move in one direction and simply accumulate on one side of the playa. There's no reason distance above sea level should matter.

NOTES:

**?** **The Writing Test is optional!**
*(but you really should take it)*

# #

## HOW MANY?

**40** minutes
1 issue
3 perspectives

40

issue 1

## How your essay is scored:

> **Writing Test** score from 1 to 36

> **Four sub-scores**
Ideas & Analysis
Development & Support
Organization
Language Use

> **ELA score** that combines
the English, Reading, and
Writing Test scores

40min

# WRITING

*The Breakdown*

**3**

*perspectives*

> **Evaluate & Analyze**
> **the perspectives**

> **State & Develop**
> your **own** point of view

> **Explain** how
> **your point of view relates**
> to the given perspectives

**Do...**
write a lot.
**Three perspectives
plus your own**
is a lot of ground to cover.

**Don't...** stress the essay.
It's not a factor in
your overall test score.

# Introduction

**The good news?**
　　You finished the Science section!
**The bad news?**
　　You still have to write the essay.

Fear not! When you have Tutor Ted's help, you have a plan to attack this bad boy.

First, take a deep, slow breath as you find out that the essay does not factor into your overall score. What? Doesn't count towards my score? It's true. The essay is not factored into your ACT Composite *(1-36)* score. Not one little bit.

That's not to say that it isn't important, though. The Writing Test score *(reported on a 1-36 scale like the other sections)* **does** appear on your score report. Writing is a skill that college students use all of the time, so the essay is your chance to show college admissions officers that you are a terrific writer.

**Is the ACT essay really optional?** Yes...but you should write it.
The majority of colleges ask to see the Writing score.
You might as well stay on the safe side and write the thing.

## BASIC FACTS:

**The ACT Writing Test** *(that's the official name)* **is the last section of the test.** Students are given 40 minutes to evaluate three perspectives on an issue and present their own perspective.

The test makers are evaluating you *(and scoring you)* on **four aspects of writing:**

- ✎ Ideas and analysis
- ✎ Development and support
- ✎ Organization
- ✎ Language use

Which is pretty much everything that's involved in writing.

*Let's make ACT magic.*

**What is the ACT Writing Test, anyway?** Students are given **a topic plus three perspectives** that respond to that topic. The test instructions ask you to:

**"analyze and evaluate the perspectives given"**
**"state and develop your own perspective on the issue"**
**"explain the relationship between your perspective and those given."**

**More good news/bad news.** The good news: those instructions do not change from one test to the next. That means that every single time you write an **ACT** essay you'll answer the same question, just based on a different topic.

**The bad news is that those instructions are asking a lot of you. You have to respond to three separate perspectives, present your own perspective, AND relate it to the prompts they gave you.**

||||||||||||||||||||||||||||||||||||||||||||||||||||||||||||||||||||||||||||||||||||

## THIS BRINGS US TO RULE 1 OF THE ACT WRITING TEST:

1

RULE 1: WRITE A LOT.
You get four pages of space to write your essay. How are you going to write that much in the relatively short period of 40 minutes?

By sticking to Rule 2.

## 2 RULE 2: HAVE A PLAN.

The ACT gives you a prompt with instructions on the first page. Then they give you **one page front and back to plan your essay.**

**What are they telling you?** Yep: they want you to take some time to plan. As much fun as it might be to write a freestyle, improv jazz-style essay, **the ACT is kindly asking that you organize your thoughts.**

**Planning Your Essay.** Take a solid 5-10 minutes to outline your ideas. You'll write a longer (and better) essay if you do.

This is helpful. Here is what ACT says you should be thinking about when you plan your essay. (Turn the page to learn more about how to plan your essay.)

You may wish to consider the following as you think critically about the task:

- Strengths and weaknesses of the three given perspectives
- What **insights do they offer**, and **what do they fail to consider?**
- Why might they be **persuasive** to others, or why might they **fail to persuade?**
- Your own knowledge, experience, and **values**
- What is **your perspective** on this issue, and what are its **strengths and weaknesses?**
- **How will you support your perspective** in your essay?

# HERE IS A SAMPLE ESSAY QUESTION:

## 1. Environmental Regulation

Most environmental scientists agree that climate change is taking place as a result of increased carbon emissions by humans. Some of those scientists claim that our efforts to change our behavior in the immediate future will make the difference between life as we know it and global environmental catastrophe. Others argue that the situation is not so grim, and that we do not need to make any urgent changes to our global lifestyle. As the discussion around climate change and the resulting environmental consequences continues, we have a duty to assess the implications of any decisions we make—or do not make—regarding environmental regulation.

| Perspective One | Perspective Two | Perspective Three |
|---|---|---|
| Human beings are fundamentally concerned with our own survival, and we are also innovative. We should not limit our own progress with environmental regulation now—we are smart enough to solve our problems when they arise. | The extinction of other species shows us that there is a point of no return. Just because we haven't faced serious consequences to date does not mean they are not real and perhaps imminent. | Humans, like other animals, are consumers. We need food to eat and shelter to stay warm. Because they are necessary for our survival, we will always prioritize those needs over less immediate goals like sustainability. |

## Essay Task

Write a unified, coherent essay in which you evaluate multiple perspectives on the impact of environmental regulation. In your essay, be sure to:

- analyze and evaluate the perspectives given
- state and develop your own perspective on the issue
- explain the relationship between your perspective and those given

Your perspective may be in full agreement with any of the others, in partial agreement, or wholly different. Whatever the case, support your ideas with logical reasoning and detailed, persuasive examples.

# Have a Plan

**In the strengths and weaknesses boxes write...**

## 1 STEP 1: DRAW AN ESSAY BLUEPRINT

Draw three lines up-and-down and two lines across. Label the top row 1, 2, 3, and Me. Like so:

| 1 | 2 | 3 | Me |
|---|---|---|---|
|   |   |   |    |
|   |   |   |    |

## 2 STEP 2: BRAIN TSUNAMI

You've heard the word brainstorm before, but have you heard of a "brain tsunami?"

**Since Rule #1 of ACT Writing is "WRITE A LOT," you want to come up with so many ideas that the people sitting near you in the testing room run to higher ground to save themselves from your flood of ideas.**

**During the Brain Tsunami, you have two jobs:**
- Read the prompt and perspectives.
- Fill in the first three columns of your Essay Blueprint.

After you do those two things, you will be ready to write a lot and make all of the points you need to make to score well on the essay.

# Here is what goes in each box of the **Blueprint**.

## How to fill this guy in:

**Read the prompt** *(the big paragraph at the top of the Writing Test)* and Perspective One.

**In the Strengths/Weaknesses box, write down all of your responses to Perspective One.**
If your idea supports the given perspective, put a + sign in front of your idea. If it disagrees with the perspective, put a – sign in front.

**In the Evidence box, write down anything relevant and specific that you could discuss.**
Your evidence can be drawn from anywhere: news/current events, your school studies, even your personal experiences.

**How does evidence come into play?** You want to reference specific situations or examples that illustrate why you think a point you are making is true. If you are making a point about how cultures borrow from each other, a piece of evidence to use could be chocolate—an Aztec invention that became an institution of Europe and later an international industry.

**Repeat those steps for Perspectives Two and Three.**

Once your Blueprint is complete, look across the Strengths/Weaknesses row and **circle your strongest points—the ones you're most excited to share.**

| 1 | 2 | 3 | Me |
|---|---|---|---|
| + strengths<br>– weaknesses | + strengths<br>– weaknesses | + strengths<br>– weaknesses | Brief summary of your perspective |
| evidence | evidence | evidence | |

 **HOT TIP**
**Draw your Essay Blueprint before you start reading the prompt.**
**Why? You can start to fill it out while you are reading.**

## 3 STEP 3: BUILD YOUR PERSPECTIVE

**Architects use blueprints to build a house.** We'll use ours to build an essay.

**You're going to fill in the last spot of the Essay Blueprint, the "Me" section, with your perspective on the topic.** Your perspective can agree with a given perspective, combine elements of two or more perspectives, or disagree completely with what was given.

**The Strengths/Weaknesses that you circled should give you a clue.** How do they combine to create your point of view? Are there additional points you want to make beyond what was given? Jot a quick summary of the ideas—yours and theirs—that you want to highlight when you share your perspective.

**In the "Me" box, jot your ideas down concisely.** Bullet points and even single words might be enough here. The most important thing is that you use the pieces that were given to you plus any ideas you supply to build a perspective.

**Steps 1, 2 and 3 are the planning phase.** We recommend you spend between 5 to 10 minutes in this phase. That might sound like a big chunk of your 40 minutes. Believe us: it is a lot easier to write a well-planned essay in 30 minutes than it is to write a think-it-up-as-you-go-along essay in 38 minutes.

## 4 STEP 4: WRITE A LOT.

**Now comes the fun part.** That is, if your idea of fun is desperately trying to write down as many thoughts and ideas as you can in 30-35 minutes. You'll know you did a good job if your hand is nearly numb when you're done.

This is the structure we recommend you use. It's pretty straightforward.

**I. Introduction**
    **a.** Key factors important to your perspective

**II. Perspective One**
    **a.** Strengths + Evidence
    **b.** Weaknesses + Evidence

**III. Perspective Two**
    **a.** Strengths + Evidence
    **b.** Weaknesses + Evidence

**IV. Perspective Three**
    **a.** Strengths + Evidence
    **b.** Weaknesses + Evidence

**V. Your Perspective**
    **a.** Similarities to given perspectives
    **b.** Differences from given perspectives

## Notice that we didn't include a conclusion.

### The last paragraph should serve as your conclusion.

It should present your perspective and synthesize the ideas you shared earlier. After you do that, what is left to say? **You won't get any extra value out of repeating yourself just for the sake of having a concluding paragraph.**

## STEP 5: POLISH

**5**

**To be honest—you might not have time for this step.** If you finish writing all the ideas and points you have and still have a minute or two to spare, read through your essay and correct any grammatical issues. Keep in mind that your essay doesn't have to be perfect *(even to receive a "perfect" score of 36 out of 36).*

*If you don't get to the polishing stage,*
*don't sweat it.*

# SAMPLE ESSAY PROMPT

## Cultural Blending

The advancement of communication technologies like the internet and smart phones has made Earth a smaller place than ever, for it has enabled us to share knowledge, traditions, and ideas almost instantaneously. Increased interchanges between cultures have led to increased familiarity and even overlap between cultures around the world. Hip-hop music, which originated in the Bronx in New York City, is present in nearly every culture around the world. Some worry that cultural blending will lead to individual cultures losing their uniqueness. Since the rate of cultural blending seems to be accelerating, it is vital to explore how cultural blending affects the world in both positive and negative ways.

*Read and carefully consider these perspectives. Each suggests a particular way of thinking about the impact of cultural blending.*

| Perspective One | Perspective Two | Perspective Three |
|---|---|---|
| Human societies have always shared, stolen, and learned from one another. Anything worth sharing will quickly be assimilated by other cultures—that is simply the natural process of cultural evolution. | If the cultures of the world become fewer and less diverse, we will lose not just elements of culture like food, music, and dress, but also different ways of understanding the world. | Just like a gene pool gets stronger as it becomes more diverse, so cultures gain strength when they are mixed and remixed. Cultural blending will lead to cultures that are more robust and stable. |

## Essay Task

Write a unified, coherent essay in which you evaluate multiple perspectives on the impact of cultural blending. In your essay, be sure to:

• analyze and evaluate the perspectives given
• state and develop your own perspective on the issue
• explain the relationship between your perspective and those given

Your perspective may be in full agreement with any of the others, in partial agreement, or wholly different. Whatever the case, support your ideas with logical reasoning and detailed, persuasive examples.

## SAMPLE ESSAYS

Give these sample responses to the **"Cultural Blending"** prompt a read.

### Three essays are included:

- one that would likely score in the range of 33-36
- one that would likely score between 27-30
- one that would likely score between 21-24

---

**First up is the student whose essay would likely score 33-36.**
For the first essay, we included **a version of the author's Blueprint** so you can see how it translated into the essay.

| 1 | 2 | 3 | Me |
|---|---|---|---|
| + usefulness. We take what's helpful. | + Loss of perspective | + Stronger = useful for the time and place | Culture is alive, helps us in the present. Should preserve it but only adopt if it is useful. |
| - Inevitability. People have choice. | - Who knows if we need what we lost? Culture must be vital. | - Depends on what stronger/more robust means | |
| Chocolate | Native Americans | Story Corps | |

**This essay would likely score in the range of 33-36 out of 36**

### Begin WRITING TEST here.

Cultural blending is not a new phenomenon, though the influence of the internet has certainly accelerated it. Mankind has traveled and wandered throughout all of recorded history, and when we travel we bring our culture with us. In addition, people often seek out ways to improve their own lives. If they see a better alternative to their culture, they will adopt it. These two aspects of human nature make cultural blending an inevitable reality. It is not a dire outcome, for cultural blending offers us the chance to develop cultures that are more vital and useful to us in the 21st century.

Perspective 1 points out the long history of cultural integration. Nearly every aspect of our culture has its origins elsewhere. Chocolate, which is now more closely associated with Switzerland or France, had its origins in the Aztec empire. It came to Europe (along with the tomato and the hot pepper) after Cortez's conquest. However we feel about the destruction that Cortez brought to the Aztecs, it's clear that bringing to chocolate to Europe improved the lives of Europeans. Innovations that are shared—from chocolate to television—are adopted because they improve the lives of the recipients. One weakness of Perspective 1 is that it presents a cultural blending as inevitable, that it will and must happen. People have more choice than this perspective suggests—they will only adopt a new cultural behavior if it benefits them.

Perspective 2 suggests a graver concern of cultural blending: that something deeper and more significant will be lost beyond the visual aspects of culture. Native American culture is a demonstration of this. Westward expansion of America led to the death and displacement of Native American people. What is left of their culture is only what has been able to be preserved. Certain aspects are lost now: entire languages no longer exist. Without those languages or the people who speak them, we are simply ignorant of what we're missing. In other words, we don't know what we don't know. This also reveals a weakness in this perspective. We may not know what is lost, but that does not mean that it is something better than what we have. Vitality is important when it comes to culture. Vitality describes how much a culture applies to life as we live it now. We can (and should) mourn the loss of Native American culture, but we simply don't know if it is better than what we have now.

Perspective 3 takes an interesting tack in describing culture in terms of strength and robustness. What does it mean for a culture to be robust and stable? If those words describe cultures that fit their time and place and are helpful to the people who adopt them, then a

**If you need more space, please continue on the next page.**

316

| WRITING TEST |
| --- |

robust and stable culture is more desirable. The initial prompt describes the danger of the loss of uniqueness, which Perspective 3 does not address. Are we stronger with fewer but more robust cultures? The answer to that question depends on your definition of "stronger."

Culture is a vital tool that helps us live in the world in a meaningful way. Its most essential characteristics are its vitality and its usefulness. Those two qualities are what make a culture strong. For that reason, culture must always evolve and adapt. Given the pace of change in our world, it makes sense that culture has been evolving more quickly than ever. That evolution is simply a survival mechanism as people adapt to a new way of being in the world. Should we abandon our old cultures? No; we should document them so we can understand them. They may provide us with insight that we don't have. We should not cling to them just because they are old, however. If we do, we deny ourselves the most useful culture we can have. A non-profit group called StoryCorps travels the United States and asks people to tell stories about themselves. Frequently the stories are told inter-generationally, between a younger family member and an older one. This is a perfect example of how cultural preservation can work: the older generation informs the younger ones. The younger ones then bear the responsibility of finding their own way through the world but may borrow from the wisdom of their elders as well. Culture is a living, changing organism. It should breathe and change and not be stuck on a museum shelf and stared at. True cultural strength means having a culture that works for people in their time and place.

**What makes this essay top shelf? For one, it addresses all of the aspects of the Essay Task.** It does an especially good job of analyzing the given perspectives, looking at each one with a critical/analytical eye. The perspective of the author is well thought out; he includes some ideas about cultural blending that were not given in the prompts but seem quite pertinent. **Lastly, the essay's use of language is strong and clear.**

## 👍 COMMENTARY

**We think this essay is an example of a high-scoring ACT essay.** Does it get a 33 or does it get a 36? It depends on the grader's mood that morning. How strong was their coffee? Did the cat pee on the rug again? Impossible to say. We think this essay is good enough to get a top score, so feel free to use this as a model of a top-scoring essay.

**Let's move on to a sample essay that would likely score in the range of 27-30 out of 36.**

| |
|---|
| **Begin WRITING TEST here.** |
| Cultures blend. Even in just the past few years, cultures around the world have changed, becoming more modern and international. A song written and sung in Korean ("Gangnam Style") became popular around the world because of it's video on the internet. How they affect each other and whether that is a good thing is uncertain in the modern age. |
| The first perspective shares the idea that cultures borrowing from each other is a natural and unavoidable thing. One example of how this is true is the growth in the popularity of soccer in the united states. Previous generations of sports fans have known the "big four" sports to be baseball, football, basketball, and hockey. Now, soccer might be one of the top four. It has been the most popular sport in countries from Europe to Africa to South America for decades, and has now spread to the united states. If people enjoy soccer, there is no harm caused from it spreading to the us and becoming part of the culture. |
| Perspective Two shares a different point of view: that culture expresses a way of thinking. An example relevant to this point is hip-hop. Although hip-hop spread first within the united states and later to nearly every country in the world, it has not become a force that limit how people see or understand the world. In fact, I recently listened to a hip-hop song recorded in Farsi, the primary language of Iran. While the beat to the song was recognizable as a hip-hop beat, the nature of the lyrics reflected the concerns of youth in Iran. Not only that, but the song also included instruments like the dutar, a traditional Persian string instrument. This song shows how cultural blending can add to a culture without the culture losing its unique perspective. |
| Like the example of the hip-hop song suggests, cultures do become stronger when they adopt customs from others. For that reason, I agree with Perspective Three. American history offers examples of many different cultures that came together to form one culture. Almost every immigrant group was discriminated against when they first came to the us. Eventually, they became part of American culture and shared their own customs. Italian immigrants introduced pizza. Now pizza is a central part of American culture. Both Italian Americans and the American culture are better as a result of influencing each other. |
| Cultures throughout history have been influenced by each other, and the result is greater variety and understanding of the world. The world is getting smaller as a result of technology. As that happens, it makes sense that the cultures of the world are becoming more |

**If you need more space, please continue on the next page.**

| WRITING TEST |
|---|
| similar. Maybe the world at some point will have one unified, diverse culture. That is likely to |
| happen only if the countries of the world are working together in harmony. All the world should |
| strive to understand each other better. There is no better way to acheive that goal than to |
| exchange cultural ideas with each other. |

## 👍 COMMENTARY

**We gave this essay a score in the 27-30 range, which means it is a really good essay just one tier below the highest scoring essays.** Look back at the previous essay to draw a comparison. The higher scoring essay made two points about each of the given perspectives from two points of view, where this essay only makes one point. The points this essay makes are a little less sophisticated too: the author tends to just agree or disagree with each perspective rather than analyzing them or considering their implications. This essay is also shorter and has less sophisticated sentence structure and vocabulary than the higher scoring one. **All in all, a very good essay.**

**The next essay would likely score in the range of 21-24 out of 36.**

| |
|---|
| **Begin WRITING TEST here.** |
|       In my opinion, cultural blending is mostly good, but it should be monitered to make sure that it does not happen too quickly. All cultures learn and grow from one another as Perspective One suggests, but due to the internet that is happening faster than ever before. As Perspective Three says, cultures get stronger as they become mixed. As long as this mixing does not happen too quickly, cultural blending is always a positive step. |
|       Perspective One points out that cultures have always stolen from each other. That has been true for thousands of years. The Romans stole their mythology from the Greeks and simply renamed the gods. It is impossible to prevent such things from happening. Nothing was lost when Romans adopted it as their own. In fact, Romans now had a new way of looking at the world that they didn't have before. That is why I disagree with Perspective Two. It suggests that we will lose ways of seeing the world. What if cultural blending is just a way of adding a new way of seeing the world? I believe that is how cultural blending happens in the world. |
|       Perspective Three says that cultures become stronger when they are mixed, and I agree. Where I live in California, many different cultures interact, people from Mexico, El Salvador, South Korea and Armenia all call California home. The result is a more fun place where I can get a variety of food, from Korean barbecue to pupusas. I would rather live in a place with this variety than in a place where one culture is king. |
|       In conclusion, cultural blending has many positive benefits. The only thing that may cause concern about it is that it can sometimes happen too quickly. If a group of people joins another culture too quickly, they can forget their previous culture and feel cut off from their past. Every culture should respect their past and look to the future in order to create the most successful culture possible. |

## 👍 COMMENTARY

**If you've read all of the sample essays so far, you might see a pattern emerging.** This essay is shorter, makes fewer points in response to the prompts, and uses less sophisticated language. The best thing going here is that the author has a clear point of view of his/her own—that cultural blending is good so long as it doesn't happen too quickly. The author doesn't support that position with any concrete evidence, though, which is a weakness. **This is still a competent essay, but it's not one that is going to "wow" the graders.**

# HOW the Writing Test is scored

Let's talk about how your **ACT** essay is scored. You get a variety of scores with the essay—none of which affect the composite score of your **ACT**, just to remind you. **Among the scores you'll get:**

- ✶ **An overall Writing Test score** from 1-36.
- ✶ **Sub-scores in four categories:** Ideas and Analysis, Development and Support, Organization, and Language use.
- ✶ **An ELA score** that combines the English, Reading, and Writing test scores.

**You might be saying, "that's a hilariously large number of scores."** You're right! It is also flat-out amazing that none of them factor into the composite score. Sometimes you just have to shake your head.

**It's a tough task to get this essay completed in 40 minutes, so practice is your friend.** We've got **printable essay answer sheets for you on our website.** Just visit **www.tutorted.com/resources** to download a PDF version of the **ACT** essay answer sheet and other useful resources.

---

IN THE NEXT SECTION, YOU'LL FIND **EIGHT SAMPLE ESSAY PROMPTS** TO USE FOR PRACTICE.

Remember our **two key rules:**
### RULE 1: WRITE A LOT.
### RULE 2: HAVE A PLAN.

### Plus, the five steps of the plan:
- ▣ Step 1: Draw an Essay Blueprint
- ▣ Step 2: Brain Tsunami
- ▣ Step 3: Build Your Perspective
- ▣ Step 4: Write a Lot
- ▣ Step 5: Polish

*Go try it out for yourself!*

# 1. Environmental Regulation

Most environmental scientists agree that climate change is taking place as a result of increased carbon emissions by humans. Some of those scientists claim that our efforts to change our behavior in the immediate future will make the difference between life as we know it and global environmental catastrophe. Others argue that the situation is not so grim, and that we do not need to make any urgent changes to our global lifestyle. As the discussion around climate change and the resulting environmental consequences continues, we have a duty to assess the implications of any decisions we make—or do not make—regarding environmental regulation. .

| **Perspective One** | **Perspective Two** | **Perspective Three** |
|---|---|---|
| Human beings are fundamentally concerned with our own survival, and we are also innovative. We should not limit our own progress with environmental regulation now—we are smart enough to solve our problems when they arise. | The extinction of other species shows us that there is a point of no return. Just because we haven't faced serious consequences to date does not mean they are not real and perhaps imminent. | Humans, like other animals, are consumers. We need food to eat and shelter to stay warm. Because they are necessary for our survival, we will always prioritize those needs over less immediate goals like sustainability. |

# 2. Animal Rights

For centuries, animals have been used for transportation, food, clothing, entertainment, and research. In recent years, the treatment of animals has come under greater scrutiny as animal rights activists, such as the organization PETA (People for the Ethical Treatment of Animals), have gone to great lengths to attempt to reduce adverse treatment of animals. While there is a general public consensus that animals should not be mistreated, it is important to acknowledge our dependence on animals for scientific research, as it allows us to create life-saving cures and treatments. Given our reliance on animals for human progress, it is important to examine where we should draw the line in the name of animal welfare.

| **Perspective One** | **Perspective Two** | **Perspective Three** |
|---|---|---|
| Humans are earth's most dominant species. It is simply impossible to assign the same rights to animals as to humans; otherwise, human society will not advance at the pace it needs to. | If we try hard enough, modern science can advance in other ways than through animal testing. We should not need to torture innocent animals to progress as a society. | How we treat animals demonstrates how much we respect our world, which indirectly expresses how much we respect ourselves. Mistreat animals and we essentially mistreat ourselves. |

## 3. Charitable Actions

It is easier than ever to be charitable. People can make a donation by adding a dollar or two to their grocery bill when prompted at checkout, or by responding to a request for donations via social media. Weaving opportunities to be charitable into people's everyday lives results in greater overall participation; however, are all charitable contributions created equal? Donating our time through volunteer work requires greater time and effort. Does volunteering have a greater impact? Given the increased presence of requests for charity in people's lives, it is worth examining the implications of these new, more efficient ways to give.

| **Perspective One** | **Perspective Two** | **Perspective Three** |
|---|---|---|
| Many people do not have the time and energy to participate personally in charity work. Making it easier for people to give provides an opportunity for everyone to be involved. | When we give to charity by simply pushing a button or "liking" something on social media, we get a false sense of accomplishment causing us to feel like we have done something more significant than we have. | Overwhelming people with a multitude of opportunities to give to charity can backfire. "Donor fatigue" will actually lead people to give less. |

## 4. Speaking Freely

One of the most central aspects of a free and democratic society is the ability of citizens to speak, write, and express themselves openly. There are now more ways than ever to express oneself freely: from posting a personal opinion on a blog to advocating for a particular cause through an online video. At the same time there are some limitations set on freedom of speech. For example, many schools impose rules that prevent students from wearing clothing with potentially offensive images or words. With social media and other technologies providing additional platforms from which to express their views and ideas, it is important to consider the need for rules and limitations to free speech.

| **Perspective One** | **Perspective Two** | **Perspective Three** |
|---|---|---|
| Specific restrictions on what people can write or say are biased because they represent one group or person's opinion. We should be careful not to allow restrictions on speech to turn into censorship. | Speech can be hostile, and it can even stir people to cause physical harm to others. In a civilized society, people should be protected from speech that threatens them emotionally or physically. | It is impossible to set enforceable rules or limitations on free speech due to the vast number of opportunities and platforms people have to express themselves in the 21st century. |

## 5. Bias in the News

The way people receive the news has changed in the past two decades. The number of television and online news organizations has expanded while the number of daily newspapers has declined. No matter how the news is delivered, the style of presentation can communicate more than just the facts. Many viewers complain that some news outlets consistently present a biased rather than a neutral version of reality. Because our understanding of current events can significantly shape our larger worldview, it is important to consider whether news organizations can (or should) aim for neutrality.

| Perspective One | Perspective Two | Perspective Three |
|---|---|---|
| Our idea of reality is influenced by our own experiences and beliefs. The news media cannot avoid this bias. Instead, they should share with viewers the nature of their unique perspective. | There are undeniable facts. News organizations should be careful to report "just the facts" and avoid editorializing or interpreting those facts. | The biased presentation of news has helped to divide us. We now live in a world made up of people armed not only with different opinions but with different "facts." |

## 6. What Schools Teach

The traditional model of education that is common in public schools across the U.S. focuses on knowledge acquisition. Recent research suggests that character traits such as determination and resilience (the ability to recover quickly from a difficult situation) are better indicators of future success than knowledge. In school, however, helping students develop such attributes often takes a back seat to teaching core subjects. Given the importance of education to the future success of our society, it is worth examining carefully what we teach.

| Perspective One | Perspective Two | Perspective Three |
|---|---|---|
| School is a place where children should learn what they cannot learn elsewhere, like algebra and history. Children should learn skills like resilience but not in the school setting. | The smartest person in the world cannot succeed without the ability to overcome failure. If the purpose of schooling is to prepare students for future success, then resilience and persistence should be taught in school. | Personality traits cannot be taught directly but can be developed. Schools should help cultivate these traits through traditional academic work. |

## 7. Digital Privacy

In the digital era, privacy and anonymity are complex topics. Because digital communication passes through IP addresses and channels like Twitter or Gmail, it can be easily monitored. The Government and other entities such as corporations, advertisers, and data aggregators have the ability to acquire all kinds of information about private citizens. As our reliance on the Internet increases, it is important to consider the threat to our rights to digital privacy.

| **Perspective One** | **Perspective Two** | **Perspective Three** |
|---|---|---|
| The collection of personal data by the government is in the service of the greater good and should be allowed. | Privacy standards of the pre-Internet era were much stricter than what we tolerate today. It is a federal crime to open someone's mail; the same standard should apply to emails and tweets. | A policy that allows the violation of other people's privacy requires thoughtful oversight. governments should be monitored carefully by citizens to ensure that it does not cause harm. |

## 8. Designer Children

Advances in the science of reproduction and fertility have given rise to concerns regarding the possibility of "designer children." In the present day, parents attempting in-vitro fertilization can choose the sex of their baby and test for genetic diseases. In the near future, parents may be able to select for traits like eye color and height. Are "designer children" simply the next step in medical advancement or do they represent a dangerous attempt to alter our genetic makeup? With the possibility of selecting nonmedical traits on the horizon, it is important to consider the implications and significance of this development.

| **Perspective One** | **Perspective Two** | **Perspective Three** |
|---|---|---|
| Creating "designer children" can help ensure the survival of our species by allowing us to select the necessary traits to achieve optimal health and success. | Only wealthy parents will be able to afford to genetically engineer their children. As a result, the gap of inequality between rich and poor will widen. | Genetic factors may be controlled, but they do not guarantee how a child will turn out. Psychology shows that the environment influences children as much as genetics. |

What do you think? Is the **ACT** simpler now than it was when you started?

The next thing you need to do is apply your newfound knowledge and strategies by practicing.

**Our companion volume, "Tutor Ted's ACT Practice Tests"** has three realistic practice tests with explanations based on the strategies in this book. **We highly recommend it.** *(Of course we do.)*

Like we said in the beginning, knowledge and strategy will turn you into a confident and successful test taker. The next step is practice. Put your knowledge and strategy into action. **It's not magic; it's common sense.**

NOT MAGIC... just common sense.

## So go practice.

And get in touch with us! We love to hear from our students. You can find us in all of the usual places on the Internet, or you can email us at sayhello@tutorted.com.

**I would say,** **"good luck,"** **but you're really not going to need luck.**

TED

Made in the USA
Lexington, KY
24 June 2016